Instructor's Resource Manual

Seeing the Pattern

Readings for Successful Writing

Instructor's Resource Manual

Seeing the Pattern
Readings for
Successful Writing

KATHLEEN T. McWHORTER
Niagara County Community College

Prepared by
Gail Hanlon

Bedford/St. Martin's
Boston ▪ New York

Manufactured in the United States of America.

0 9 8 7 6
f e d c b a

For information, write: Bedford/St. Martin's, 75 Arlington Street, Boston, MA 02116   (617-399-4000)

ISBN: 0-312-41903-1

EAN: 978-0-312-41903-5

This manual is intended to assist both new and experienced instructors in using *Seeing the Pattern* more effectively and to save time in developing courses that use this text. Rather than suggest how to teach first-year composition, the manual offers a wide variety of tips, strategies, and approaches, allowing instructors to choose methodology that is compatible with their teaching style and philosophy.

Unit 1, "Resources for Teaching Composition with *Seeing the Pattern*" (p. 1), offers practical suggestions for developing a composition course using the text. The first section, "Teaching with *Seeing the Pattern*" (p. 3), introduces the textbook; includes organizational tips; discusses course goals, relationships with students, journal writing, and collaborative activities; and offers suggestions on how to use computers and software. To assist instructors further, "Developing Your Course Plan" (p. 17) presents sample course plans and a sample syllabus. Because so many students enrolled in first-year composition courses lack certain basic writing and reading skills, a section on teaching underprepared students has been included: "Helping Underprepared Students Improve Their Skills" (p. 23) describes both cognitive and affective characteristics of underprepared students and discusses instructional accommodations. It also offers suggestions for developing basic writing skills, building students' reading skills, and fostering critical reading and thinking. At the end of this section is a bibliography of books and articles for instructor reference.

Unit 2, "Teaching Tips and Suggested Answers for Individual Chapters in *Seeing the Pattern*" (p. 33), is designed to help instructors new to the book as well as those who are looking for new ways of teaching familiar readings. This section includes introductions to each chapter in the text. In addition, specific teaching suggestions are included for each reading in Chapters 5 through 10, along with suggested answers to the apparatus that accompanies each reading. These answers are not intended to be definitive; rather they are brief, sample responses designed to both aid instructors teaching a reading for the first time and stimulate discussion in the classroom while opening up a dialogue between instructors and students.

I wish to thank the authors who contributed sections to this manual. Michael Hricik of Westmoreland County Community College prepared "Teaching with *Seeing the Pattern*" and "Developing Your Course Plan." I am especially indebted to Gail Hanlon, who contributed to all aspects of the manual and prepared the teaching tips and suggested answers to the apparatus for all the readings in the book. At Bedford/St. Martin's, I thank Laura Arcari, Beth Ammerman, Laura King, and Harold Chester. Without their contributions, this manual would not have been possible.

Kathleen T. McWhorter

Contents

Resources for Teaching Composition with *Seeing the Pattern*

Teaching with *Seeing the Pattern*

Seeing the Pattern has been designed with instructors' needs in mind. To get the most out of this text, however, you'll need to organize in advance, keep up with your responsibilities for the course, preview chapter contents and assignments, and structure the course in a balanced way. If you make every effort to chart a plan as you begin, you will find that the end result of the course will be much more satisfying. This *Instructor's Resource Manual* will give you practical advice for using *Seeing the Pattern* and for maximizing the use of your time. It will also help you identify appropriate course activities to support your objectives.

Planning and Organizing Your Course

Before you even begin your semester or quarter, try to decide how you will meet the requirements specified by your department, division, or academic area. Typically, the department chair or an administrative assistant will be able to provide you with any departmental guidelines and syllabi from previous terms. This information will assist you in planning your syllabus, particularly if this is your first term with *Seeing the Pattern* or if this is your first term teaching this course. See pages 17–23 of this manual for sample course outlines and advice on writing a syllabus.

When you develop a course syllabus, it is usually a prudent strategy to make a weekly outline of assignments, with due dates for first and revised drafts of essays, as well as for other assignments or journals. (See the sample syllabus on p. 18 of this manual.) For yourself, try to make a more detailed outline in which you develop a fairly accurate class plan of how the activities for the term will be coordinated. For instance, you will want to determine if and when you will be scheduling student conferences, a library orientation, or visits to the writing center or the learning assistance center. If you are planning to visit any of your college's services, contact the appropriate person at the start of the term to get added to their calendar.

Finally, make sure that you connect your class activities throughout the term. For instance, as you make a detailed term plan, try to look back at the essays, in-class writings, discussions, and other activities to see if you can link them. You should attempt to move from lower-level rhetorical skills to higher-level skills by using a coordinated plan throughout the term. This plan will assist you in focusing on long-term goals and objectives. Likewise, if you have an especially busy week at a certain point in the term, you will find that you have a basic idea or outline of what should be done for the next week.

If at all possible, try to develop your notes for the first two weeks of the class even before the term begins. The first two weeks always seem to be overwhelming, so you are always better off having a plan already prepared. In addition, your level of confidence will be much higher going into the course if you have clear objectives and activities in mind. The impression that you give to your students in those initial weeks can be lasting.

Considering Your Primary Goals for the Course

When you are planning your course syllabus—and as you progress through the term—you should consider the four or five most critical skills that students should master. Consult the departmental course syllabus or course description to determine the most critical skills. If you're uncertain about this, ask a more experienced faculty member.

Focusing on Expressive and Informative Writing

If your course focuses primarily on expressive writing, you need to concentrate on writing that exhibits a clear and consistent main idea. You will typically assign a sequence of essays that exhibit logical progression, cohesiveness, and meaningful connection of ideas. The course will likely focus on basic editing, sentence construction, and paragraph-level writing. During the course you will help students develop a fuller awareness of the various rhetorical patterns of development as you assign progressively difficult readings. Strive to develop some higher-level thinking, reading, and writing skills as the term progresses. Keep in mind that you should see improvement in the students' writing and their organization of ideas. Writing involves thinking, and revision involves reseeing, so students will usually became more reflective and focused in their writing by the end of the term.

Many instructors begin a course based on expressive writing with either a narrative or a descriptive essay. Of course, if your department allows, you may choose another option. Whatever you do, try to avoid going beyond the initial limitations of your students. If you discover that your students are struggling with a particular essay, consider extending its due date. However, not all students will master every pattern of development, so you will need to move on. Keep in mind, though, that if you get too far off schedule, your whole term plan will start to unravel. Always strive to have your students meet the minimum number of essays or assignments established by your department.

Likewise, with informative writing, you will focus on essays such as comparison and contrast, classification or division, definition, and cause and effect. The focus here is to inform the reader more fully, with or without material from sources. These types of essays can work well without sources if students choose a narrowly defined topic at the start. The informative essays help students make the transition between personal writing and more involved research writing, such as argumentation. These essays help students develop skills in looking beyond their own experiences as they synthesize outside information to use in their essays.

Focusing on Informative and Research Writing

In a course that focuses on both informative and research-oriented writing, you will typically divide the course into two segments; be sure to allow more time for the research-oriented essays. For such a course, follow the main strategies mentioned in the previous section for the first part of the term, and then start to focus on developing the use of sources in writing. An excellent starting point is a less difficult research-oriented essay, such as a comparison and contrast or definition (with two or three sources). (See Chapters 9 and 11 in *Seeing the Pattern.*) Some instructors assign a definition paper by asking students to find several dictionary definitions of a particular word (for denotations) and then the same number of books or periodicals in which the word is used (for connotations) to show how the definitions differ. Other instructors assign an essay comparing and contrasting two authors who write in the same genre, with students using two or three reference books as sources.

Keep in mind that you should introduce more complex readings (both student and professional) with sources as you move through this section of the course. Try to place particular emphasis on analysis or interpretation of essays, synthesis of several essays, and evaluation of both sources and student essays. The writing in the second half of the course will help students develop a high degree of independent thought and will facilitate these levels of thinking as well. You want to help students feel comfortable in moving to a research paper and developing stronger reading skills for future academic success.

When you are working on papers with sources, you should allow more time for peer review, conferences, and revisions. It can be a good strategy to require a rough draft, a revised draft, and then an edited draft. If you do this, you will discover that students will have stronger final drafts and less tendency to procrastinate. The critical point with a course that includes research isn't just the writing but the level of thinking as the term progresses. You should require more detailed comments on the peer-edited essays and ask for more detailed responses to the professional essays and journal assignments.

Establishing a Good Relationship with Your Students

Developing a good relationship with your students is important. You will learn about your students through their writing and your discussions with them, so you need to develop a level of trust and understanding from the start.

Getting to Know Your Students

At the very beginning of the term, get acquainted with students by handing out 3½- by 5-inch index cards or an information form that elicits basic information from them such as contact information, writing courses they have taken so far, the types of reading they enjoy, and their strengths and weaknesses in writing. This activity will allow the students to see that you are personally interested in them. Also, you will get to know their names more quickly.

Clarifying Your Expectations

Many students who take a freshman-level course will be uncertain what is expected of them. It is helpful to focus on major and minor expectations in the first week. For instance, you may want the assignments for the class to have particular headings. If you have other specific expectations, go over these while reviewing your syllabus or during the first week of class. It's always a good idea to limit class rules to several points: be on time, work hard while in class, ask questions when something is unclear, and treat classmates and instructor with respect. Students often appreciate when you set limits because they know what you will allow and what you will not accept.

Discuss evaluation practices and their consistent application throughout the term. Do this at the start of the term so that the students understand your system of weighting grades and averaging the components with essays, peer reviewing, journals, portfolios, homework, class participation, quizzes, and so on. Try to be as specific as possible about how you will grade the essays and the prewriting, first draft, and revised draft. If you factor peer reviewing into the class participation grade or into some other category, be sure to mention that fact early in the course so that students will learn to give more specific comments from the start of the term. It helps to include this breakdown in the course syllabus, but you should also refer to it at several points during the term.

Most institutions have some type of attendance policy. However, you should allow some flexibility on this because exceptions or specific situations may occur for which you will have to allow a student some leeway. If your institution has a specific policy, try to follow it for consistency. Some institutions have no attendance policy, and you will have to develop some standards of your own. A very reasonable policy is to allow students to miss no more than 20 percent of the allowed classes; after that, you can impose a penalty on their in-class grade. Give consistently scheduled and unscheduled assignments and quizzes throughout the term. Missing one or two of these won't cause problems; missing more than that will impact a student's grade. If a student has not attended class for an extended period of time, it is advisable to contact that student directly or have a faculty-initiated withdrawal form sent to that student.

Setting Your Classroom Tone

When working with a new class, you should initially set the tone or atmosphere that you would like to maintain throughout the course. Don't be concerned with trying to emulate another instructor who is very successful with students. Be comfortable with your own style because it is a big part of your personal identity. If you develop a very informal and relaxed approach early on and then switch to a demanding style, you will encounter problems with students. The best approach is to start off with a more demanding style and then loosen up as you get to know the class.

Also make sure you inform your students how they should submit and organize essays and revisions. At the very least, it's a good idea to require students to put prewriting, peer reviews, and drafts of an essay into a manila folder for submission. This strategy forces students to be more organized, and it is easier for you to follow the flow of their work.

Anticipating Problems and Using Services at Your Institution

During each week of the term, you will typically encounter at least one type of academic, personal, or classroom-centered problem that you must deal with to keep a student or your class focused. In such cases, you should attempt to utilize the resources of your institution. Your school will likely have a writing center or an academic skills center. Don't personally try to tutor each student with writing-related problems. Refer students with writing difficulties to the writing center instead. Likewise, students who are having difficulties with study habits or organization can be referred to the academic skills center. If you have serious concerns about a particular student, you may want to take on a more personal role to ensure that he or she gets the needed help in a timely manner.

If a student approaches you to indicate a concern about a busy work schedule in relation to the course assignments, you may want to recommend that this individual consult with financial aid for a student loan. This is especially critical in the first three weeks of class because this is the time when a student may decide to withdraw from all classes rather than explore other options.

If you have a student with personal issues, especially those involving psychological concerns (such as depression or a total lack of focus), you should advise the student to make an appointment with a campus counselor or psychologist. As an English instructor, you can certainly be an empathetic listener, but you should always be cautious when offering advice. A student who demonstrates clear signs of depression or has other serious problems should be referred to counseling as quickly as possible.

Finally, you have several choices in dealing with class behavior problems. Some of the most common situations are these: arriving consistently late to class, talking excessively while you are talking, and attempting to dominate the class discussion. The best way to resolve these situations is to address them as quickly as possible with an oral comment. However, if they can't be addressed effectively in this manner, it's advisable to discuss the problem with the student after class. Be firm and direct, but initially try to ask a series of questions to determine the root of the problem. Talk about the possible consequences of continuing the behavior. After this initial meeting, give the student one other opportunity. Then, if the problem persists, consider taking administrative action as indicated in the faculty handbook of your institution.

Staying Organized as the Term Progresses

At the start of the term, you need to develop some basic strategies for staying organized. You should keep a copy of the course syllabus and your detailed course outline on the wall next to your desk and one taped to the inside cover of *Seeing the Pattern*. You can refer to both of these as the term progresses.

Keeping Consistent Records

It is always a good strategy to organize the overall content of the class. You won't be able to establish totally objective grades or criteria for all assignments because there is certainly a level of subjectivity in a writing course. However, you should track daily attendance, check off the submission of prewriting and multiple drafts, give points for major in-class assignments, and record all the grades for revised essays. Be sure to establish a clear policy on how many revisions you allow and what your essay grading policy is.

Whatever grading policies you establish, you should give students an accurate estimate of their class grade at several points during the term. This will help to reduce disagreements at the end of the term and allow you to catch any errors that you have made in recording grades. Many English instructors are now using spreadsheets for tracking grades. If you record grades the traditional way, you may want to photocopy your class grades at several times during the term in case you lose your grade book.

Finally, when you feel that you are struggling to keep up with the paper load, you should keep in mind that all essays, journals, or assignments don't need to be graded with equal thoroughness. For the graded essays, you might want to focus on several criteria in your own comments and then use peer reviewing to cover other areas. For the non-graded assignments, you can give a Credit or No Credit grade and focus on one or several areas for commentary.

Meeting Individually with Students

It can be beneficial to have at least two conferences with each student during the term. You can use these conferences to discuss a student's overall progress or to discuss the development of a particular essay. If you do use class time for conferences, it is time well spent. You can have the students do peer reviewing or collaborative small-group work while you are holding conferences, you can use this time for an out-of-class assignment in addition to the conferences, or you can choose to meet with students outside of class.

Using *Seeing the Pattern* Effectively

If you spend a limited amount of time early in the term—and as the term progresses—to explain the critical sections of *Seeing the Pattern*, you will find that your students will better understand key writing concepts. Be sure to inform your students that there is an introduction—"Using *Seeing the Pattern* to Improve Your Writing"—at the front of the textbook that includes information about the book and its features. Consider assigning this section or taking some time in the first day of class to go through the book's features, showing students what is in the book and explaining how to use it.

Beginning with Part 1

Because *Seeing the Pattern* is designed to be flexible, you can choose which chapters you would like to cover and in what order. You might want to use the writing process chapters first (Chapters 2–4), reserving Chapter 1 until you begin assigning the patterns of development in Part 2. You could spend two weeks with Chapter 2 ("Planning Your Essay") and one of the patterns of development, such as Chapter 5 ("Narration") or Chapter 6 ("Description"), so that you focus more strongly on prewriting with the initial essay. On the other hand, you may want to cover Chapters 1–4 by themselves or in conjunction with the first major writing assignment. In particular, you may want to use Chapter 4 at more than one point in the course. For specific suggestions on using the first four chapters, see pages 49-58 of this manual.

Using the Visual Features of *Seeing the Pattern*

You will notice that an excellent feature of *Seeing the Pattern* is the visual nature of the text. Illustrations and diagrams offer a visual approach to writing and engage today's more visual students. Each chapter in Parts 1 and 2 begins with a Writing Quick Start to give students a preview of the major objectives of the chapter and the pattern of writing. The initial exercises in each chapter act as a critical starting point for writing and discussion.

The graphic organizers in each chapter are especially valuable for spatial learners, but this feature of the book should be helpful to all students. Graphic organizers are diagrams that *visually* present the relationship among ideas within a piece of text. Many students, especially underprepared students, have difficulty recognizing the organization and overall structure of what they read. They fail to recognize hierarchical and coordinate relationships and consequently have difficulty remembering what they read. Graphic organizers offer a meaningful conceptual framework that enables students to understand relationships and make connections with their existing knowledge. According to cognitive psychologist David P. Ausubel, creating these kinds of graphic organizers—which he has termed *advance organizers*—builds bridges, or "ideational scaffolding," that enables readers and learners to construct and reconstruct meaning within text (148).

Graphic organizers work effectively because they encode information in memory in two ways—verbally and spatially. Thus, they provide two different layers of cueing, or two memory paths; if one fails, the other may work. Graphic organizers in *Seeing the Pattern* can be used as both reading and writing strategies. For each method of development, students are shown two graphic organizers. The first demonstrates the relationship among the unique elements of the particular type of essay and also functions as a model. The second applies the model organizer to a specific essay included in the chapter. Viewing a created graphic organizer and then creating their own graphic organizer facilitates students' comprehension and recall. Later in the chapter, students are also asked to complete a graphic organizer for one of the readings in the chapter. You may want to experiment with having students fill out graphic organizers or make their own organizers at various phases in their reading process.

In *Seeing the Pattern,* graphic organizers can also be used for the revision of writing. When a student draws a graphic organizer of an essay he or she has written, the structure and relationship of ideas or lack thereof becomes apparent. Lack of supporting ideas also becomes immediately obvious, as does misplaced or irrelevant information. Some students may find these tools more helpful than others and may like to work with organizers on a regular basis. Assign at least one organizer exercise online and then make them optional if only a few students prefer to use them. (Interactive versions of the graphic organizers are available online at www.bedfordstmartins.com /seeingthepattern.)

Revision flowcharts clearly indicate places where a student's draft might need to be revised. Presented in a visual format with directional arrows, a revision flowchart asks the student to identify and evaluate his or her own thesis and underline and evaluate topic sentences, among other revisions, moving slowly, section by section, through the paper. After using a few of these flowcharts, students will begin to recognize key areas and learn to apply questions such as "Does your thesis clearly state the generalization that your examples support?" to their own writing.

Annotated professional and student essays provide excellent models for students to evaluate because key sections and points (such as the thesis statement) are clearly highlighted. Modeling is a very effective method for helping students to improve their writing because they are more apt to critique a "student essay" than a professional one, at least until they become accustomed to the process and can move on to model professional essays. This kind of clearly marked text is also visually stimulating and easier to comprehend by students whose learning styles are visual in nature.

Throughout *Seeing the Pattern,* bulleted and numbered lists are elements that make the text visually accessible and aesthetically pleasing. See, for example, the What to Look for, Highlight, and Annotate sections where Understanding the Reading activities and Examining the Characteristics of [Narration] Essays summarize what to look for as the student reads a particular rhetorical mode. Each idea is clearly and simply stated. You might like to recommend that students highlight or flag any list they find themselves consulting frequently—there is a directory of lists on the inside back cover of the book.

Using the Reading Apparatus in Part 2

The reading apparatus in Part 2 will help you to motivate students to read assigned essays more carefully so that they will be prepared to discuss or write about the essays in greater detail in class. Once students become accustomed to working with these questions, either as take-home work or as in-class work, they will begin to read more actively, highlighting and annotating their text and looking up vocabulary words in anticipation of doing the assignments.

Understanding the Reading

These questions focus on the content rather than the form of each essay. If you find that students are not reading the assigned essays actively, remind them to read and reread closely, annotating and highlighting as they go along. If they are still not reading closely enough, assign these Understanding the Reading questions beforehand. You may also use Understanding the Reading to give quick pre-discussion quizzes. If you prefer not to give quizzes, you can ask students to read and answer these questions before class discussion; this allows them to formulate their ideas on paper before venturing into group discussion.

Visualizing the Reading

This section provides an excellent opportunity for students to evaluate what they have read, in a visual outline format, in a table, or in response to a visual image. Each one is designed to ask the questions that pertain to the unique characteristics of the chapter's rhetorical pattern. Visualizing the Reading can be used as a take-home assignment or as an in-class assignment when you feel that the discussion has been lagging or that students are not reading closely enough. Visualizing the Reading is also useful for work in pairs.

Examining the Characteristics of [Illustration] Essays

Each of the Examining the Characteristics sections is specifically tied in to the chapter's rhetorical mode. The questions will get students thinking about how, for example, illustration essays are strengthened by a series of striking examples, or how comparison and contrast essays must be organized point by point or subject by subject. It is useful to assign students to think about one of these questions as they read the essay so that they focus in on the particular characteristics of the rhetorical mode.

Building Your Word Power

This section ties in closely with active reading. You may find that students do not understand the connotations of words and figurative phrases, even after reading an essay closely. Assigning one or two questions from Building Your Word Power is an excellent way to make sure that students begin to slow down their reading pace enough to assess the meaning of figurative language and colloquial phrases in addition to unfamiliar vocabulary words. You may have to reiterate how important it is to look up unfamiliar words and phrases throughout the semester. Building Your Word Power can be used as quizzes before opening up a class discussion of the essay to ensure that all students become accustomed to looking up unfamiliar terms. These questions also stimulate good discussions about connotation, denotation, and tone.

Building Your Critical Thinking Skills

Each of these sections focuses on a different thinking skill—for instance, evaluating sources, making inferences. First there is a brief description of the thinking skill, and then a series of questions focuses in on the skill under consideration. Students then evaluate the reading based on the sources it provides, the inferences they can draw from it, and so on. You might find it useful to dovetail your lecture with the critical thinking skill that follows each reading—talking briefly, for example, about "evaluating sources" (being able to recognize incomplete or unreliable information) before the essay is discussed in class. When students write prior to engaging in class discussion, they are usually better prepared to articulate their ideas. It is best to have students spend ten minutes writing (or doing a focused freewrite) about the thinking skill before initiating class discussion.

Reacting to the Topic: Discussion and Journal Writing

These questions offer fodder for in-class discussion relating to the topic of the reading. You might use these topics for in-class writing opportunities or have students respond to them in their journals, either in class or at home.

Applying Your Skills: Writing Assignments

The six writing assignments included for each reading in the book offer a wide range of topics and modes, from brief personal essays to longer research assignments. The first assignment in each set is for paragraph-length writing, which offers a useful way to initiate students to writing in the mode in a short, accessible format. Because of their brief length, these assignments are ideally suited for in-class exercises. You will also find here at least one Combining Patterns assignment and an Internet Research assignment relating to a topic covered by the reading.

Assigning the Patterns of Development in Part 2

When you focus on Part 2 of the book, you will discover that, as with other parts of the text, these chapters are designed to be flexible. Some instructors cover fewer chapters, but in greater detail. This approach can be effective, helping students see the range of potential that exists within that particular pattern of development. Some instructors cover many of the patterns of development in less detail and assign a larger amount of short papers or assignments during the term.

Another excellent possibility is to pair together or cluster professional and student essays that are related thematically. For instance, an instructor could develop an assignment emphasizing synthesis, using a cluster of readings or a series of related themes throughout the term. If you are interested in organizing your course this way, refer to the thematic table of contents included in *Seeing the Pattern*.

When using Part 2 of the book, you may decide to focus on one or two patterns of development in conjunction with Chapters 1–4. If you are teaching expressive writing, you may want to start off with narration or description. Many instructors like to begin with illustration or classification and division as a way of getting students to organize their thoughts from the very start. You could also assign a limited number of chapters in Part 2 and discuss those in greater detail. It is especially critical early in the term to help students work through the section on writing an essay using the pattern of development. This section appears at the end of the introduction to the mode in Chapters 5–14. With the first one or two essays, you can work with students as a class or in small groups as they develop their essays. Typically, you would work on the prewriting stage in class as journal exercises. Drafting, revising, and editing can be done outside of class or in conjunction with peer review. Most instructors look at a first draft and a revised draft of an essay, but you can also have students do peer reviews of drafts in progress. During this process, you can act as a guide or adviser, but don't feel that you always have to be the authority on writing in the class. You will find that some of your best students are sharp and perceptive in their editing skills and in providing feedback. You can develop any additional questions or comments on the essays in progress that you like, but for consistency you may want to use the specific questions in the revision flow-charts, which are part of the introductions to the mode for each chapter in Part 2.

Using Part 3

Designed in part as a reference for students, you may find it helpful to refer or assign students all or part of this section of the book. If you include research writing in your course, Chapter 15 offers a brief guide to using and evaluating sources along with a comprehensive list of documentation models in MLA style. Chapter 16 provides a unique key to academic success.

If you are using sources in essays, consider scheduling a library orientation before getting started. Spend part of at least one class talking about evaluating sources for use in an academic essay. The sources that a student chooses can have a major impact on the overall quality of the finished essay, especially if only two or three sources are used.

You might want to refer students to Chapter 16, "Keys to Academic Success," in Part 3 early in the term. This chapter gives special attention to study skills, providing practical survival strategies for college work before class, in class, and while studying. It also reinforces necessary study, reading, and work habits that underprepared students need special help with.

Integrating Grammar Coverage into the Course

Consider giving mini-lessons on some major writing errors throughout the term. You may find it useful to review in class the Seven Common Errors to Avoid section in Chapter 4 at the beginning of the term. Also, each of the chapters in Part 2 includes an Editing and Proofreading section that alerts students to common grammatical errors associated with a particular pattern of development. By using these sections individually or in class, you can help strengthen your students' writing skills. A useful collaborative activity is to mark different-colored stars on the top of student essays based on the types of errors they contain, then pair students who have stars that are the same color. This technique allows students to see the same writing errors that they make themselves in another writer's paper. At times, the errors that students regularly overlook in their own writing will be easier to see in another student's paper.

Using Journals in the Course

You can use journals in several ways in conjunction with *Seeing the Pattern*. The Reacting to the Reading: Discussion and Journal Writing questions in Chapters 5–14 are designed to support journal writing. These questions can help you to integrate journal writing into the course in a consistent way. You can also use journal writing with the Focus on the Topic prereading activities in Chapters 5–14. To encourage prewriting, you might consider having students use their journals to develop their ideas for writing. Consider encouraging students to use a loose-leaf binder for a journal so that pages can be added.

Keep in mind that you don't always have to collect all of the journal assignments and preliminary essay work. To reduce the paper load, you can take ten minutes at the end of a class to walk around the room and scan student journals. Also, use peer review for journal entries in connection with student essays. If you do collect journals, you have several options. You can give a Credit/No Credit grade when you check journals every week or two, and a letter grade at two points during the course. If you count the journal as equivalent to an essay, as many instructors do, you might want to grade the journals at two points during the course and average the grades. You should grade the journals periodically so that students will put more effort into them. When they do, they will also realize your emphasis on the development of ideas in preparation for writing an essay. When grading journals, you should focus on students' quantity of entries and focus, but not so much on the quality of their thinking. Try to reward effort and consistency rather than just the detailed insights, which students will learn to develop further as your class proceeds.

Using Computers and Software

Links to Exercise Central are available at www.bedfordstmartins.com/seeingthepattern. This collection of online exercises is the largest available. It is thorough, simple to use, and convenient for you and your students. Exercise Central includes multiple exercise sets at a variety of levels, as well as an interactive reporting feature that guides students to appropriate exercise sets, thus ensuring that their practice time is well spent. Students receive customized, immediate feedback for all of their answers, including an explanation of why they are correct or incorrect—feedback that turns practice into learning experience.

Grammar diagnostic. This diagnostic quiz is provided as a self-study tool. Its purpose is to help students identify which areas of English grammar, usage, style, punctuation, and mechanics they have already mastered but need more practice with. Once students know which topics they need to focus on, they can use the exercise sets in Exercise Central to practice them.

Tracking. Exercise Central makes it simple for students to track their progress and for you to monitor your students' progress and activity. Whenever students sign in, they can check their customized lesson plan to see which topics they have mastered and which exercises they have completed.

Reporting. To simplify the task of course management, the reporting feature of Exercise Central allows you to monitor the progress of individual students or of the class as a whole; if you choose the latter option, you can see the results for a single exercise set or for all exercise sets at once. If you have several classes or sections, you can even set up customized reports that will display results for each class or section separately.

The first time you sign in to Exercise Central as an instructor, you will be asked to register by supplying some information about yourself, your class, and your institution. Once the registration process is complete, you will receive a password by email. When you sign in using this password, you will gain access to the instructor's area of Exercise Central. Complete instructions for using the standard reports and creating customized reports are available at Exercise Central, which you can access at www.bedfordstmartins.com/seeingthepattern. You may want to distribute to your students the following step-by-step instructions for accessing, logging on, and bookmarking the Exercise Central Web site.

A Student's Guide to Accessing Exercise Central in Ten Easy Steps

1. Enter **www.bedfordstmartins.com/seeingthepattern** into the address field of your browser.

2. Click on the **Exercise Central** link.

3. When the welcome screen opens for Exercise Central, click on the **Student** link.

4. Once the login screen opens, **Bookmark** the page.

   For Internet Explorer:
   - Click on **Favorites** on the top bar of the browser screen.
   - Click on **Add to Favorites** in the pull-down menu.
   - When the "Add Favorite" pop-up box appears, type *Exercise Central* in the **Name** field.
   - Click **OK**.

   For Netscape:
   - Click on **Bookmarks** at top of the browser screen, just below the address field.
   - Click on **Add Bookmark** in the pull-down menu.

5. In the first field of the login box, enter your **First Name**.

6. In the second field of the login box, enter your **Last Name**.

7. In the third field of the login box, enter your instructor's email address: _____.

8. In the fourth field of the login box, re-enter your instructor's email address: _____.

9. Click **Start**.

10. Click on **42-Item Diagnostic Quiz** or the appropriate exercise topic your instructor has assigned to begin.

Winding up the Course

As you move into the final weeks and days of your class, you will be slowing down the pace of assignments and essays, but don't allow students to become overly lax. Try to maintain the structured, organized class you started with at the beginning of the term. You will need to stress to students the importance of finishing off the term in a strong manner. Just as the first two weeks are critical for overall success, the last two weeks can definitely make a difference in a student's grade.

Be sure to complete the class evaluations given by your department, division, or academic area. You may also want to request a brief, anonymous evaluation of your own. Try to look for certain patterns or trends, either negative or positive, in determining your overall performance in the class.

If time allows, try to collect final essays before the last week of class. Alternatively, if you collect them on the last day of class, either meet on the assigned finals day or give students a time, date, and location where you will be available to return papers with their final grades. By doing this, you will reduce extra work for yourself during the next term if a student questions a final grade. When you return papers, also give each student an overall assessment of his or her progress in the course. Try to make this final conference a positive experience.

Developing Your Course Plan

When developing a course plan, you need to choose a structure that is appropriate for the level of your students' abilities and the guidelines of your department. You also need to consider the goals of the course. In addition, knowing the length of instruction (ten weeks or fifteen weeks) and the terms (one or two) will help you plan an appropriate course structure.

Writing a Course Syllabus

The syllabus is an important document in the classroom. It is the contract between the instructor and the students as to the topics, policies, and procedures of the course. The syllabus should contain all relevant information pertaining to the course, so that students will know exactly what is expected of them. Likewise, all course-related information such as the instructor's office hours, email address, and phone number should be included, so that students know how and when to get in contact with the instructor. Because the syllabus becomes the "policies and procedures" manual of the course, all pertinent material must be included. The following is a sample syllabus with a course plan for a fifteen-week semester course that includes research.

Sample Syllabus for a One-Semester Course That Includes Research

I. General Information

Course Title: English Composition I   *Course Number:* ENG 161
Prerequisite: English 070 or placement test   *Semester:* Fall
Instructor: John Gillam   *Phone:* (724) 555-7890
Email: gillam@indiana.edu   *Office Hours & Location:* MWF 3–5
English Department offices, Ryan Hall

II. Text

McWhorter, Kathleen T. *Seeing the Pattern.* New York: Bedford/St. Martin's, 2006.

III. Course Description

This course covers the fundamentals of college writing, including the paragraph, the expository essay, and the research essay. Emphasis is placed on developing a coherent thesis, writing concisely and clearly, and adapting one's writing to a particular audience. This course also emphasizes self-editing, mechanics, and grammar. (taken from college catalog)

IV. General Course Objectives

1. The student will learn to write well-organized and well-researched papers.

2. The student will learn to recognize her or his common grammatical mistakes.

3. The student will become familiar with different patterns of expository writing.

4. The student will be able to use several different writing patterns.

V. Specific Course Objectives

1. The student will write papers using the following strategies: illustration, process analysis, classification and division, comparison and contrast, definition, cause and effect, and argumentation.

2. The student will edit and proofread for errors in grammar, punctuation, mechanics, and spelling.

3. The student will be tested on reading comprehension.

4. The student will critically analyze readings that use specific writing strategies.

5. The student will use the Internet as a tool for research.

6. The student will write a research paper using appropriate documentation.

VI. Classroom Procedures

Absences: The student is responsible for attendance. Attendance affects performance, and all students are expected to take part in class discussions and peer-review editing sessions. Each student is expected to be present and is responsible for class notes and assignments. If absent, the student is responsible for arranging an appointment with the instructor to discuss the notes and assignments missed.

Format for papers: Papers must be typed double-spaced using a 12-point font. Be sure to keep a copy of each assignment for yourself.

VII. Disability Statement

If you need to have special arrangements made due to a physical or learning disability, please notify the instructor as soon as possible. (Disclosure of the type of disability is not required.)

VIII. Grading

All papers must be turned in on the due date. Late papers will be lowered one letter grade. No papers will be accepted after the last day of class. Please save all papers in a folder to be collected periodically.

IX. Tentative Schedule

Week of Sept. 5:   Course Introduction
                   Ch. 1 ("A Guide to Active Reading," especially Using a Graphic Organizer)

Week of Sept. 12: Writing Assessments
                   Ch. 2 ("Planning Your Essay," especially Developing and Supporting your Thesis Statement) and Ch. 16 ("Keys to Academic Success")

Week of Sept. 19: Ch. 3 ("Drafting Your Essay")
                   Draft of Essay #1 due

Week of Sept. 26: Ch. 7 ("Illustration") and Ch. 15 ("Finding and Using Sources")
                   Draft of Essay #2 due

Week of Oct. 3:   Ch. 8 ("Process Analysis")
                   Peer review of Essay #1 or #2
                   Revision of Essay #1 or #2 due

Week of Oct. 10: Ch. 8 ("Editing and Proofreading")
                   Final draft of Essay #1 or #2 due

Week of Oct. 17: Ch. 9 ("Comparison and Contrast")
                   Draft of Essay #3 due
                   Peer review of Essay #3

Week of Oct. 24: Ch. 10 ("Classification and Division") and Ch. 15 (*continued,* especially Evaluating Internet Sources)
Draft of Essay #4 due
Peer review of Essay #4
Final draft of Essay #3 due

Week of Oct. 31: Ch. 11 ("Definition")
Draft of Essay #5 due
Peer review of Essay #5
Final draft of Essay #4 due

Week of Nov. 8: Ch. 12 ("Cause and Effect")
Draft of Essay #6 due
Peer review of Essay #6
Final draft of Essay #5 due

Week of Nov. 15: Ch. 13 ("Argumentation") and Ch. 15 (*continued,* especially Avoiding Plagiarism)
Library Orientation
Final draft of Essay #6 due

Week of Nov. 22: Ch. 13 (*continued*) and Part III "Student Resource Guide"
Working thesis and research questions due

Week of Nov. 29: Ch. 13 (*continued*)
Summary and paraphrase due

Week of Dec. 6: Ch. 14 ("Combining Patterns")
Research paper draft due

Week of Dec. 13: Ch. 14 (*continued*)
Peer review of selections from research paper drafts

Week of Dec. 20: Ch. 14 (*continued*)
Final research paper due

Single-Quarter Course Plan

This plan consists of a ten-week quarter including five written essays: one expressive, one informative, and three argumentative. Other essays or chapters can be substituted based on individual preferences.

Week 1   Ch. 1 ("A Guide to Active Reading") and Ch. 2 ("Planning Your Essay")

Week 2   Ch. 3 ("Drafting Your Essay") and Ch. 16 ("Keys to Academic Success")

Week 3   Ch. 5 ("Narration") or Ch. 6 ("Description") and Ch. 4 ("Revising and Editing Your Essay")

Week 4   Ch. 4 (*continued*) and Ch. 12 ("Cause and Effect")

Week 5   Ch. 12 (*continued*)

Week 6   Ch. 13 ("Argumentation")

Week 7   Ch. 13 (*continued*) and Ch. 15 ("Finding and Using Sources")

Week 8   Ch. 14 ("Combining Patterns") and Part III (Student Resource Guide)

Week 9   Ch. 14 (*continued*)

Week 10 Ch. 14 (*continued*)

A Course Plan Based on Expressive Writing

This plan is based on a fifteen-week semester that focuses on writing from personal experience. Students begin by narrating and describing past events. They then move on to writing about current topics and finally to problems and solutions based on field research.

Week 1   Ch. 1 ("A Guide to Active Reading")

Week 2   Ch. 2 ("Planning Your Essay," especially Prewriting to Start the Assignment)

Week 3   Ch. 3 ("Drafting Your Essay") and Ch. 4 ("Revising and Editing Your Essay")

Week 4   Ch. 4 (*continued*) and Ch. 5 ("Narration")

Week 5   Ch. 6 ("Description")

Week 6   Ch. 7 ("Illustration")

Week 7   Ch. 8 ("Process Analysis")

Week 8   Ch. 9 ("Comparison and Contrast")

Week 9   Ch. 9 (*continued*)

Week 10 Ch. 11 ("Definition")

Week 11 Ch. 12 ("Cause and Effect")

Week 12 Ch. 13 ("Argumentation")

Week 13 Ch. 13 (*continued*)

Week 14 Ch. 14 ("Combining Patterns")

Week 15 Ch. 14 (*continued*)

A Course Plan Based on a Thematic Approach

This plan follows the various patterns of writing, from narration to argumentation. Students will learn to follow the various patterns, while reading essays and doing guided assignments based on different writing patterns over a fifteen-week period.

Week 1   Ch. 1 ("A Guide to Active Reading")

Week 2   Ch. 2 ("Planning Your Essay," especially Prewriting to Start the Assignment), and Ch. 16 ("Keys to Academic Success")

Week 3   Ch. 3 ("Drafting Your Essay") and Ch. 4 ("Revising and Editing Your Essay")

Week 4   Ch. 4 (*continued*) and Ch. 1 (*continued,* especially How to Use a Graphic Organizer)

Week 5   Ch. 5 ("Narration")

Week 6   Ch. 6 ("Description")

Week 7   Ch. 7 ("Illustration")

Week 8   Ch. 8 ("Process Analysis")

Week 9   Ch. 9 ("Comparison and Contrast")

Week 10 Ch. 10 ("Classification and Division")

Week 11 Ch. 11 ("Definition")

Week 12 Ch. 12 ("Cause and Effect")

Week 13 Ch. 13 ("Argumentation")

Week 14 Ch. 14 ("Combining Patterns")

Week 15 Ch. 14 (*continued*)

A Course Plan Based on Research Writing

This plan concentrates on the steps involved in research writing. Students will do guided assignments based on different writing patterns while conducting research.

Week 1   Ch. 1 ("A Guide to Active Reading," especially Using a Graphic Organizer)

Week 2   Ch. 2 ("Planning Your Essay," especially Developing and Supporting Your Thesis Statement) and Ch. 16 ("Keys to Academic Success")

Week 3   Ch. 3 ("Drafting Your Essay")

Week 3   Ch. 4 ("Revising and Editing Your Essay")

Week 4   Ch. 7 ("Illustration") and Ch. 15 ("Finding and Using Sources")

Week 5   Ch. 8 ("Process Analysis")

Week 6   Ch. 9 ("Comparison and Contrast")

Week 7   Ch. 10 ("Classification and Division") and Ch. 15 (*continued,* especially Evaluating Internet Sources)

Week 8   Ch. 11 ("Definition")

Week 9   Ch. 12 ("Cause and Effect")

Week 10 Ch. 13 ("Argumentation") and Ch. 15 (*continued,* expecially Avoiding Plagiarism)

Week 11 Ch. 13 (*continued*) and Part III (Student Resource Guide)

Week 12 Ch. 13 (*continued*)

Week 13 Ch. 14 ("Combining Patterns")

Week 14 Ch. 14 (*continued*)

Week 15 Ch. 14 (*continued*)

Helping Underprepared Students Improve Their Skills

The first-year college classroom is continually evolving. Over the years, instructors have welcomed increasing numbers of adult students, ESL students, and minority students. Now instructors are finding growing numbers of underprepared students who lack many of the academic skills that traditional first-year college students possess. This section will describe underprepared students and offer teaching suggestions for helping these students become successful college writers. It will also discuss how to strengthen students' reading and critical thinking skills. Although the discussion must necessarily focus on the academic deficiencies of underprepared students, it is important to point out that these students have as many positive qualities as traditional students. Underprepared students also make substantial and worthwhile contributions to a writing classroom — adding a variety of perspectives, new experiences, and diverse viewpoints.

Identifying the Characteristics of Underprepared Students

Underprepared students are challenging but rewarding. They often require special attention and may learn and think differently from other students. Instructors of underprepared students not only must examine what and how to teach but also must discover new ways to help these students learn.

The accommodations described in this section are not limited to underprepared students. You may find that these strategies will help capable students learn more easily and develop a more positive attitude toward writing instruction.

Identifying Negative Academic Self-Image

Many underprepared students regard themselves as academic failures. Some think they lack the ability to learn and, specifically, the ability to learn to write. Many students think of themselves as unable to achieve or compete in an academic environment. This attitude may be largely a result of numerous failures they have experienced in previous educational settings. Consistent, then, with their past history, they expect little of themselves and may seem negative, defeated, or disengaged even before the course begins.

Designing Instructional Accommodations. Refer students to Chapter 16, "Keys to Academic Success," in Part 3 for advice on improving academic self-image. Try to design assignments, especially initial ones in the term, so that the students experience immediate success. The first opportunity to practice a newly learned skill should also demonstrate success. For example, the first assignment in learning to use descriptive language might involve asking students to write a list of words describing but not naming an interesting object you bring to class. No matter what a student writes, it will be correct, and it will demonstrate to the student that he or she can use descriptive language.

Recognizing Lack of Self-Direction

Underprepared students often lack goals and direction in their pursuit of a college education as well as in the management of their lives. They may have few or no long-term goals; their short-term goals are often unclear and changeable. As a result, these students tend to lack the discipline or focus to attend class, complete assignments, or work independently on long-term projects.

Designing Instructional Accommodations. Refer students to Chapter 16, "Keys to Academic Success," in Part 3 for advice on becoming self-motivated. Make assignments immediate and short-term. Establish clear due dates and supply regular feedback. Distribute a written course syllabus that details all requirements, your grading system, and as many due dates of assignments as possible. Check frequently to be sure that students complete assignments, do homework, and "stay with" the course. For graded essays, it may be helpful if you require students to submit their work at various stages of the writing process so that you can approve their thesis statement and then their first draft, for example.

Distinguishing a Passive Approach to Learning

Partly because of their lack of experience in and success with academic environments, underprepared students often exhibit a passive approach to learning. They seldom ask questions, initiate action, or pursue solutions to academic problems. Instead, they follow procedures as well as they are able to understand them, wait to be told what to do, and take whatever action seems expected. They seldom initiate study plans, seek help from instructors, or ask questions to clarify assignments.

Designing Instructional Accommodations. Refer students to Chapter 16, "Keys to Academic Success," in Part 3 for advice on becoming an active learner. Initiate class discussions and construct collaborative activities that require involvement and problem solving to encourage and shape more active learning. Often a forthright discussion of active versus passive learning characteristics is effective as well. To encourage students to ask questions and to improve their ability to do so, direct students at the beginning of class to write at least two or three questions they hope the course will answer or several statements of what they want to learn.

Coping with Negative Attitudes toward Instructors

Throughout their previous negative educational experiences, many underprepared students have come to associate instructors with unpleasant or uncomfortable learning environments. As a result, students are often closed, unresponsive, or evasive with their instructors.

Designing Instructional Accommodations. Refer students to Chapter 16, "Keys to Academic Success," in Part 3 for advice on communicating with instructors.

Establishing a framework of trust is difficult but necessary. Try to encourage openness, directness, honesty, and patience. Give careful, detailed explanations of course requirements, and listen willingly to students. Once you have established your authority and made sure that there are no behavior problems, you may find it helpful to present yourself as a person who experiences successes and failures just as students do.

Recognizing Lack of Familiarity with College Life and Academic Procedures

More than traditional students, underprepared students are confused and frustrated by the strangeness, formality, and seeming unfriendliness of the academic environment. Many underprepared students are the first in their families or among their friends to attend college; therefore, they lack the advantage of practical advice and support that many students receive from family and peers. They are unfamiliar with class schedules, college policies, and instructors' expectations.

Designing Instructional Accommodations. As a means of establishing trust as well as building familiarity with college life, offer as many practical "how-to-get-around" tips as possible. Also, as events occur on campus, take a few minutes to explain them. For example, when drop-and-add day begins, explain what is going on; when advance registration for the next term begins, alert the class and explain the procedures involved.

Identifying Lack of Time-Management Skills

Many underprepared students may lack the ability to plan and organize their time. Others may be working too many hours at part-time or even full-time jobs, and they may have numerous family responsibilities as well. Some underprepared students — especially those coming directly from high school, where their time is tightly structured — may have difficulty adapting to the relatively unstructured college environment. Underprepared students also tend to have high absentee rates. Their absenteeism is, of course, related to other characteristics such as lack of self-direction and poor time management skills. In addition, many underprepared students are overcommitted. They are working many hours at part- or full-time jobs and have not yet found a balance among family life, work, friends, and academic responsibility.

Designing Instructional Accommodations. Refer students to Chapter 16, "Keys to Academic Success," in Part 3 for advice on time management. You can help students by structuring your course consistently. For example, make essays always due on Fridays and in-chapter exercises always due on Mondays. Make deadlines and due dates clear, distributing them in writing and also announcing them in class. Establish also a clear, firm absence limit. You may have to make exceptions in obvious emergencies, but a firm absence policy is important. Do not accept late papers without penalty, and include a class participation component in your grading system.

Compensating for Lack of Experiential Background

Owing perhaps to inadequate preparation in high school or an immature approach to learning while in high school, underprepared students sometimes lack basic knowledge expected from college freshmen.

Designing Instructional Accommodations. Refer students to Chapter 16, "Keys to Academic Success," in Part 3 for advice on communicating with instructors. The immediate solution is, of course, to fill in gaps of knowledge as they arise by providing needed background information. Point out to the class that glosses added to the professional readings in the text supply information students may need to understand the reading.

Recognizing Avoidance of Reading

Many underprepared students choose not to read, because reading is not their primary method of obtaining information. Some find reading difficult, non-interactive, and time consuming; consequently, a few will try to "get by" without reading assigned essays.

Designing Instructional Accommodations. Refer students to Chapter 16, "Keys to Academic Success," in Part 3 for advice on using a syllabus. To encourage active reading, make sure that you accompany any given reading assignment with an activity that will engage the students and produce tangible results. In the headnote for most essays in the text, for example, students are directed to identify and highlight a particular feature of the essay. Use also the prereading questions before each reading to help focus students on something specific to read for in the essay.

Identifying Lack of Perseverance with Academic Tasks

Some underprepared students have difficulty persevering with lengthy or complicated academic tasks and multi-stage processes. Their goal is to complete a task as quickly as possible; as a result, they tend to jump immediately to the final step. These students, then, may skip prewriting, planning, and organizing their ideas and may begin by writing what they perceive to be a nearly final draft.

Designing Instructional Accommodations. Refer students to Chapter 16, "Keys to Academic Success," in Part 3 for advice on staying focused. Offer incentives for students to work through the writing process. Award a specific number of points for the submission of prewriting and so forth.

Developing Basic Writing Skills

Many underprepared students lack certain basic writing skills. They make errors in sentence structure (especially comma splices, fragments, and run-ons) and in grammar, punctuation, and mechanics. The reasons for these deficiencies are diverse. Some students never learned these basic skills in high school. Others have been out of school and have forgotten standard conventions. Still others are unaware that correctness is important and write carelessly, ignoring conventions.

Valuable instructor and classroom time need not be consumed addressing basic writing problems since students can learn to correct their own problems by using Exercise Central (p. 16).

Using the "Editing and Proofreading" Section in Chapter 4

This section of Chapter 4 includes writing instruction designed to explain basic rules and principles of grammar, punctuation, mechanics, and spelling in a straightforward, nontechnical manner. Numerous hand-edited examples are provided to assist students who learn better by studying examples than by reading rules. Exercises are also included to help students determine whether they understand and can apply each rule or principle.

Using Exercise Central

Exercise Central is an extensive bank of exercises on a variety of topics in grammar, punctuation, and mechanics. Students who need further practice on a given problem can access additional exercises at www.bedfordstmartins.com/seeingthepattern. A more detailed description of Exercise Central appears on page 16 of this manual.

Strengthening Students' Reading Skills

Many underprepared students do not read at the college level. As a result, they find assigned textbooks and essays challenging and sometimes frustrating. To assist such students, *Seeing the Pattern* contains numerous features to guide students through essays in the text, while providing them with skills and strategies for improving their reading skills. Numerous tables, flowcharts, bulleted lists, and diagrams both emphasize and condense important information.

Chapter 1 ("A Guide to Active Reading") provides a framework for improving students' reading skills. It dispels misconceptions students may hold about reading, presents a step-by-step guide to reading actively, and offers suggestions for understanding difficult text. This chapter can be taught in class, assigned for students to work through independently, or assigned selectively to students who demonstrate reading problems. Chapter 15 ("Finding and Using Sources") also provides useful information on reading critically.

Building Active Reading Strategies

Many students are passive readers; they do not interact with the ideas they read, and they fail to make connections between the ideas presented in the text and their own knowledge and experience on the topic. They accept ideas rather than question and evaluate them. Further, they do not monitor their comprehension or initiate strategies that will improve it. Unless directed to do so, many students do not preview before reading; highlight as they read; or review, synthesize, or summarize after they read. The section How to Read Actively in Chapter 1 offers students a step-by-step process for approaching a reading assignment. They learn to preview before reading, activate background knowledge, establish a purpose for reading, read with an intent, highlight and annotate, and review after reading. This guide can be applied to all essays in the text as well as to readings or textbook assignments in other academic courses. In fact, the process is a variation of the well-known SQ3R system, developed by Francis P. Robinson in 1961 and used ever since as a means of strengthening both reading and recall of expository text. Encourage students to use the five active reading strategies in all of their academic coursework.

The text contains several other features that promote active reading. Headnotes and prereading questions that accompany readings direct students to search for a particular element or apply specific skills. In each chapter, students are directed to draw a graphic organizer of at least one of the chapter readings, thereby encouraging the application of active reading strategies. Chapters 6–14 offer specific suggestions for reading essays based on each method of development, showing students how to adapt and apply the active reading strategies to specific types of reading materials. In these chapters, three of the seven types of questions (Understanding the Reading, Visualizing the Reading, and Examining the Characteristics of [Narration] Essays) that follow the readings enable students to evaluate their reading strategies and guide them in analyzing the essay.

Using Graphic Organizers

Many underprepared students have difficulty recognizing the organization and overall structure of what they read. They fail to see how ideas within the text connect and develop. Since material that is perceived as organized is easier to recall than that which is not, these students often have difficulty remembering what they read. Graphic organizers diagram these relationships *visually*, creating a meaningful conceptual framework that allows underprepared students to recognize patterns within the text. (For more on graphic organizers, see p. 9 of this manual.)

Strengthening Vocabulary Skills

Underprepared students often need to improve their vocabulary as well as their comprehension. The essays in *Seeing the Pattern* offer ample opportunity. Many of the essays contain words that may be vaguely familiar to students but are not part of their speech or writing. In many essays, glosses are provided for terms and references that are likely to be unfamiliar. Building Your Word Power questions following each reading have students analyze the use of language and require them to define vocabulary words from the reading, thus placing a continuing emphasis on vocabulary development. Here are a few suggestions for helping students improve their vocabulary.

1. Encourage students to develop a word awareness. You can do this by bringing to their attention a particularly well-chosen word, an apt phrase, or a high-impact word as you discuss professional essays in the text.

2. As you read student essays, mark a place or two where a more forceful or more descriptive word or phrase is needed.

3. Encourage students to keep a computer file or notebook of new words they want to begin to use in their own writing or speech.

4. Show students how to figure out the meanings of words from context clues. A few quick examples from one of the chapter essays is often sufficient to get them started.

5. Refer students with serious vocabulary problems to the college's academic skills center for further instruction.

Fostering Critical Reading and Thinking

Underprepared students often lack critical reading and thinking skills. They accept a writer's ideas at face value and fail to interpret, evaluate, and react to ideas. *Seeing the*

Pattern promotes critical thinking and reading in several ways. The readings in chapters 5–14 include Building Your Critical Thinking Skills questions that introduce students to important critical thinking concepts, such as tone, evaluating sources, and bias. Students must then apply this skill to the essay they have just read. The chapter apparatus also includes a Reacting to the Reading section that guides students in developing a critical response to each reading.

You can promote critical thinking in the classroom in the following ways.

1. Establish an open environment in which students are welcome to ask serious questions freely at appropriate times.

2. Serve as a role model. Ask critical questions often and encourage students to explore them with you.

3. Correct the misguided notion that critical thinking means only to find fault and that it emphasizes the negative.

4. Use a problem-solving paradigm to teach critical thinking. Use daily classroom problems, such as a fire drill that results in the class missing a scheduled in-class revision workshop, to guide students through the stages of (1) gathering information, (2) defining the problem, (3) identifying possible solutions, (4) evaluating solution paths, and (5) making a decision.

5. Require generalization. Give students practice in seeing how a specific writing skill can apply to a wide range of situations. Ask the class, for example, when a narrative might be useful in workplace settings, or in what college courses comparison and contrast might commonly be used.

Works Cited

Ausubel, David P. *Educational Psychology: A Cognitive View.* New York: Holt, 1968.
Robinson, Francis P. *Effective Study.* New York: Harper, 1961.

Teaching Tips and Suggested Answers for Individual Chapters in *Seeing the Pattern*

Part 1: Skills for Success in Reading and Writing

Part 1 is a guide to active reading and writing and provides a broad overview of the relationship between the two. Because this is a subject that students may initially consider unnecessary and simplistic, it may be challenging to help them to recognize how important it is to re-learn or refine their previous understanding of what it means to "read" an essay and to "write a good paper." Therefore, you will probably find it helpful to devote several class sessions at the start of the term to Part 1 of *Seeing the Pattern* in order to dissuade students from the idea that they can simply go on reading texts and writing papers exactly as they did in high school. Although you may at first encounter resistance to the idea that they need to re-learn how to read an essay and write and revise their papers, over time, as their writing improves, first-year students will begin to appreciate the writing and reading skills they develop in your introductory class.

CHAPTER 1 A Guide to Active Reading, p. 3

Chapter 1 is devoted to the idea of "active reading," also called close or critical reading. It is important to establish the connection between reading and writing critically early in the semester. If you take the time early on to reinforce the idea that analytical reading and writing are closely related, your students' ability to read, think, and write critically will develop more readily over the course of the semester. You may find it especially worthwhile to devote some class time to the concept of critical thinking, emphasizing that college-level writing depends upon the ability to analyze readings and to support opinions with evidence from a text (or texts). The section entitled Changing Some Misconceptions about Reading on page 4 is a good way to open up a discussion of critical thinking. This kind of discussion will help your students understand that they are being asked to engage in a new level of scholarly thinking.

Before giving the first reading assignment, you should review the Strategies for Reading (p. 5) with your students. This section outlines five active reading strategies that you may want to encourage your students to follow on a regular basis. You might, for example, want to go through the seven Guidelines for Previewing (p. 6) aloud with your students to show them how to "preview" the essays you assign in class. One way to make use of this feature would be to go down the list with them, asking them what kind of information a reader can glean from each of the previewing suggestions listed. To reinforce the usefulness of these techniques, you might also want to use the list in conjunction with the annotated essay by Etta Kralovec, "No More Pep Rallies!" (p. 7). Encourage your students to go through the previewing steps for every assigned reading throughout the semester.

Many first-year students simply do not understand why they should highlight key points (p. 10) and annotate their impressions (p. 10), or why they need to look up and remember the meaning of unfamiliar vocabulary words (p. 21). Remind them that college-level courses require a new kind of reading and that rereading or "reviewing" (p. 11) will foster a more sophisticated level of thinking. You might want to ask them to show you their copy of *Seeing the Pattern* at the beginning of the first few classes after you have discussed highlighting and annotating. Observe whether or not they are underscoring and writing in the margins. If you are still not seeing much annotation, remind them of what you would like to see. You might want to show them your own text, which is undoubtedly marked up, as an example of what you expect to see. Once they are highlighting and annotating their texts, ask them to share a word or idea they underscored (or questioned) with the class. Ask them to explain why they marked it and what they learned from doing so.

Another important concept that you may wish to introduce to your students is the idea that a text can be looked at visually, *before being read,* as if it were an object. Surprisingly enough, many students are completely unaware of the meaning of "key elements" (pp. 9–10) such as headings and type size or font differences. Point out that design and the textual formatting of titles, headnotes, headings, subheadings, and so on indicates various kinds or levels of headings. For example, "No More Pep Rallies!" (p. 7) uses highlighting and annotations to visually show the parts to look for when previewing a text. This essay can be used to show students how to apply the active reading strategies explained in the chapter. Let students know that you will be questioning them about or asking them to identify key elements, such as thesis statements, in every reading you assign during the semester.

Because all students will at some point encounter texts that are difficult to understand, it is a good idea to show them the table titled Difficult Readings: Specific Problems and Strategies for Solving Them (p. 12). Explain how they can use this table to identify the problem they are having (in the left-hand column) and then find strategies for reading and comprehension to address this difficulty (in the right-hand column).

You may want to go over the section Using a Graphic Organizer (p. 13) carefully, as these visual representations of an essay's content and structure are used throughout *Seeing the Pattern.* Many students find graphic organizers very helpful for identifying the flow of ideas in an essay. The graphic organizer is also a useful device for slowing down a student's pace as he or she reads a text. Identifying the thesis statement and other key aspects of the essay and seeing them arranged visually into sections may help students who have difficulty understanding how a text is organized. As they fill in the boxes, they can visualize the text in a new way, organized into parts: *introduction,* with background material and thesis; *body,* with topic sentences and key details; and *conclusion,* with restatement of thesis. By learning to slow down, reread, and pick apart a reading in order to fill out the graphic organizer, students will eventually find themselves able to structure and revise their own writing with greater ease.

Finally, if you plan to have your students work with the visuals included in *Seeing the Pattern* or in other texts, you may want to take a little time to discuss Reading Visuals (p. 18). Students are generally comfortable with and eager to discuss visuals but may have given little thought to how to think critically about them. As an in-class exercise, you may ask students to apply the Five Questions to Ask about Visuals to an image that appears with one of the readings in this text or elsewhere.

Chapter 2 Planning Your Essay, p. 23

Chapter 2 gives an overview of different prewriting strategies and then explains how to use these techniques in order to develop and support a thesis statement. Many students consider prewriting a pointless exercise, preferring instead to write a single draft in just one sitting—something that they often did in high school. In order to prevent this tendency to skip the preliminary phases of developing an essay, you may want to assign papers in a step-by-step fashion. Ask students to hand in their papers, phase by phase, over a period of weeks. For example, you might ask them to hand in their freewriting first, followed by any notes they jotted down, their narrowed topic, thesis statement, outline, first draft, and so on. Reiterating the advantages of using this technique throughout the semester will increase students' willingness to employ prewriting and will result in more carefully thought out and executed essays.

This chapter addresses many of the aspects of the first draft that cause students difficulty, including considering audience and tone. The two examples shown on page 27 of a student writing about an orientation session, first to a friend and then in the school newspaper, illustrate vividly how tone is transformed by the idea of audience. You may find it useful to assign Exercise 2.1 to help students discern the often subtle differences in tone and point of view, depending upon their audience. First-year students often have difficulty with the idea of "audience," asking what is meant by it since the only person who is going to see their writing is you, the instructor. You may need to review this topic over several class periods, explaining that it is necessary to assume that the audience needs some background even if they are familiar with the subject. It is often worthwhile to generate some discussion about this idea, experimenting with various audiences, from journal writing to freewriting that will be read aloud in class.

Learning to narrow down a topic is another skill that first-year students tend to have difficulty with. Exercises 2.4 (p. 32) and 2.5 (p. 33) can be used in class to give students practice in setting the parameters of paper topics. Once they've developed an understanding of how to successfully narrow and define a topic, they will be ready to move on to the thesis statement, one of the most difficult of all concepts to teach. Be prepared to show your students how to refine their thesis statements throughout the term. Tools on thesis development included in *Seeing the Pattern* that you may find especially useful include the list of Guidelines for Writing a Thesis Statement (pp. 38–39) and Exercise 2.8 (p. 39), which will help your students work toward a better understanding of what makes an effective thesis statement. Explain, too, that although many of the professional writers whose work appears in this text use "implied" thesis statements, it is best to begin by perfecting the explicit thesis statement (p. 39).

Chapter 3 Drafting Your Essay, p. 47

Chapter 3 explains how to outline and organize a first draft, beginning with a clear method of organization. As an introduction to this topic, you may want to refer students to the graphic organizer on The Structure of an Essay: Parts and Functions included at the start of the chapter (p. 49). Students may better grasp this subject if they work through a draft of their own using the Essay in Progress exercises included in this chapter. By applying the various stages of drafting an essay to writing of their own, students will better see how important an organizational plan is to the development of their essay.

By using the examples from the student essay discussed in this chapter, "The Value of Volunteering," your students can observe three different ways to develop their ideas: using an informal outline (p. 51), preparing a formal topic outline (p. 51), and creating a graphic organizer (p. 52). You may find it helpful to have the students create an outline or graphic organizer for all of the writing they do for the course. By requiring this step, you give students the opportunity to review and make changes to the organizational plan for their essay before they begin drafting it.

Once your students understand the importance of developing an organizational plan, they are ready to begin drafting their essay. Their writing will likely be strengthened if you spend some time in class working through the section on Writing Effective Paragraphs (p. 54). This section begins with a discussion on What Well-Focused Topic Sentences Must Do (p. 54). Mention to your students how closely the purpose of a topic sentence relates to that of a thesis statement. The list of Guidelines for Writing Topic Sentences on pages 55–56 can serve as a useful guide for students as they draft paragraphs for their essays, and the list of Guidelines for Writing Specific Paragraphs on page 58 will be of use in coaxing students to develop paragraphs that are more specific and interesting. Finally, in order to show students how to link their ideas within and between paragraphs, you should spend a little time discussing Connecting Supporting Details with Transitions and Repetition (p. 59). Commonly Used Transitional Expressions (p. 60) offers a handy list that will help your students' writing flow more clearly from topic to topic.

You will probably want to review the structure of an essay throughout the term, letting students work in pairs or small groups to evaluate their own writing on a regular basis. The Guidelines for writing effective introductions and conclusions (pp. 61–62 and 63–64) are especially useful tools; you will likely refer students to this material over the course of the term as needed. Knowing that other students will be reading their writing motivates students to write well, so you may want to devote some class time every week to peer review. Remember that what seems obvious to you, such as the function of a title (to "announce your subject" and "spark readers' interest"; pp. 64–65), often needs to be explicitly pointed out to first-year students. Even after you have done so, their titles may remain generic and vague (for instance, "Red States versus Blue States: A Comparison and Contrast Paper") for the first few weeks. Refer to the list of Five Tips for Writing Effective Titles (p. 000) over and over, and have students evaluate each other's titles in pairs, until you see results.

Chapter 4 Revising and Editing Your Essay, p. 70

Chapter 4 provides an overview of the revising and editing process. The revision process is one of the most difficult of all phases to explain to beginning students. Many of them simply do not understand what revision entails, no matter how many revision checklists you give them. Even if you assign first and second drafts, they will often only make whatever changes you explicitly marked on their copy. It is important, therefore, to stress early on the importance of revision. You may need to remind your students, over and over, what editing entails. Remind them that most professional writers edit their own work through countless drafts, even before submitting it to a professional editor, who then edits it yet again. As way of example, you might explain to the class the steps that you take to revise your own writing. It may be more real for students if they understand that all writers work through multiple drafts before finalizing a piece of writing.

Encourage students to visit you during office hours to discuss their drafts, or if time allows, set aside time in class to meet with students individually to discuss their drafts and how they might be improved. In addition, you might use peer review (p. 75). Go over the Peer Review Questions (p. 76) so that each student understands her or his responsibility as a critic and what elements to evaluate. Engaging students in an active discussion about their writing can open up their minds to a more critical evaluation of the strengths and weaknesses of their work, leading to stronger revisions.

You will probably find it helpful to have students apply the skills in this chapter to their own writing by using the Essay in Progress activities included throughout this chapter. You may also want to have students apply the Questions to Ask as You Revise (p. 71) to all of the writing that they do in the class. These questions will make the process of revision clearer and more enjoyable for them. Other useful tools include the revision flowcharts Evaluating Your Thesis Statement, Topic Sentences, and Evidence (pp. 73–74) and Evaluating Your Paragraphs (pp. 74–75). These visual features walk the students through the process of revision, step by step. It breaks the process of revision down to a series of parts and helps them to see, for example, that they can add in "transitional words" or "transitional sentences" (p. 118) if they forgot to insert them earlier.

This chapter also addresses the idea that revision means making one's sentences more concise, clear, and beautiful. Using the lists Improving Your Sentences (p. 77) and Improving Your Word Choice (p. 79), alone or in pairs, students can improve their work at the sentence level while creating interesting and lively writing. They can also begin to address common grammatical issues, comparing their work against the Common Errors to Avoid (p. 81). If particular issues need attention (for instance, confusing shifts), either on an individual level or by the entire class, you might want to assign other grammatical exercises in addition to those provided in this book. One resource for supplemental exercises is Exercise Central at www.bedfordstmartins.com/seeingthepattern. Gradually, as students grow accustomed to revising their work and studying lists like the Common Errors included here, they will begin to recognize their own mistakes. They will also begin to catch their errors more quickly in the revision process.

Part 2: Readings for Writers

Chapter 5 Narration: Recounting Events, p. 93

The narrative essay is usually familiar to most first-year college students because it involves storytelling of the kind they hear every day. You might want to begin with a definition of *narration,* that is, a story that makes a point. When presented as a story, the narrative essay becomes much more accessible to students who are apprehensive about expository writing. Another way to explain a narrative is to see it as an answer to the question, "What happened?" You will want to emphasize that creating a story is not just a matter of saying, "This happened, then that happened." Every narrative needs to be propelled by a strong narrative line. The narrator (or story teller) uses language to shape the narrative or tell the story in the most effective way. Pacing and point of view are important. The writer must leave out irrelevant details and organize the narrative to best effect (chronologically, spatially, or otherwise). Stress also that while a narrative is essentially a story, it is also a story that makes a point. This point is crucial because students will need to make a point in their own narratives through the use of a clear thesis statement.

This chapter includes a wide range of narratives. The annotated essay, "Right Place, Wrong Face" by Alton Fitzgerald White (p. 94) recounts events in a straightforward, chronological way — the tension mounts as readers see the author's belief in the justice system being dashed. Sherry Amatenstein's narrative, "Talking a Stranger through the Night" (p. 112), sets up tension through the use of foreshadowing when she prays not to get a suicide caller as she mans a crisis hotline in New York City. When the call comes in, she then finds herself absorbed in making sure that the caller wants to live. Although the phone call takes hours, the author selects only those lines of dialogue that are crucial to the reader's sense of the progress being made. The tension is based on the question in the reader's mind, "Will the suicide caller stay on the line or hang up and kill herself?"

Amy Tan's "Fish Cheeks" (p. 118), Langston Hughes's "Salvation" (p. 122), and Cherokee Paul McDonald's "A View from the Bridge" (p. 127) are all tightly woven sketches that employ key moments and key lines of dialogue to further the action and heighten the tension. Each piece is written in straightforward chronology (alternating summation and action), and each uses vivid sensory details to make the story come alive. Toni Cade Bambara's "The Lesson" (p. 133) is a short story that relies heavily upon colloquial language to reveal character, contrast races and classes, suggest emotion, and further the action. All of these readings offer models of narration that students can emulate in their own writing.

Alton Fitzgerald White, "Right Place, Wrong Face," p. 94

Alton Fitzgerald White, a young, successful black actor who lives in Harlem, is arrested as a suspect when the police respond to a call describing "young Hispanics with guns" (para. 6). Ironically, at the time of the story White is playing the part of Coalhouse Walker Jr.—a black man who is similarly abused—in the Broadway play *Ragtime,* yet the event takes White by surprise and causes him to lose faith in the justice system. He had naively expected to be treated with "consideration" (2) by the police.

In opening up a discussion about this essay, you might ask students about their knowledge of New York City, especially Harlem and mid-town Manhattan where White works. For background, be sure to point out that although Harlem has a reputation for being dangerous, it has many safe neighborhoods for black middle-class professionals, such as the neighborhood White lives in. You might want to initiate a discussion about situations in which black men are wrongly considered suspects by police officers. This scenario is one that is documented and well known in the black community; most black men are warned early that such a thing might happen in their lifetime. You might want to discuss the reasons that White identifies himself not as black but simply as an actor from Cleveland, Ohio, who was raised to be a "gentleman" (1) and to have "manners" (2).

As you work through the section on Characteristics of Narrative Essays (p. 97), you might return again to the White essay. The annotations clearly mark the points of conflict, tension, and climax and other narrative techniques used by White. You might have students add additional annotations of their own to mark notable passages of dialogue and physical description as well as events that build suspense and further the narrative.

Aphonetip Vasavong, "You Can Count on Miracles," p. 108

This student essay tells the story of a crucial moment in Aphonetip Vasavong's life. The dramatic story of her family's escape from political persecution in Laos has all the elements of a good narrative. Because her family must leave secretly, at night, without telling their neighbors where they are going, the conflict is dramatic. When eight-year-old Vasavong gets lost in the woods but cannot risk calling out for help, a rabbit appears suddenly to "lead" (para. 6) her to her family. The rabbit's mysterious assistance lends Vasavong's story an almost mythological quality. Students will no doubt enjoy analyzing this narrative since it is a real-life story that could, perhaps, have been told with even greater skill. It might be useful to assign students to break into small groups to rewrite the story so that it has maximum impact. Tell them that they can fictionalize, adding in details such as active verbs, dialogue, and sensory details (especially sounds). Instruct them to try to maintain Vasavong's voice and basic story line. Have them rewrite the ending so that it has greater impact.

Responding to "Students Write," p. 108

1. Students are likely to have different views on the effectiveness of Vasavong's thesis. While overall Vasavong's essay presents a strong narrative, her thesis is not very effective, sounding almost like a cliché. Encourage students to revise this thesis into a more meaningful statement that makes a clearer point about the events of the essay.

2. The author doesn't really elaborate on the idea of "coincidences that are so unusual and meaningful that they could not have happened by chance alone" put forth in the first sentence. Given the prominence of this point at the start of the essay, students may note that idea could be expanded upon. Because most students are likely to be unfamiliar with the situation in Cambodia during the 1980s, more historical and background details about Laos and the Communist regime would have been helpful. Still other students might ask why an eight-year-old girl would be left at the end of the line. Wouldn't an adult or older child be put there to make sure that everyone was safe?

3. Most students are likely to say that Vasavong very effectively establishes conflict and creates tension. To move beyond this, have students identify how she creates tension and encourage them to identify any points in the essay where points of tension and conflict could be improved.

4. Vasavong uses foreshadowing with the mention of the rabbit in the first paragraph. Because this use of foreshadowing is related to the essay's thesis, you might want to link this discussion to that of question 1.

5. To encourage critical analysis of the title, introduction, and conclusion, refer students to the relevant sections of Chapter 3 that explain the Do's and Don'ts of writing effective titles, introductions, and conclusions. While answers will vary, most students will probably agree that the title is satisfactory because it conveys the author's belief that the rabbit guiding her way was a kind of miracle. Likewise, students are likely to agree that the introduction is good because it foreshadows the rabbit's part in the story. The conclusion, however, is somewhat weak because Vasavong does not adequately explore the meaning of the rabbit leading her to safety not being "attributed to chance alone" (para. 6). In analyzing the conclusion, encourage students to reflect again on the essay's thesis and how the thesis and conclusion might have been strengthened by a more clearly stated point about Vasavong experiences.

Sherry Amatenstein, "Talking a Stranger through the Night," p. 112

Amatenstein's narrative vividly establishes how the events of a single night spent staffing a crisis hotline changed her view of the world. The first two nights quickly diminish the author's idealism as she deals with problem callers, one after another. Then, on the third night, a dreaded suicide call comes in, after only a brief training session on how to handle such emergencies. Several hours later, Amatenstein has successfully calmed the caller's fears and possibly averted a suicide. After she hangs up, Amatenstein realizes how the process of helping the suicide caller made her feel more connected to the human community, a moment of true epiphany for her.

In discussing this essay, you might want to provide some background information about the issue of suicide and how it is prevented or addressed by psychologists and others. A discussion about volunteering or helping those less fortunate, and where such altruism fits into our culture, might also be useful. Ask students to share their experiences volunteering and how their expectations were met or foiled. In particular, ask if any of them want to share an experience in which helping someone else helped them as well.

Understanding the Reading, p. 114

1. Amatenstein reveals that she is the child of Holocaust survivors and has always wanted to "ease other people's pain," especially after 9/11 (para. 1).

2. She receives calls from "men who wanted to masturbate," "repeats" who called over and over again to relate their "horrific childhoods," and callers who "railed" or were "abusive" if she wouldn't give them advice (3). These early conversations made Amatenstein less idealistic about her work at the crisis hotline and less sympathetic toward the people calling.

3. Examples of how the author was helpful to Sandy, the suicide caller, include: the caller was able to think of "an interest in books on spirituality" (8), which gave her pleasure; she kept talking for two hours even though her throat hurt from crying (8–10); after hearing Amatenstein read a prayer, Sandy said she thought she'd be all right for the night (10); and she asked about when the narrator would be staffing again (11).

4. Amatenstein learned that because she herself had been feeling lonely "[d]espite having people in my life" (13), the experience with Sandy meant just as much to her as it did to Sandy. Through this experience the author learned that connecting with "another troubled soul in New York City" (13) was of greater value than the material comforts of her own life.

Visualizing the Reading, p. 115

Possible answers include:

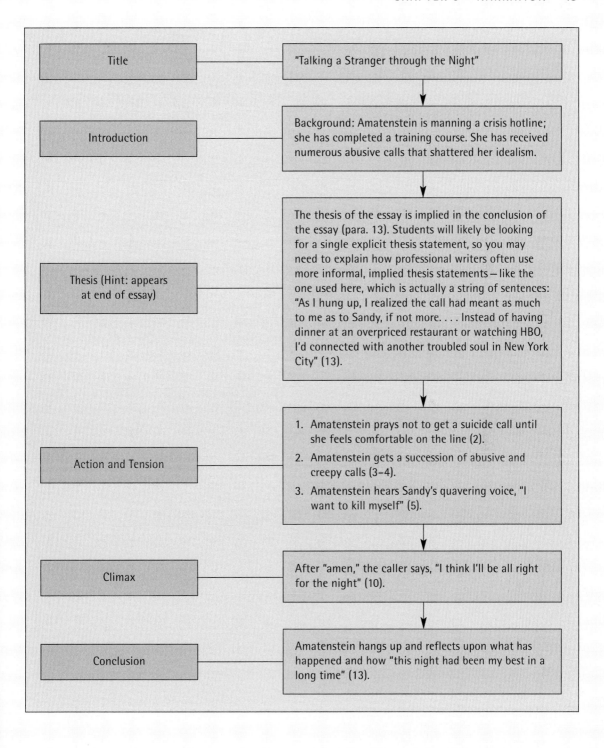

Title	"Talking a Stranger through the Night"
Introduction	Background: Amatenstein is manning a crisis hotline; she has completed a training course. She has received numerous abusive calls that shattered her idealism.
Thesis (Hint: appears at end of essay)	The thesis of the essay is implied in the conclusion of the essay (para. 13). Students will likely be looking for a single explicit thesis statement, so you may need to explain how professional writers often use more informal, implied thesis statements—like the one used here, which is actually a string of sentences: "As I hung up, I realized the call had meant as much to me as to Sandy, if not more. . . . Instead of having dinner at an overpriced restaurant or watching HBO, I'd connected with another troubled soul in New York City" (13).
Action and Tension	1. Amatenstein prays not to get a suicide call until she feels comfortable on the line (2). 2. Amatenstein gets a succession of abusive and creepy calls (3–4). 3. Amatenstein hears Sandy's quavering voice, "I want to kill myself" (5).
Climax	After "amen," the caller says, "I think I'll be all right for the night" (10).
Conclusion	Amatenstein hangs up and reflects upon what has happened and how "this night had been my best in a long time" (13).

Examining the Characteristics of Narrative Essays, p. 114

1. Amatenstein's dialogue is crucial to the narrative, a point that will likely be clear to most students. She uses it sparingly for effect. The first line of dialogue is the suicide caller's voice, and thereafter every statement is selectively chosen to heighten tension. The next few lines are either the suicide caller or the narrator trying to draw her out, trying to help her remember reasons why she might want to live. The resulting effect is one of tension that draws readers in as they read on to discover the fate of the suicide caller.

2. Amatenstin includes sensory details: the taste of peanuts, the sight and sound of the "Oprah" show, the smell of leaves (para. 10). The author likely chose to include these because they are familiar details that most readers can relate to, that remind them of the simple joys of life. The details contribute to the narrative because they personalize Sandy while showing how the narrator reaches out toward her over the course of their conversation.

3. The main narrative technique that the author uses to make readers care about the suicide caller is the use of key lines of dialogue. Amatenstein also recounts the tragic events in Sandy's life: her parents disowned her, she had a bone-crushing fall and then was hit by a cab, and her boyfriend died of cancer (5–6). And the author includes physical description such as: "Sandy's . . . quavering voice" (5), "Since she was handicapped, she couldn't even walk to her window to jump out" (5), and "Now she was in constant pain" (6). Students are likely to cite the narrative techniques of dialogue, recounting events, and first-person point of view as tools that Amatenstein uses to draw readers into the story about Sandy. The author also builds and creates tension through the use of foreshadowing. At the start of the essay, she notes: "I prayed I wouldn't get [a suicide call]" (2). Through this technique, she establishes a conflict: the threat of suicide. The tension is sustained by the question of whether the suicide caller will stay on the phone long enough to change her mind.

4. The implied thesis is effective because it makes a clear point about what the experience of aiding Sandy meant to the author. The use of an implied thesis statement at the end is more satisfying because it is less predictable than an explicit thesis placed early in the essay.

5. Students are likely to find the conclusion satisfying because it has an element of surprise. While Amatenstein had hinted earlier in the essay about her own loneliness, the clear connection that she draws in the conclusion between her own troubles and that of a stranger make for a moving and satisfying conclusion.

Building Your Word Power, p. 115

1. The picture created by the simile "I tossed life-affirming statements at her like paint on a canvas" (para. 7) is that of a splattered abstract expressionist painting.

To help students who are having trouble with this simile, you might want to show them a picture of a painting done by an abstract expressionist like Jackson Pollack.

2. To "fan the spark" (7) means to blow on a coal or ember to make a fire burn brighter.

Building Your Critical Thinking Skills: Inferences, p. 116

1. The events of September 11 might have made the author appreciate all the help New Yorkers gave each other in the wake of the disaster. Being a New Yorker herself, September 11 might also have made Amatenstein think more about how community is strengthened when people help one another in an emergency.

2. One can infer that the author's parents experienced a lot of emotional suffering that she witnessed but was unable to alleviate as a child.

3. The author, a journalist, has a network of friends, family, and colleagues in the city but still finds New York "isolating" (para. 4) and "lonely" (13). A possible inference that students might make regarding Amatenstein's comment in paragraph 13 about eating in an "overpriced restaurant" is that the narrator finds her life in New York to be superficial.

Amy Tan, "Fish Cheeks," p. 118

Amy Tan is best known for *The Joy Luck Club* (1989), a novel about four Chinese American mother-daughter relationships. In "Fish Cheeks," she sketches a brief autobiographical scenario full of conflict. As a teenager, Tan is apprehensive about her family's Chinese customs and ethnic foods when her mother invites to dinner a white boy Tan has a crush on. Tan's shame prevents her from recognizing that her mother has served Tan's favorite foods, including fish cheeks, at what her mother no doubt sees as a special occasion for her daughter.

You may find it useful to break the class into small groups to discuss American cultural norms and how notions of the "melting pot" and ethnic differences fit into the American ideal. Have each group report back to the class about their findings. You might also have students freewrite about their own family's unique customs. Be sure to emphasize the need to respect other cultures and to recognize that even though some cultural groups are more assimilated than others, every ethnic group in America (including those descended from the pilgrims) has its own unique practices and traditions.

Understanding the Reading, p. 119

1. Tan is upset because she is worried about what Robert will think of "our shabby Chinese Christmas" (para. 2). She thinks that he will see her in an exoticized

Chinese context, in which her relatives will seem "noisy" (2) and ill mannered by American standards and the food will seem disappointingly un-American.

2. Students are likely to have different notions about why Tan's mother chose to serve a traditional Chinese menu. One possibility suggested by the text is that she wanted to teach her daughter a lesson about not being ashamed of her Chinese heritage. In paragraph 7, Tan's mother states this clearly when she says, "You want to be the same as American girls on the outside. . . . But inside you must always be Chinese. You must be proud you are different." The other possibility suggested in paragraph 8 is that her mother chose a Chinese menu full of Tan's "favorite foods" in order to make Tan happy while treating their guests to an authentic Chinese meal.

3. In paragraphs 5 and 6, the minister and his family respond in the ways that Tan predicted in terms of not understanding the different Chinese customs associated with food (such as helping oneself to communal dishes while using one's own chopsticks rather than waiting for food to be passed, in accordance with American etiquette [5]). The son, Robert, grimaces when he sees a whole fish replete with eyes (5); Robert is embarrassed when Tan's father burps in order to be polite and explains about the "Chinese custom to show you are satisfied" (6); and Robert's father, the minister, then manages "to muster up a quiet burp" (6).

4. The author comes to realize years later that she was so ashamed of being Chinese that she did not even recognize that the dishes on the table that night were her "favorite foods" (8). She had so desired to be identified with American customs and values that she overlooked the importance of her Chinese heritage. In maturity, Tan is able to appreciate her mother's "lesson" (8) and how important it is to be proud of being different.

Visualizing the Reading, p. 120

Possible answers include:

Narrative Characteristic	Examples
Makes a point or thesis	Implied: Tan learned to be proud of her Chinese heritage.
Uses dialogue	1. "Amy, your favorite" (para. 5) 2. "It's a polite Chinese custom to show you are satisfied" (6). 3. "You want to be the same as American girls on the outside. . . . But inside you must always be Chinese" (7).

Includes sensory details	"slim new American nose" (1); "shabby Chinese Christmas" (2); "noisy Chinese relatives" (2); "pulling black veins out of the backs of fleshy prawns" (3); "[a] slimy rock cod with bulging eyes" (3); "licked the ends of their chopsticks" (5); "belched loudly" (6)
Recounts action	1. Mother preparing the meal (3) 2. The arrival of the minister's family (4) 3. The dinner, ending with the shameful burping episode (5–6) 4. Tan's gift from her mother along with her lesson (7)
Builds tension	Tension builds over the course of the essay as Tan's shame and embarrassment intensify. Examples from the text include: "What would Robert think of our shabby Chinese Christmas?" (2); "I saw that my mother had outdone herself in creating a strange menu" (3); "Dinner threw me deeper into despair" (5); "offering me the tender fish cheek. I wanted to disappear" (5); the burping incident stuns Tan "into silence for the rest of the night" (6).
Presents a sequence of events	Every paragraph in the essay has forward momentum, introducing a new sequence in the linear story line. For example, paragraph 1 identifies that the story takes place "the winter I turned fourteen"; paragraph 2 presents the next sequence, opening with: "When I found out that my parents had invited the minister's family over for Christmas eve dinner, I cried"; and so on.

Examining the Characteristics of Narrative Essays, p. 119

1. Tan's purpose may be to help other "outsiders"—that is, new immigrants or others whose cultural or ethnic backgrounds are not considered mainstream—to develop pride in their own cultures.

2. The questions create tension as the readers anticipate Tan's embarrassment. This serves to heighten the readers' surprise at the end of the essay when they realize that their sympathies with Tan's predicament have been falsely aligned and that Tan came to realize how wrong she was to feel such shame over her Chinese heritage.

3. Dialogue, because it is used so sparingly, represents crucial moments in the text. The first two lines of dialogue—both of them remarks that Tan's father makes at the table (para. 5, 6)—represent the most shameful moments for the narrator. The final lines of dialogue come from Tan's mother (7) and convey a lesson to the young Tan about being proud of being Chinese. All the lines of dialogue in the essay reveal that the author's parents were most likely aware of her shame throughout the dinner and acted in such a way as to teach their daughter to appreciate her "otherness" and to not shy away from her Chinese heritage.

4. The mother's advice in paragraph 7 about being proud of being different and her statement to Tan that "Your only shame is to have shame" makes for an implied thesis. It is more effective here than a traditional thesis statement because it more subtly acknowledges the narrator's inner conflict. It also reveals her parents' recognition of her desires and conflict even as they combat it by refusing to be more "American" for their daughter.

Building Your Word Power, p. 120

1. The allusion is to the Virgin Mary, Christianity, and the Christmas holiday—associations that are not traditionally associated with Chinese culture. The color white links Robert with the Caucasian race and with the concept of purity. Given that this essay is written years after the events of the story took place, this description could be read as an expression of Tan's "virginal" love for him at the time, or alternately, as a slightly sarcastic description of a boy whom she perhaps grew to disdain later in life.

2. The use of hyperbole in paragraph 3 illustrates Tan's distorted perspective of the dinner created by her fear and shame.

Building Your Critical Thinking Skills: Point of View, p. 120

1–3. Tan's use of first person is effective because the fourteen-year-old perspective is full of self-consciousness and exaggerated emotion and drama. Examples from the text include her wish for a "new American nose" (para. 1) and, when she ignores Robert, writing, "I pretended he was not worthy of existence" (4). This kind of self-consciousness and embarrassment about one's parents is a common experience for teenagers, and students are likely to understand and relate to it. Certainly, it is conceivable that Tan chose to use the first person precisely for this reason; it works to "dupe" the reader into siding with Tan's fourteen-year-old self, only to present an alternative, more mature understanding of the events of the story at the end of the essay. If the third person had been used, readers might have learned more about the parents' knowledge of Tan's embarrassment. Readers might also have learned whether or not Robert liked Tan and what he thought of her family.

Langston Hughes, "Salvation," p. 122

In this short essay, Hughes creates a vivid picture of himself as a child, suffering the social and religious pressure to convert and "see Jesus" at a revival. Having taken the phrase literally, Hughes waits expectantly for Jesus to appear to him in the flesh. But, after a long time, the oppressive heat and the pressure of his aunt, the minister, and the congregation all praying and pleading with him to be saved finally forces him to lie about seeing Jesus.

Because of Hughes's expert use of tension to create drama and suspense, this essay might usefully be studied with a graphic organizer. The class might break into small groups to analyze it, step by step, noting where the conflict occurs, how tension is heightened, and how Hughes uses dialogue and other narrative techniques to heighten tension. Remember when discussing this essay that your students are likely to have different reactions to it depending on their own religious beliefs. Encourage students to express their personal views and reactions, but make sure that the discussion remains respectful of these different views and beliefs.

Understanding the Reading, p. 124

1. The special meeting for children was designed to bring them into the church, to be "brought to Christ" (para. 1) in order to save their souls.

2. Westley is different from Hughes because he doesn't suffer the same sense of moral conflict in deciding to lie about seeing Jesus. Because Westley's father is an immoral person (a "rounder" [6]), one might infer that Westley doesn't see anything wrong with lying.

3. The aunt thinks Hughes is overcome by his experience of having been saved, but actually he is crying because he has lost his faith in Jesus since Jesus didn't come and because he lied to his aunt and the congregation.

4. Hughes learns that he is capable of being pressured to lie. The events of the story also force him to reevaluate his own religious beliefs, leading him to no longer believe in Jesus.

Visualizing the Reading, p. 124

For students unfamiliar with revival meetings, this picture serves to capture some of the religious fervor that many parishioners experience at such events. As Hughes describes, revivals are full of "much preaching, singing, praying, and shouting" (para. 1), and this picture certainly matches the author's description of a revival. Additional details from the picture that could add meaning to Hughes's essay include a raising up of the arms to the heavens, closing one's eyes to feel the spirit of God, and the collective emotion and rejoicing of a revival.

Examining the Characteristics of Narrative Essays, p. 124

1. Hughes's narration reveals the feeling of social pressure to conform and his belief that Jesus will appear to him in visible form.

2. You may find it useful when discussing this question to create a list on the chalkboard as students suggest details from the text. Students might note: "a wonderful rhythmical sermon, all moans and shouts and lonely cries and dire pictures of hell" (para. 3); "And the little girls cried" (3); "old women with jet-black faces and

braided hair, old men with work-gnarled hands" (4); "And the whole building rocked with prayer and song" (4). Note that students may have slightly different images of the revival meeting and the people there, depending on their own religious experiences and beliefs.

3. The conflict for Hughes is that he can't "see" (7) Jesus. He feels ashamed that he isn't saved but doesn't want to lie about it like Westley does. The narrative technique that Hughes uses to great effect to build and sustain tension is the use of dialogue. Examples include: the preacher calling out "Won't you come? Won't you come to Jesus?" (3); Westley giving up and saying "I'm tired o' sitting here. Let's get up and be saved" (6); and Hughes's aunt sobbing "Langston" (9). Hughes also uses transitional words to great effect to illustrate the excruciating passage of time: "Still I kept waiting to *see* Jesus" (5); "Finally all the young people had gone to the altar and were saved" (6). Students will likely see how the action of the story creates tension: the fact that everyone had gone up to be saved but Hughes and Westley; and then after Westley gives up, how Hughes was alone with the "mighty wail of moans and voices" (7).

4. Auntie Reed's dialogue reveals her highly emotional and very religious perspective. The preacher's words reflect the high-minded, persuasive, and stylized language of an evangelical revival preacher. Westley's utterance of the blasphemous "God damn!" (6) reveals his casual, colloquial language and nonreligious attitude.

5. Hughes's thesis is implied: that he lost whatever faith he had in Jesus in the process of pretending to be "saved." It is effective because it reveals a child's perspective and literal understanding of the world, a child's expectation and misunderstanding that cannot be fully explained to an adult.

Building Your Word Power, p. 125

1. The idiom "by leaps and bounds" (para. 1) means rapidly.

2. The metaphors "sea of shouting" and "waves of rejoicing" (13) mean that the congregation is moving or acting as a single, unified mass like the ocean, rather than as individuals. They are swept up in the enthusiasm of the moment.

Building Your Critical Thinking Skills: Connotative Meaning, p. 125

1. In the context of the story, *saved* has a negative connotation because it is only about the appearance of being saved. Hughes, who is so clearly truthful and sincere, cannot be saved, while Westley, who is a nonbelieving liar and a sinner, is believed to be saved. To "save further trouble" (para. 11), Hughes finally lies and is then falsely believed to be saved. Ironically, he is not a sinner at the beginning of the story but becomes one (a liar) in order to be recognized as saved.

2. Hughes thinks Jesus will appear visibly before him, whereas his aunt means that he will experience Jesus in his soul and "see the light," or finally understand and believe in Jesus's teachings.

Cherokee Paul McDonald, "A View from the Bridge," p. 127

Cherokee Paul McDonald recounts an ordinary day that is made extraordinary by an encounter with a blind boy. As the narrator is jogging along the water, a young boy with a fishing rod asks for his help. Pausing reluctantly, the jogger soon becomes engaged as he watches and ends up coaching the boy as he reels in a large silver tarpon. The jogger doesn't realize that the boy is blind until late in the story when the boy asks him to describe the fish he has reeled in. As he describes the fish, the jogger finds himself fully engaged in the process, straining to describe it fully. In the process, he finds himself "seeing" in a new way.

Students will benefit from a close reading of this well-crafted essay. You might consider asking them to reread it, searching for clues to the boy's blindness as if it were a mystery story. Ask them to also seek out points in the essay where they can identify a shift in the author's attitude toward the boy (especially changes in tone). They might also want to look for narrative transitions that signal a change in focus. By now, this narrative arc in which the narrator has an "epiphany" of some sort has probably become familiar to your students. Ask them to evaluate the effectiveness of this particular epiphany. You might then havwe them freewrite about a similar moment in their own lives.

Because of the relationship between seeing in "Salvation" (p. 122) and seeing in this essay, you may find it useful to discuss these two essays in conjunction. In addition to the narrative techniques used by the two authors, you might discuss the larger points that each author makes about "seeing" and how the two endings—one optimistic and one pessimistic—contrast to one another.

Understanding the Reading, p. 129

1. The jogger is initially annoyed to be interrupted by the boy. His attitude toward the boy changes as he becomes interested in watching and advising the boy while he reels in the catch. When the jogger realizes that the boy is blind, he is amazed at how good a fisherman the boy is, forcing him to reconsider how one "sees" the world around him.

2. Clues to the boy's blindness are his odd "wrap-around sunglasses" (para. 3); his "fumbling" with the rod (4); his inability to see the shrimp by his foot (8); his failure to realize that the fish is still hooked (20); his failure to reply when the jogger exclaims "Whooee, is that a nice fish or what?" (25); and most telling, his remark "Hey, mister, tell me what it looks like" (29).

3. Because the boy is such a good fisherman and is able to do so many things without seeing, the jogger can't tell initially that the boy is blind.

4. The jogger means that by having to describe the fish to the boy he became more aware of both the fish's beauty and that of the world around him, making him realize his own good fortune in being able to see.

Visualizing the Reading, p. 129

Possible answers include:

Narrative Characteristic	The Boy	The Jogger (narrator)	The Fish
Physical description	1. "He was a lumpy little guy with baggy shorts" (para. 2) 2. "stupid-looking '50s-style wrap-around sunglasses" (3)	1. "I puffed on by, glancing down into the empty bucket as I passed" (4). 2. "hands on my hips and the sweat dripping from my nose" (7)	1. "the silver is . . . made up of *all* the colors" (33) 2. "He has all these big scales, like armor" (35)
Dialogue	1. "Could you tell me what he looks like, mister?" (32) 2. "I don't want to kill him" (37).	1. "What do you want, kid?" (7) 2. "Whooee, is that a nice fish or what?" (25)	n/a
Events	1. The kid "dropped the baited hook" (13). 2. "The kid cranked like mad, and a beautiful grin spread across his face" (22).	1. The narrator climbs down the seawall (27). 2. The narrator takes the fish off the hook (37–38).	1. The tarpon jumps "almost six feet out of the water" (14). 2. The tarpon swims slowly off (38).

Examining the Characteristics of Narrative Essays, p. 130

1. The title implies that only the jogger can see the literal view from the bridge. But on a figurative level, his view is transformed by understanding the blind boy's perspective (or vantage point).

2. The first impression readers get of the boy is of a somewhat sloppy kid, odd and unstylish. The words the narrator uses to describe him and his clothes in paragraphs 2 and 3 include: "lumpy," "baggy," "faded," "falling down," "shaggy," and

"stupid-looking . . . sunglasses." Later, as his view of the boy shifts, he presents the boy as skilled and competent: "The kid played it perfectly" (24); "the kid kept the rod tip up and the line tight" (24).

3. As the narrator begins to use more descriptive language (33–36), readers sense that he is more compassionate and kinder than he seemed at first. The tone changes from one of impatient questioning to one of encouraging, coaching, listening, and helping. Events also slow down as the narrator becomes more contemplative.

4. The implied thesis is that the boy teaches the narrator to see. Students will have many different possible explicit theses, but one common explicit thesis would be something like: "I thought I knew what was important in life, but my experience with the blind boy taught me to really see the beauty in this world and to appreciate everything around me."

5. Your students are likely to have different perspectives on the effectiveness of the author's conclusion. Some will find it moving and satisfying, while others might find the author's expression of faith in the boy's optimism to be somewhat clichéd. A different, feasible conclusion might be to end at paragraph 47 with the boy's words, without the narrator's response.

Building Your Word Power, p. 130

1. Some of the fishing terms McDonald uses are: *rod and reel* (para. 4), *bait bucket* (4), *baited hook* (13), *tarpon* (14), *line* (16), *reel* (16), *crank* (16), *drag setting* (16), *rod tip* (17), and *slack* (21). You might want to ask if any students in the class fish; if yes, perhaps they could explain to the rest of the class what some of this jargon means.

2. Both figures of speech use militaristic language: "silver missile" creates a picture of a rocket shooting upward; "scales like armor" implies a suit of mail that is tough but flexible.

Building Your Critical Thinking Skills: Symbolism, p. 131

1. The bridge creates a vista or view, enhancing the narrator's ability to see, yet the child can't see. Also, the language that the jogger uses to describe the fish to the child creates a bridge of communication between them.

2. Most students will probably agree that the boy represents innocence. Examples from the text to support this view include: the boy trusts the jogger even though he is a stranger (para. 5); the boy doesn't want to kill the fish (37); and the boy believes he will become a sports fisherman (47). While initially his blindness suggests vulnerability, as the story proceeds his disability suggests the classic idea of blindness representing greater insight.

3. You are likely to get a broad range of answers from students to this question. One possible answer is that the fish symbolizes the goals people pursue in life, the things that make life worth living.

Toni Cade Bambara, "The Lesson," p. 133

Toni Cade Bambara's short story is told from the perspective of a young black girl, Sylvia, who goes on a day trip to F.A.O. Schwarz toy store with an educated neighbor, Miss Moore, and other neighborhood children. During the cab ride to the Upper East Side, Sylvia silently mocks and criticizes Miss Moore for her educated language and her constant attempts to teach the children about arithmetic and economic rights, among other things. But seeing the price tag on a sailboat that reads "one thousand one hundred ninety-five dollars" (para. 25) stuns Sylvia into realizing that there is a great deal about economic disparity that she does not know. She is still reluctant to accept Miss Moore as a mentor but goes off alone to think over what she has seen.

The tone of this essay is so clearly driven by Sylvia's tone of voice, colloquial language, and dialogue that it might be worthwhile to begin a discussion about the effect created by a narrator such as Sylvia. You might want to ask students, for example, about her use of the word *hate* when she talks about Miss Moore and how Sylvia's humor and frank observations contribute to the reader's impression of her. You could ask students to break into groups that "liked" or "didn't like" Sylvia as a character. Ask them to report back as a panel to the group about why they did or didn't like her, using examples from the text. The same exercise could be done for the character of Miss Moore.

Understanding the Reading, p. 139

1. As the story progresses, readers learn that Sylvia is street smart and clever but doesn't like school or respect education. She is disdainful of people like Miss Moore who ask her to think too much and who are, in her view, condescending. She lives a sheltered life in Harlem and although she wants money, she doesn't understand that she has to earn it (para. 3). The young age of the narrator is evidenced by her desire for fun and excitement ("I'd much rather go to the pool or to the show" [2]). While she defensively mocks anything she doesn't understand, her character is redeemable and capable of learning and contemplation, as readers learn at the end when she goes off alone to contemplate what she has learned during her trip to F.A.O. Schwarz (58).

2. Sylvia seems to resent being asked to think by Miss Moore. It is implied that she and the other children may feel that Miss Moore and her educated ways are condescending toward them.

3. The outing makes the children recognize the profound social and economic differences between them and the wealthy white people who frequent a store like F.A.O. Schwarz.

4. The lessons taught are about social, economic, and racial inequality.

Visualizing the Reading, p. 139

Possible answers include:

Event, Action, Dialogue, or Description	Significance
1. Miss Moore is the only woman on the block with no first name. (para. 1)	This suggests formality and distance; it also suggests respect.
2. "I'm really hating this nappy-head bitch and her goddamn college degree." (para. 2)	Sylvia hates what Miss Moore represents: education and civility.
3. Sylvia decides she needs the cab driver's tip more than he does. (para. 3)	Sylvia doesn't understand what it means to earn money.
4. "I feel funny, shame." (para. 40)	Sylvia realizes that she is different from the wealthy people who can afford to buy such expensive toys, and this realization makes her feel embarrassed to be there.
5. "'You sound angry, Sylvia. Are you mad about something?'" (para. 43)	Sylvia doesn't want to acknowledge how her inequality makes her feel. She would rather make fun of Miss Moore and remain seemingly unaware of her status as a poor, black girl from Harlem.
6. "Where we are is who we are, Miss Moore always pointin out." (para. 44)	This suggests that being in the "ghetto" limits one's social status.
7. "Imagine for a minute what kind of society it is in which some people can spend on a toy what it would cost to feed a family of six or seven." (para. 49)	This comment is about values and social inequities. It is a reason to be angry and determined, not ashamed. Miss Moore suggests here that one needs to be educated in order to be empowered.

Examining the Characteristics of Narrative Essays, p. 140

1. Given that this may be the first short story that students encounter in your class, it may be worthwhile to explain the difference between thesis statements and themes. The broad theme in Bambara's story is that social injustice is harmful

and that some people don't have a fair chance — whether because of lack of education, lack of money, or the color of their skin — to get ahead economically.

2. The slang, dialect, and swearing create a vivid characterization of a young girl who is at odds with society and her elders. Students are likely to have different reactions to this style of writing — some may be offended and critical of the protagonist, others may be sympathetic to her immaturity and obvious disadvantages associated with her status as a poor, uneducated, African American girl.

3. The conflict of the story is the protagonist not wanting to learn the lesson and to remain ignorant. The tension is sustained through Sylvia's resentment of Miss Moore. The climax occurs when Sylvia goes off alone to think about what she has learned (para. 58).

4. Had a third-person perspective been used, readers could have seen how Miss Moore felt about Sylvia's attitude. Readers also would have had more insight into Miss Moore's motives for taking the children to F.A.O. Schwarz and how she hoped to educate and influence them.

5. Place is important in "The Lesson" not only because the action of the story occurs as the characters move from Harlem to the Upper East Side (Fifth Avenue), but also because the two neighborhoods offer a concrete example of the social inequalities between the residents of these two New York City neighborhoods. Readers know Harlem by Bambara's details about "the junk man" and "the winos who cluttered up our parks" (1). These details are contrasted by the descriptions of "everybody dressed up in stockings" and "One lady in a fur coat, hot as it is" (3) used to convey the atmosphere on Fifth Avenue.

Building Your Word Power, p. 141

1. The connotation of "real money" as used in paragraph 2 by Miss Moore is the real value of money — how money is used and how far it goes, or doesn't go, toward buying things.

2. This metaphor paints a vivid picture of Miss Moore working as one would in a factory or a mine with her hands, using them much as worker would as she tries to teach with her gestures.

Building Your Critical Thinking Skills: Colloquial Language, p. 141

1. The period may be the 1950s because the prices are so low for everyday items like a taxi ride (para. 3), a model sailboat (27), or bunk beds (44). Other elements of the story that date the piece include references to pinafores (2), paperweights (13), and a blotter and letter-opener (18).

2. Miss Moore has a college education; as a result, her language is more formal and standard than that used by the children who are uneducated and live in a ghetto. The stark differences between the language used by Miss Moore and that used by the children set up a profound difference between them, a difference that Sylvia keenly feels and rebels against.

3. Students are likely to sense how crucial the use of colloquial language is to the story because of the way it describes and defines the different characters. Most students will find Sylvia humorous because she is witty, has a sharp eye and a foul mouth, and makes amusing observations. She is particularly good at sizing up other people's characters in a sarcastic manner. For example, she says: "You got some ole dumb shit foolishness you want somebody to go for, you send for Aunt Gretchen" (1).

Chapter 6 Description: Portraying People, Places, and Things, p. 144

The descriptive essay is enjoyable for most first-year college students because it involves vivid, sensory details and can be written in the first person. You might want to begin with a definition of *description*, that is, writing that appeals to the senses through the use of vivid detail. You might also want to briefly discuss how narration and description overlap, because they are most often presented together. Give students lots of examples of what you mean by "vivid" and "precise" details, using the examples in this chapter to help them recognize when a description is dull and vague. You will also want to emphasize the idea of "significant detail," the concept that not every single detail is as important as another. Explain how tiresome it would be if a writer told a story in which every single detail he saw or heard or tasted was thrown in. Remind students that they are already familiar with the use of descriptive language through the stories they hear or tell on a daily basis to their friends or families. You might ask them to think, for example, of someone they know who is a particularly good story-teller. How does this individual use details to create a vivid impression?

Just as you did when you talked about narration, you may want to explain that the storyteller shapes the narrative in a descriptive essay artfully by arranging the story-line in the most effective way possible. The author accomplishes this by choosing only those details that create a single dominant impression and point of view. A storyteller or writer must organize the story or narrative to best effect (chronologically, spatially, or from least-to-most or most-to-least importance).

The revision flowchart included in this chapter (pp. 156–158) will help students understand what revising or editing a descriptive essay entails. As mentioned in Part 1, revision is often a difficult concept for first-year students to grasp, so using the revision flowchart throughout the semester will increase their understanding of the editing process. Because students often work harder to polish a descriptive passage when they know that they will be sharing it with the other students in the class, you might want to have them read each other's work on a regular basis. Using the flowchart to evaluate each other's work in pairs may also increase their interest in the process.

In this chapter, Jeremy MacClancy's essay, "Eating Chilli Peppers" (p. 144), assembles an array of sensory details, using similes to describe the stimulating sensations hot peppers create. In "The Discus Thrower" (p. 163), Richard Selzer also uses many similes, comparing his amputee patient to a bonsai tree, a log, and a sailor on deck. Eric Liu, in "Po-Po in Chinatown" (p. 174), uses similes and vivid details to compare his grandmother's voice to Yoda's and her talkativeness to a tidal wave, among other things. The readings in this chapter also offer a range of perspectives from which to discuss point of view. MacClancy uses the third person to lend his informational piece about the use of hot chillis a formal but conversational tone. Mary Brave Bird's "The Sweat Bath Ritual" (p. 169) also has an educational purpose, but it is written in the first person. Eric Liu, Gary Soto in "Piedra" (p. 180), and Maya Angelou in "Sister Flowers" (p. 185) all use the first person to describe powerful experiences from childhood and young adulthood. Liu's and Angelou's pieces are detailed portraits of individual people who had a great influence on them; Selzer also focuses on a single person, a patient who affected his life as a doctor.

Jeremy MacClancy, "Eating Chilli Peppers," p. 144

As the graphic organizer on page 151 shows, Jeremy MacClancy's essay moves from a description of hot peppers as painful and thrillingly stimulating to an argument that they are beneficial. He uses lots of active verbs to convey the taste of the peppers and the exciting physical and psychological sensations they cause. Because he is an anthropologist and because this essay was written as an informative piece, he uses the third person to educate the reader about crosscultural eating habits and motivations for eating chillis, comparing the pleasurable side effects to a drug high. He also outlines the more productive crosscultural use of hot peppers in folk medicine.

MacClancy's essay can be used to illustrate how even informative or academic essays can be made more lively and compelling through the use of active verbs, varied sentences (p. 148), and figurative language (p. 149). Remind students that they will be doing similar work when they begin to write comparison and contrast and other more analytical essays.

Danielle Cruz, "I Survived the Blackout of 2003," p. 159

Danielle Cruz's essay provides an example of unpolished student work. It is useful for students to see such work, in addition to the professional essays that make up the bulk of this anthology, because students often hesitate to find fault with the work of professional writers. Essays like Cruz's give them an opportunity to read critically, looking for "flaws," just as they will when they do peer revision. The marginal annotations and highlighting included for this essay help students to recognize structural transitions, the thesis statement, and other key elements of the piece.

Responding to "Students Write," p. 161

1. Cruz's dominant impression is positive. It is stated implicitly in the first sentence of the essay when she describes how her outlook on the world has been shifted by her experiences during the blackout of 2003 that affected New York City and much of the Northeast.

2. Some effective sensory descriptions in Cruz's essay include: "the comforting rumble of the AC" (para. 1); "a bag of half-frozen okra for a pillow" (6); and "the sweet smell of lavender [candles]" (6). As a class or in small groups, have students improve upon less effective details, such as the description of a neighbor as a "familiar-looking woman" (2).

3. Comparisons include the blackout of 2003 with the events of 9/11 (2) and "dog-walkers pushing through the crowd like salmon headed to spawn" (3).

4. Questions that Cruz does not address include: What caused the blackout? What was Cruz doing in New York? It would also be helpful to know more about her occupation and where she came from.

5. The title is satisfactory but not very original. In the introduction, it might be useful to include more about where Cruz came from and what she was doing in New York City. The conclusion is good — it conveys her positive impression of the spontaneous sense of community created in the aftermath of the blackout.

Richard Selzer, "The Discus Thrower," p. 163

Selzer's essay describes a few brief, fairly unproductive encounters between a doctor (the narrator) and his dying amputee patient. As his doctor, Selzer is curious about the patient but remains detached. Selzer knows that the patient is dying alone and angry—alienating the nurses by repeatedly throwing his plate at the wall—yet he doesn't communicate with him. Instead, Selzer "spys" on or observes him for clues about his background and his behavior. Sparse dialogue conveys the lack of communication between them.

Encourage students to read this piece several times, looking carefully at Selzer's tone, which may be difficult for many students to comprehend. You might want to talk briefly about the issue of patient care in the United States and what is expected or not expected of doctors and other medical professionals. You might also ask students to consider a doctor's mandate to "cure," and how that might be thwarted when he or she knows that a patient is terminal. You might have students break into small groups to discuss the role of empathy in the doctor/patient relationship—has it been shown, for example, to enhance healing? Students could share an experience of feeling cared for (or not cared for) and how it influenced their progress.

Understanding the Reading, p. 165

1. According to Selzer, the patient is blind and legless, and something "vile" is making his skin turn brown (para. 2). Over the course of the essay, readers never learn what caused his amputations or his blindness and, ultimately, his death.

2. The head nurse is upset because the patient won't eat, throws his plate, and in a word, is "Nasty" (27). She wants the doctor to do something about the situation, but Selzer only stalls her, saying, "We'll see" (30).

3. The patient exhibits delight, laughing when he throws his plate (34).

4. Selzer learns of the patient's death from the head nurse, who feels that his death is a "blessing" (49). Selzer reacts to the man's death much as he has throughout the essay: unemotionally. He returns to the man's room "a spy looking for secrets" to view his body, lying there "grave, dignified" (50) in bed.

Visualizing the Reading, page 165

Possible answers include:

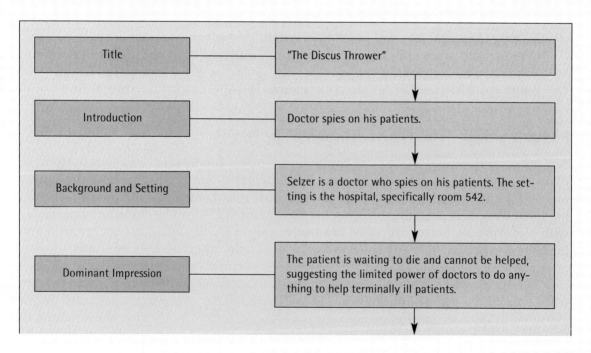

Title	"The Discus Thrower"
Introduction	Doctor spies on his patients.
Background and Setting	Selzer is a doctor who spies on his patients. The setting is the hospital, specifically room 542.
Dominant Impression	The patient is waiting to die and cannot be helped, suggesting the limited power of doctors to do anything to help terminally ill patients.

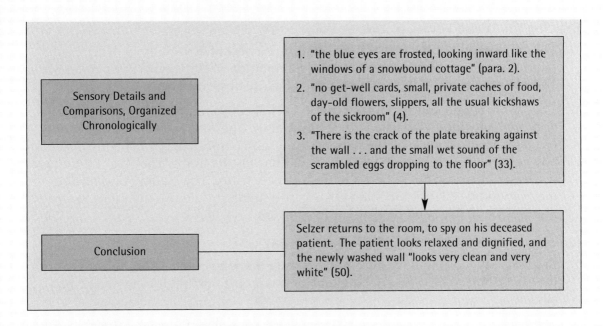

Examining the Characteristics of Descriptive Essays, p. 166

1. The dominant impression is that the patient in the bed is unhappy (except when he throws his plate) and waiting to die. Selzer's purpose for writing might be to describe his own sense of helplessness as a doctor when he cannot do anything to save a patient.

2. Encourage students to reread the essay, highlighter in hand, to mark all the places where Selzer uses effective sensory details. Examples include: a body like a "bonsai" (para. 2), and dreaming of a time "when his body was not a rotting log" (19). Selzer also uses sound to effectively describe key events: the patient's laughter "could cure cancer" (34); "the crack of the plate breaking against the wall" (33).

3. The author's vantage point as a doctor is somewhat effective because Selzer knows that the patient is in the "last stage" of his illness (2). However, despite what most people would consider an insider's vantage point, the reader receives only hints about the disease but doesn't know what caused the amputations or the blindness or why the patient has no visitors.

4. After the patient's death, Selzer notices that the wall where the patient had thrown his plate every day is very clean. Earlier, the hospital room was described as empty of personal effects (4); after the patient's death, it is described as "very white" (50). The overall sense is one of peace and tranquility, contrasting with the earlier descriptions of a very ill man who is detached and angry at his predicament.

Building Your Word Power, p. 166

1. The connotation of *spy* (verb) in paragraph 1 is to watch secretly in order to obtain information. In paragraph 50, the connotation of *spy* (noun) is a person who seeks to obtain secret information through close observation.

2. The "snow-bound cottage" image (para. 2) is effective because the patient's blind eyes are like windows glazed with ice and snow. The "bonsai" (2) analogy is only partially accurate because the patient's limbs are truncated; but his body is not really in miniature, it is more like a tree that has lost its limbs. The "log" (19) image works well because the patient's body is mostly trunk. The "sailor" (20) analogy may sound less effective to students because sailors would use their legs to steady themselves on deck and the patient has no legs.

Building Your Critical Thinking Skills: Tone, p. 167

1. Students are likely to have different views on the tone of the essay. Selzer's overall tone is distanced or neutral, though some students may find it to be sad or pessimistic.

2. The dialogue, used sparingly by Selzer, is also neutral, not very emotional or expressive, except for the nurse's and aide's remarks (para. 27, 36, 41), which exhibit frustration, bewilderment, and anger.

3. Expect different responses to this essay, depending on how students react to the perceived tone. Because the author's tone is generally unemotional and distant, many readers may feel somewhat unsympathetic to the patient. But some readers may also feel a little curious about the patient, perhaps even slightly sympathetic to him, because he is alone, is unable to connect with the staff, and does not complain. The tone will also affect how students perceive the doctor, who remains a mysterious figure throughout. Some will likely be offended by his somewhat "cold" actions, while others will find his behaviors and quiet contemplation to be caring and understanding in a quiet and respectful way.

Reacting to the Topic: Discussion and Journal Writing, p. 167

You might want to have students break into two large groups to discuss their feelings about the doctor's attitude toward and efforts to help the patient. They could then form panels (pro and con) to defend or criticize the doctor's bedside manner.

Mary Brave Bird, "The Sweat Bath Ritual," p. 169

Mary Brave Bird is best known for her autobiographical book *Lakota Woman* (1990). In "The Sweat Bath Ritual," she gives a first-person, informative description of her experience of the sweat lodge ritual. Her aim is to inform others about the ritual in a literal way and also to convey some of its psychological and spiritual benefits.

Although she is Native American, the story begins at a time when she did not know much about traditional ways. Because the story is presented in chronological order, sometimes summarizing a series of events, the reader learns along with the author what the ritual feels like, what it entails, and what it means.

You might want to have the class freewrite for a few minutes and then break into small groups to discuss how they would feel about engaging in a ritual like this one. Would they, for example, enjoy being a cultural anthropologist or a travel writer, traveling around the world to participate in and learn about ceremonies such as this one? Why or why not? Have them report back to the class about their feelings. They could also freewrite about a similar experience when they were first exposed to an unfamiliar cultural practice, such as the time they attended their first bar mitzvah or a formal dinner where they had to negotiate several kinds of forks and plates.

Understanding the Reading, p. 171

1. Mary Brave Bird goes to a sweat lodge because she had not yet participated in this ancient ceremony. By experiencing this ceremony, which "precedes all sacred ceremonies" (para. 3), she hopes to have a better understanding of both this and the other Native rituals of her tribe.

2. The interior of the sweat lodge is dark. The dome is formed of willow sticks that are tied with red strips of cloth. There is a circular fire pit in the center (4).

3. The white limestone rocks that are placed in the lodge are covered with a "spidery network of green moss," which is supposed to "represent secret spirit writing" (5).

4. At first the author felt that she wouldn't be able to withstand the heat because it "hurt" (10), but afterwards she felt elated and connected to the Indian community and to the spirit world. Through her experience, Mary Brave Bird learns about the transformative power of ritual (10).

Visualizing the Reading, p. 171

The physical description of the lodge as written by Brave Bird is actually clearer than what one can see in this image. This may come as a revelation to some students, given the power that most undergraduates likely ascribe to visuals over text. However, the physical experience of being in a sweat lodge is vividly shown in this photograph. Students are likely to comment on the reddish glow of the fire, the sweat glistening, and the almost religious experience this man is undergoing. You may wish to contrast the emotion shown here with that shown in the picture of a revival meeting that accompanies "Salvation" on page 122.

Examining the Characteristics of Descriptive Essays, p. 172

1. You may find it helpful to create lists of details that appeal to the senses of smell, taste, touch, sound, and sight. Examples include: smell—"Green cedar . . . filling

the air with its aromatic odor" (7); taste — "catch the sacred smoke with their hands, inhaling it" (8); touch — "My body tingled" (10); sound — "we can hear the river's voice" (3); and sight — "spidery network of green moss" (5).

2. This essay is organized chronologically in terms of the author's first sweat. Brave Bird presents herself as a newcomer, presumably like most readers, because even though she is Native American, she has never experienced the sweat ritual. This perspective makes her essay a highly descriptive and informative account. The chronological method of organization is effective because it enables the reader to participate in Brave Bird's experience as she does, from her fear that she won't be able to handle the heat, to her sense of relief and elation once the ceremony has ended (para. 10).

3. Some comparisons that Brave Bird uses include: comparing the lodge to an "igloo-shaped hut" (7), an effective comparison in terms of shape if not in terms of temperature; the simile "like inhaling liquid fire" (10), a vivid description of the extreme heat within the lodge; and the analogy "newly born" (10), a slightly clichéd but apt explanation of the transformative power of the experience. These and other comparisons help the reader to see that although the ceremony entails some discomfort, it is ultimately rewarding and transformative.

4. The author's background contributes the idea that even a Native American can be skeptical about the value and power of traditional Native ritual. In writing this essay, Brave Bird may have intended to foster respect for Native spirituality among both Native and non-Native people.

Building Your Word Power, p. 172

1. Seeing with the "eye in one's heart" refers to experiencing the world with a loving, nonjudgmental attitude.

2. "Liquid fire" would pour down one's throat, into one's belly, causing the severe discomfort that Brave Bird is describing.

Building Your Critical Thinking Skills: Evaluating Authors, p. 172

1. You might want to use this section to underscore the importance of scanning (or previewing) a writer's biographical information before reading an essay. Have students consider how the information included in the headnote shaped their reading of the piece. Ask also how this essay would be read differently, for example, if the headnote described Brave Bird as a white anthropologist.

2. The first three paragraphs of Brave Bird's essay explain why she is eminently qualified to write about this experience: she is a Native American, she has experienced other traditional rituals, and she wishes to experience the sweat lodge ritual for the first time in her "family's sweat lodge" (para. 3).

Eric Liu, "Po-Po in Chinatown," p. 174

Eric Liu describes a series of visits to see his grandmother in Chinatown in New York City. He does not say where he himself lives, but it is clear that his visits to her in Chinatown are somewhat of a pilgrimage to an unfamiliar and exotic territory. Although there is an element of familial obligation to Liu's visits, he also appears to enjoy seeing this woman who represents his family's origins. Her attachment to the past and to all things Chinese, from language and politics to food, makes his visit feel like a voyage to another century.

The vividness of the portrait Liu creates is a result of his close attention to sensory details. You might want to begin a discussion of this essay by having students freewrite about the sensory impressions they retained after reading the essay. Then have them freewrite again, but about the main ideas that underlie the essay. Ask them to think about Liu's main purpose in writing. This may develop into a discussion of the intellectual or rhetorical purpose that often underlies a descriptive essay such as this.

Understanding the Reading, p. 176

1. Liu's relationship to his grandmother is a mixture of obligation and fondness. The distance between them is reflected in the languages they use (she speaks the Sichuan dialect of Chinese), their age difference, religion (she is a devout Christian), and geographic distance (she doesn't visit his house). Despite these differences, their closeness is evidenced throughout the essay. Examples include their shared laughter as they do exercises together (para. 7) and the way Liu holds her close at the end of the visit (9).

2. Po-Po seems very fond of Liu. She wants to share her ideas with him, especially her knowledge about China (5). There is a clear affection shown by Po-Po toward Liu, as illustrated through the way she always entertains him with stories (5), feeds him a huge lunch, and gives him money when they part (9).

3. Po-Po appears to live very modestly, though whether this is through a frugal nature or by necessity, Liu does not say. Examples from the text to support this include the fact that she lives in public housing (1), wears old glasses, uses a lawn chair for furniture, and has a frayed toothbrush (3). Her life revolves around the Chinese American community, and her primary interests have to do with China and her Christian faith.

4. Students are likely to have different responses to this question. One possible view is that the author is commenting on the value of the Chinese tradition of respect for one's elders. Another possibility is that Liu is commenting on assimilation and the varying degrees to which Chinese Americans adapt to, embrace, or reject American life.

Visualizing the Reading, p. 177

Possible answers include:

Characteristic	Examples
Active verbs	1. "*shuffled* to the kitchen" (para. 2) 2. "*scurrying* with excitement" (2) 3. "I *gorged* myself" (4)
Sensory details (sound, smell, touch, sight, taste)	Sound: "she chattered excitedly" (5) Smell: "broiled fish" (4) Touch: "stroke her knotted back" (9) Sight: "the filmy, clouded mirror" (3) Taste: "stir-fried shrimp still in their salty shells" (4)
Varied sentences	"With an impish smile, she proclaimed my American name in her Yoda-like voice: *Areek.* She got a kick out of that" (2).
Comparisons	"Yoda-like voice" (2); "like a performer" (5); "like a child" (5)
Connotative language	"to attack this meal" (4); "torrent of opinions" (5); "tidal momentum" (5)

Examining the Characteristics of Descriptive Essays, p. 177

1. The implied dominant impression that Liu creates is one of a garrulous, expressive, and lively elderly woman. Her talkativeness is revealed in the following quotes: Po-Po "chattered excitedly" (para. 5); "she would take a sip of 7 UP and swerve back to something in the news" (5); her words created a "tidal momentum, relentless" (5); and "If there was a lull" (7).

2. Occasional Chinese words and phrases are used throughout such as when Liu and his grandmother meet (2), when Po-Po invites him to eat (3), and when Liu describes the food she prepares (4). The understanding of the Chinese words used will be clear to students from the context. In some cases the actual meaning is defined ("*Lai chi ha,* Po-Po would say, inviting me to eat" in para. 3), while in other cases it is implied by the context of the situation (for instance, when Po-Po greets her grandson in para. 2). The use of Chinese is effective because it becomes another descriptive element, adding detail to our impression of the elderly Chinese women.

3. The method of organization is chronological. The details range from his arrival at Po-Po's door to a physical description of her and her apartment to what they eat for lunch and talk about afterwards. The essay concludes with a description of their parting hug and words.

4. The descriptive details used for Po-Po convey the sense of an energetic, happy, and expressive woman. Examples include: "scurrying with excitement" (2); "She offered a giggle" (2); and "she would chuckle" (8). She is also very generous, feeding her grandson a "banquet's worth" of food (4) and giving him "a little red envelope of money" at their parting (9). She is also, as previously mentioned, talkative ("she chattered excitedly" [5]), strong willed ("If I interjected, she'd cut me off" [6]), religious ("she revealed to me her own way of prayer" [9]), and loving (*"How I wish I had wings so I could see where you live"* [9]).

Building Your Word Power, p. 177

1. *Attack* and *gorged* (para. 4) suggest that Liu considers it his duty to show his appreciation by making a valiant effort to eat the enormous amount of food that Po-Po prepares. Po-Po's expression of disappointment is likely intended to goad him into eating even more.

2. Answers will vary. It may be fun to have students try to act out Po-Po's mannerisms as described by Liu.

Building Your Critical Thinking Skills: Selective Omissions, p. 178

1–2. You might want to have students break into pairs to discuss questions 1 and 2. Then have each pair report their ideas to the class.

3. To enhance student understanding of the essay and the Chinese culture that it explores, you might consider asking students to do some Internet research in advance. Have each student choose a subject touched on in the essay (for instance, Chinatown in New York City, manners, food, Aung San Suu Kyi, or the latest developments in Taiwan), and ask them to write a paragraph and deliver a short presentation about that aspect of Chinese culture to the class.

Reacting to the Topic: Discussion and Journal Writing, p. 178

1–2. You might want to prepare a short talk to accompany this essay by researching traditional Chinese American attitudes toward elderly relatives. You might also want to ask students to do some research into the attitude toward elders in another, less industrialized culture than that of the United States. Then initiate a discussion about what it means to honor the elderly. How might contemporary U.S. culture as a whole be judged according to Chinese or other standards? You could combine this discussion with Assignment 4 under Applying Your Skills, page 178.

Gary Soto, "Piedra," p. 180

Gary Soto creates a vivid vignette of a summer day spent by the Piedra River in California with his family. This particular day is significant to Soto because it is when he realized that he would one day leave his family's world to experience another kind of life. The essay, full of details about the natural setting, alternates between summary and moment-to-moment depiction of the day's events. Because of this, it is an excellent resource for teaching both narration and description. To capitalize on the features of "Piedra," you might want to have students analyze how narration and description overlap in this essay. Have students break into pairs or small groups and then identify the points at which Soto uses key elements — such as transitional words, summary, sensory details, and dialogue — to craft his piece and create a dominant impression about this ordinary yet momentous day.

"Piedra" is rich with sensory details that make Soto's experience of this day come to life for the reader. To explore this descriptive technique further, you might have students break into pairs to interview each other (for five minutes or so) about all of the sensory details they can recall as they describe scenes from the essay. You might then have them jointly write a paragraph based on the list they created together and share their writing with the class.

Understanding the Reading, p. 181

1. Soto visits the banks of the Piedra River with his family. Through the course of the essay, readers learn that the Sotos are Mexican (para. 2), that Soto's mother wants her children to study hard so that they can go to college (2), that Soto has a stepfather (4), that Soto's parents look tired (5), and that Soto plays fairly well with his sister and brother (5).

2. The children play both physically active and imaginative games as they explore the natural setting together, whereas the parents remain physically inactive, not really exploring the landscape or even interacting with each other (5).

3. Soto dreams about the lives of rich people like the Griffins (2), especially romantic daydreams about the Griffin daughters (3). He also dreams on the mountain that he will have a chance to live a better life (7). Details such as his romantic interest in the Griffin girls suggest that Soto is entering puberty.

4. Soto spent the afternoon venturing off alone to climb a mountain beyond a No Trespassing sign. The essay does not state definitively why climbing the mountain was important to Soto, so students are likely to have different answers to this question. One possible answer is that through this time alone he acquired some perspective on his own life and the possibilities that exist beyond "the badness" in his life so far (7).

Visualizing the Reading, p. 182

The person in the photograph interacts with the river actively by rowing out on the flat, smooth water. The image creates a feeling of serenity. Soto's interaction with the

Piedra River differs in that he experiences it from the shore only. He hears it roar noisily and crash over rocks (para. 1), then can no longer hear it from the top of the mountain where it looks "thin as a wrist" (7). Despite this difference, the relationship to the bodies of water that both Soto and the rower in the picture have is fundamentally the same: the proximity to water is soothing and beneficial.

Examining the Characteristics of Descriptive Writing, p. 182

1. The sound of the Piedra River is conveyed by "the roar of water" (para. 4), "the river loud at our side" (5), and how the "gushing water spilled noiselessly" as Soto climbs further and further away from it (7). Other senses appealed to include taste (of coffee and cigarettes [5]; "hot dogs and barbeque chips and soda" [6]); touch (lizards that "ran along our fingers" [5], "hugging my knees" [7]); smell ("mowed pasture" [2]); and sight ("gray-cold current" [1], "glittery sand and soggy leaves" [5]).

2. The details Soto uses for the river are vivid, sensual, and active, indicating how the river appealed to his senses. Words like *splayed, leaped,* and *feed* (1) all indicate these qualities. These details contribute to a dominant impression of Piedra as a place of peace and happiness.

3. Soto's vantage point is moving—first in the car, then next to the river, then from the mountain top. It is effective because it allows him to illustrate that just as he moves physically through the events of the essay, he is moving beyond his current situation metaphysically, growing up and away from his family in various ways.

4. Students are likely to find the ending with its solo hike to be effective because it is a bit unexpected and it presents a moment of adolescence when one strikes off on one's own that they can relate to. The conclusion describes a moment in time when Soto is able to take his dreams of escape to another level. "I will have my chance" may mean different things to different students. One possibility is that Soto will have an opportunity to be happier than his parents (for instance, to become better educated, to have a better job, to meet people from other socioeconomic groups, and so on).

Building Your Word Power, p. 182

1. The phrase "*those* people" (para. 2) has a negative connotation. It means that Soto's mother does not want to associate with or be associated with Mexican migrant workers.

2. The phrase "itching with rust" (2) creates an image of a red skin rash.

Building Your Critical Thinking Skills: Point of View, p. 183

1–2. Soto uses first-person point of view. This point of view reflects more than the boy's experience because it incorporates his mother's comments about the need to get good grades (para. 2), the view presented in romance novels he has read (3), the fishermen "shushing" the children (5), and his brother and sister calling him names (6).

3. By using a first-person point of view, Soto tells nothing about what his family members were thinking during that day at the river or about their family background.

Maya Angelou, "Sister Flowers," p. 185

In this passage from a memoir, Maya Angelou creates a portrait of an older, educated black woman who changed her life, indirectly helping her become a writer. "Sister Flowers" describes a difficult period of Angelou's life following a childhood rape and how her association with Mrs. Bertha Flowers helps her emerge from this dark time. Angelou describes her admiration for the gracious, well-educated Mrs. Flowers; the shame she felt because her mother was not as educated or polite; and her delight when Mrs. Flowers gave her personal attention and encouragement. This selection is an excellent one to have students dissect, reading it several times to hone their understanding of how this master memoirist constructs and artfully shapes the past so that it follows logically, delivers a sense of immediacy, and conveys a dominant impression about the role of Mrs. Flowers in her life.

Understanding the Reading, p. 189

1. Marguerite feels ashamed of her mother's interactions with Mrs. Flowers because her mother is informal and does not use proper grammar (paras. 7–10).

2. Mrs. Flowers appeals to Marguerite because she is gracious and aristocratic (2), educated, and "as refined as whitefolks" and "more beautiful" (12).

3. Mrs. Flowers wants Marguerite to open up and express herself because "[w]ords mean more than what is set down on paper" (24). She tries to instill this in Marguerite by reading aloud to her (37).

4. Through her lessons with Mrs. Flowers, Marguerite learns about the beauty of language (42) and the power of feeling liked and respected for being herself (44).

Visualizing the Reading, p. 189

Possible answers include:

Sense	Examples
Sight	1. "Her skin was a rich black that would have peeled like a plum if snagged" (para. 3) 2. "flat round wafers, slightly browned on the edges and butter-yellow in the center" (34)
Taste	1. "The sweet vanilla flavor" (39) 2. "Southern bitter wormwood" (42)
Touch	1. "snag her skin" (3) 2. "the rough crumbs scratched the insides of my jaws" (34)
Smell	1. "The odors in the house surprised me" (28) 2. "The sweet scent of vanilla" (29)
Sound	1. "soft yet carrying voice" (6) 2. "She was nearly singing" (37)

Examining the Characteristics of Descriptive Essays, p. 190

1. Angelou is communicating the idea that Sister Flowers represented another way of life because she was educated and refined. It also shows that Sister Flowers's kindness and interest in Angelou allowed her to blossom as a person and begin to heal from the effects of the rape.

2. Angelou describes Mrs. Flowers's appearance (2), her voice (6), her gait (8), and her house (32). She uses a least-to-most-important organization of the details.

3. Angelou's dominant impression of Sister Flowers is one of refinement. Details include: "printed voile dresses and flowered hats" (para. 2), "gloves" (3), a soft voice (6), "Like women in English novels" (11), "beautiful" (12), and "spoke each word with . . . clarity" (22).

4. Angelou describes her mother in terms of her poor grammar (10) and the activities of the aristocratic white women in novels who "walked the moors . . . sat in front of roaring fireplaces, drinking tea" (11). This is in contrast to her more reverent description of Sister Flowers.

Building Your Word Power, p. 190

1. "I sopped around" suggests that Angelou sulked around. "[L]ike an old biscuit, dirty and inedible" implies that Angelou felt both unattractive and no longer desirable because of the taint of the rape.

2. The phrase "mother wit" means folk wisdom.

Building Your Critical Thinking Skills: Details, p. 190

1–3. Answers will vary. You may want to invite students to share their answers with the class.

Chapter 7   Illustration: Explaining with Examples, p. 192

The main aspect of the illustrative essay—giving a series of examples to support an idea—should be familiar to most first-year college students because it is something that they likely do themselves in the course of everyday conversation. You might want to begin with a definition of *illustration*, that is, backing up one's thesis with examples. Illustration is an essential skill for your students because they will be required to provide examples, or evidence, whenever they write a paper in college. Good writing is characterized by generalizations that are well supported by specific examples. Explain to the class that examples are the evidence, anecdotes, facts, quotations, and statistics that back up a thesis. Just as in narration and description essays, the examples in an illustration essay must be organized in a meaningful way.

The graphic organizer on page 200 will help students visually see how to organize the examples in an illustration essay. The revision flowchart on pages 205–206 will help them revise their drafts to make sure that the examples used are relevant, representative, and of interest to readers. In this chapter, the Editing and Proofreading section (p. 204) emphasizes the need to make verbs consistent in tense and to use first, second, or third person consistently as well. This section also describes and illustrates sentence fragments, a common problem for first-year students. The student essay, "Internet Hoaxes" (p. 207), has each topic sentence highlighted so that students learn where a topic sentence can be located. This will help them see that each topic sentence is a generalization followed up by examples. The chapter also covers the idea of introducing *alternative viewpoints* (p. 237) in order to provide a more balanced presentation of a given issue.

Each essay in this chapter uses a series of illustrations or examples to lend credibility to its thesis. For example, Bill Bryson's "Snoopers at Work" (p. 193), declares that Americans are being spied upon and that this violation of privacy is considered legal. He then delivers a series of examples of legal violations—taking place everywhere from changing rooms to office cubicles—backing up his thesis with examples that prove his case. In "Just Walk On By: A Black Man Ponders His Power to Alter Public Space," Brent Staples (p. 211) gives a series of vivid examples to show how he, and other black men, experience social discomfort and discrimination because white people stereotype and fear them. To build her argument that teenage boys increasingly are becoming concerned about their physical appearance, Rita Kempley (p. 217) uses a series of quotes from "experts" of various sorts. Quotations from psychologists, sociologists, authors, and others, as well as from teenage boys themselves, serve to develop her thesis. Nell Bernstein (p. 230) interviews a number of California teenagers to discover why they feel that they can "claim" any identity that they like. She asks them about "gangsta," "cholita," white, mixed-race, and other identities in order to provide examples of this new diverse community. Geeta Kothari (p. 223) uses a short autobiographical sketch to explore her national and cultural identity. She outlines a series of examples that illustrate how betwixt and between she feels as a South Asian American. From not having tuna fish salad sandwiches like her childhood classmates to not knowing how to cook Indian dishes as an adult, Kothari reveals that she felt less than American as a child and less than South Asian as an adult.

Bill Bryson, "Snoopers at Work," p. 193

Bill Bryson declares that American citizens' right to privacy does not extend to changing rooms, office email, or even the local bar after work because secret surveillance has been upheld by the courts. Although his thesis is shocking, Bryson backs it up with a rich assortment of valid and striking examples that provide convincing support. Point out to your students how Bryson uses helpful transitions to keep the reader apprised of his thesis and where he is headed (for instance, "I know this because . . ." (para. 2); "But it gets even more sinister than that . . ." [11]).

You might want to do some research on the issue of privacy and how it is defined by law so that you can preface this essay with a short talk. For discussion or debate, you might ask students to consider how much privacy they think people should be willing to forgo and under what circumstances. You might ask them to freewrite on the meaning of the phrase "innocent until proven guilty" or break into small groups to discuss "the right to privacy."

The graphic organizer for Bryson's essay (p. 200) provides students with the thesis at the heart of the essay and also identifies the examples he provides, one by one. It might be helpful to go over this graphic organizer with the class slowly and carefully. Review each of Bryson's examples to evaluate their effectiveness; this will prepare your students to analyze other essays that are less clearly outlined. You could initiate a discussion about the pattern in which examples are presented—does it progressively illuminate the importance of the issue of privacy? Does the pattern gradually introduce examples that might persuade a skeptical reader that there is something seriously wrong with this erosion of American privacy?

Melissa Parker, "Internet Hoaxes: A Multiplying Problem," p. 207

In this student essay, Parker compiles extensive evidence for her thesis that Internet hoaxes are damaging in numerous, often overlooked ways. You might initiate an interesting discussion about the kinds of appeals made by other types of hoaxsters—from greed to altruism. Ask students to brainstorm examples of hoaxes they have heard of and to analyze the underlying appeal. Have them write a short piece about the list of hoaxes they compile, organizing them into a pattern, such as from least to most damaging.

Responding to "Students Write"

1. Parker's thesis statement is sound and reflects the same organizational format used in her essay.

2. Answers will vary. The introduction provides useful background information, but it could be more interesting with the addition of an example in which someone was duped.

3. To assess the quantity and quality of examples used, have students create a list of each example. Next to each one, student's should rate its effectiveness in terms of supporting Parker's thesis. This exercise should lead into a larger discussion about the types of examples used and their appropriateness.

4. Students will likely find these statistics thought-provoking. This example could have been even more effective had Parker added in the "average hourly wage."

5. The conclusion reemphasizes the key points by reiterating the essay's main idea that hoaxes are more than just a nuisance.

Brent Staples, "Just Walk On By: A Black Man Ponders His Power to Alter Public Space," p. 211

Staples eloquently illustrates the irony that he, an educated journalist and so-called "softy" (para. 2), should be constantly mistaken for a criminal, as many black men are. He opens his essay with the startling phrase "My first victim was . . .," and then he proceeds to give examples of all of the times he has been mistaken for a mugger or rapist since that first experience of being mislabeled as a threat at the age of twenty-two. His willingness to consider the issue of racial profiling with an open mind, to probe the possibility that his first experience might have been caused by his clothing, or the late hour, or something else; his eloquent writing style; and his genuine concern for women (who have real reason to fear men on the street at night)—all add to the strength of his examples. From Chicago to Soho, he has experienced white people's fear and suspicion and has smothered his rage and shame to develop a series of effective personal remedies. In order to reduce the fear he creates in white people, he now employs various calming strategies, from keeping his distance to whistling classical music whenever he walks down the street at night.

Understanding the Reading, p. 213

1. Staples has the power to alter public space because he is a black man and black men are often feared by the general public as potential rapists, muggers, and other criminals. This ability makes his life at times awkward and humiliating. Such power can even be dangerous because if he does something as simple as run into a building, he is likely to be perceived as a criminal, and if the police are called, his life could be in danger.

2. Staples managed to escape the violence of Chester, Pennsylvania—the "angry industrial town" where he grew up—by becoming one of the "good boys" (para. 6).

3. Staples attributes his survival to his timidity and his ability to stay out of the way and not get involved in fights or criminal activity (7).

4. To make his presence less threatening to others, Staples has learned to "take precautions" (11): he walks around people on subway platforms, walks past lobbies if the people inside look afraid, is "congenial" (11) to the police, and whistles classical music (12).

Visualizing the Reading, p. 214

Possible answers include:

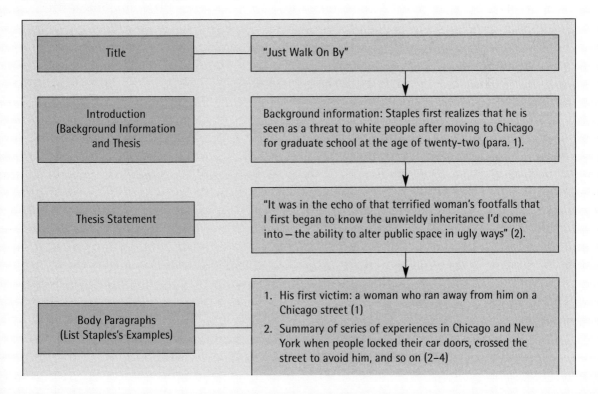

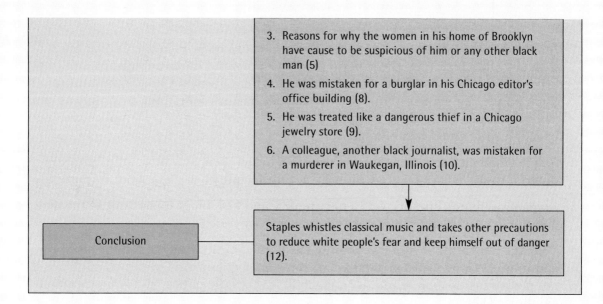

3. Reasons for why the women in his home of Brooklyn have cause to be suspicious of him or any other black man (5)

4. He was mistaken for a burglar in his Chicago editor's office building (8).

5. He was treated like a dangerous thief in a Chicago jewelry store (9).

6. A colleague, another black journalist, was mistaken for a murderer in Waukegan, Illinois (10).

Conclusion

Staples whistles classical music and takes other precautions to reduce white people's fear and keep himself out of danger (12).

Examining the Characteristics of Illustration Essays, p. 214

1. Staples's thesis appears in paragraph 2: "It was in the echo of that terrified woman's footfalls that I first began to know the unwieldy inheritance I'd come into — the ability to alter public space in ugly ways." His thesis is adequately supported by the series of examples — both his own experiences and those of friends — presented throughout the essay.

2. Staples is presumably writing for a white audience, since most people of color probably already know about this phenomenon. His purpose is to let people know what it is like to be a black man whose motives are constantly questioned by strangers. The examples that support his thesis are chosen to educate rather than to condemn. This is evident in the way Staples respectfully acknowledges other possible reasons — such as the justifiable fear of women who encounter strange men at night — for why people might be afraid of him late at night.

3. Answers will vary. One particularly striking example is the episode when he was mistaken for a mugger in his editor's building; this event must have been deeply humiliating to him as a professional (para. 8).

4. Examples of descriptive language used by Staples: "with a beard and billowing hair" (1), "the *thunk, thunk, thunk, thunk* of the driver . . . hammering down the door locks" (3); "as though bracing themselves against being tackled" (5). Such vivid descriptions enable the reader to experience Staple's sensory perception of white people's fear.

5. Answers will vary. For example, the topic sentence in paragraph 7 ("As a boy, I saw countless tough guys locked away; I have since buried several too") is followed by examples from his life of guys he knew who died ("a teenage cousin, a brother of twenty-two, a childhood friend").

Building Your Word Power, p. 214

1. "Warrenlike streets" has a connotation of a dark, narrow maze.

2. "Unwieldy inheritance" suggests the heavy burden of being perceived as a criminal that comes with being a black man in America.

Building Your Critical Thinking Skills: Cause and Effect Relationships, p. 215

1. According to the author, his appearance and proximity made the white woman run in fear: a tall, young black man with a beard, billowing hair, and a military jacket who seemed to be walking dangerously close behind her (para. 1).

2. The author's experience growing up in the tough city of Chester taught him to be careful and to avoid trouble. Through these experiences, he chose "to remain a shadow" (7).

Rita Kempley, "Abs and the Adolescent," p. 217

In this short piece on how pre-teen and adolescent boys are being affected by media images of beautiful, muscular teenage boys, Kempley uses a series of quotes from "experts" of various sorts, including psychologists, sociologists, authors, personal trainers, and athletic directors, as well as from boys themselves. The quotations give readers some quick insight into the attitudes of young boys, information about the status of teen culture, and anecdotal evidence that supports or contradicts it.

You might want to begin discussing this essay by taking a poll of what your students think about Kempley's theory. How did they feel about media images of teenage boys when they were in middle school or high school? Is it true, for example, that young boys formerly didn't care about their physiques? Didn't their fathers or grandfathers, for example, wish for larger muscles? Students could make a list of examples from their own experience, both pro and con, that would support or contradict Kempley's thesis. You could then have the class break into two panels to debate the issue pro and con, citing their own anecdotal evidence to support their view of the essay's thesis. As an alternative (or in addition) to this activity, you could ask students to list the pros and cons of weightlifting for aesthetic beauty and strength rather than playing other sports to maintain fitness. Encourage students to think critically about Kempley's article since its thesis is somewhat speculative, without many significant long-range statistics to support it.

Understanding the Reading, p. 219

1. According to the essay, men as a group have become very body conscious, especially teenagers and boys as young as age ten (para. 3).

2. The essay argues that media and advertising images are creating a new aesthetic ideal for boys that includes looking "ripped" (1), or toning their muscles (3).

3. The young men cited by Kempley try to achieve physical perfection through weightlifting and steroid use (23).

4. The phrase "negative treadmill" (22) refers to the ways in which the beauty culture (advertising and the media, especially girls' and women's magazines) has made many women dissatisfied with their looks and unhappy with their physical appearance. Many women spend time and money (and sometimes become anorexic/bulimic or psychologically depressed) trying to reach an ideal that they cannot attain. The negative aspects Kempley mentions specifically are buying "more products" (22) and thinking that their bodies are "flawed" (21).

Visualizing the Reading, p. 220

Students will have different views about the boy's concerns. Specific points in Kempley's essay that this image might illustrate include paragraphs 21, 22, and 23. You might also have students freewrite in response to this image in the voice of the teenage boy looking into the mirror. Then have them write in the voice of a teenage girl. Ask a few students to read their two versions aloud. How are they different? How are they alike?

Examining the Characteristics of Illustration Essays, p. 220

1. Kempley supports the generalization that boys—through media pressure and other outside influences—are becoming more interested in their physical appearance to the detriment of their health and well-being.

2. Most of Kempley's examples are quotations from "experts" of various kinds, including psychologists, sociologists, authors, personal trainers, and athletic directors, as well as teenagers and middle-school boys themselves. Because students are often accustomed to accepting any evidence offered by a professional writer as fact, you may need to prod your students to critically weigh all of the examples Kempley gives. Some are more representative than others, but some of her evidence seems weak. For example, one psychiatrist says that she is seeing more "steroids" being used by boys, but she does not give an exact percentage or even an estimate to support her statement (para. 23).

3. Answers will vary. An example of information that might have strengthened Kempley's thesis would be the inclusion of data from a long-term study showing the extent to which media imagery has changed the body image of men and boys over time.

4. While some students may like the fact that the final quote adds some levity to an otherwise serious piece, others will wish that Kempley had taken the opportunity to conclude with a more formal ending that summarized her findings and re-stated her thesis.

Building Your Word Power, p. 220

1. The metaphor "I'm just a piece of meat" means being objectified and evaluated only in terms of physical characteristics.

2. "Jocks' refuge" means a place where athletes feel comfortable.

Building Your Critical Thinking Skills: Evaluating Sources, p. 221

1. Because many of Kempley's sources are journalistic rather than academic, this question might be a good one to spend time on in class. You might want to go through the names of her sources aloud in class, one by one, evaluating each person's qualifications and engaging students in a discussion of how reliable his or her information is. This activity might lead into a discussion of academic sources and how they differ from journalistic ones.

2. Depending on your students' research experience, they may need some help in identifying where one would turn to best verify information that appears in a journalistic essay.

Geeta Kothari, "If You Are What You Eat, Then What Am I?" p. 223

South Asian American writer Geeta Kothari explores the sometimes tenuous links between food and cultural identity. Beginning with a vivid scene in which she and her mother puzzle over a can of tuna, Kothari explores her sense of being neither South Asian nor American when it comes to food. Because stylistically this essay differs from those the students have already encountered in this chapter, you may find it useful to have students reread the essay together, breaking it down into a list of examples used by Kothari in order to assess the effectiveness of her thesis and support.

With this essay as a point of departure, you might want to initiate a discussion of cultural differences in America and use food to focus in on these differences. You might discuss, for example, what group most closely represents the "American" in American food. Students could break into small groups to come up with a list of common American foods (for instance, hot dogs, hamburgers, pizza) and then develop a theory about the different cultures these typical foods came from. In the process, such an activity might challenge students to think about how certain types of Chinese food are considered American, whereas the "fish cheeks" discussed in Amy Tan's essay (p. 000) are definitely not.

Understanding the Reading, p. 226

1. Kothari's family eats lentils, rice, bread, vegetables, lamb, and other things (para. 21), but they don't eat processed foods like hot dogs, hamburgers, or pork. As a child, Kothari wanted to eat the foods that other schoolchildren eat like tuna salad and bologna (1), foods that her family finds "repugnant" (1).

2. During the hot season in India, her family is very careful not to eat certain foods like "ice cream" and "salad" and they boil their water because of the prevalence of diseases like dysentery (11).

3. The tuna fish episode indicates that although Kothari's mother did not have a lot of time or interest to explore American customs with her daughter, she wanted her daughter to be happy as she tried to "satisfy" her "longing for American food" (1).

4. The author does not want to eat red meat, which her husband likes. He accommodates her food preferences by cooking only poultry at home and eating red meat only in restaurants or at other people's houses (26).

Visualizing the Reading, p. 227

Possible answers include:

Example	What It Illustrates
Tuna story (para. 1–10)	Illustrates the difference between American and Indian foods, and reveals the mother's inability to grasp American ways.
Visiting relatives in India (para. 11–13)	Reveals her parents' cultural background and why they are cautious about certain American foods; also shows that they feel at home in India because they understand the customs.
Visit to uncle's diner in New Delhi (para.14–16)	Shows that the author dislikes her parents' restrictions about food.
Visit to Indian restaurant in New York (para. 17–19)	Reveals that Indian cuisine is finally entering mainstream, American culture, opening a bridge between the author's world and that of her friends.
Boyfriend's food preferences (para. 22–26)	Depicts the cultural differences in food preferences between the author and her boyfriend (now husband) and how they bridged them.
Author's attempts to cook Indian food (para. 27–32)	Illustrates that the author wants to get in touch with her ancestral roots by learning more about Indian food.

Examining the Characteristics of Illustration Essays, p. 227

1. The main point is that in terms of her food preferences, Kothari lies culturally in between Indian and American culture. She makes generalizations about what it means to be stuck between the two cultures through statements such as wanting to "eat what the kids at school eat" (para. 1) and "Indians eat lentils" (30).

2. Kothari uses examples from her personal experiences to support her main point. Students' answers will vary, but one example that is likely to make an impression on them is Kothari's dislike of her husband's "musky" smell after he eats red meat (26).

3. To help the reader understand difficult or abstract concepts, such as the unfamiliar food items mentioned in the essay, Kothari often explains what exactly they are, such as her descriptions of "dosa" (19) and "methi roti" (27). While this technique will be helpful for students, some may wish that Kothari had explained the differences between Punjabi and South Indian cooking a bit more (21).

4. Kothari organizes her examples chronologically.

5. Other methods of development that Kothari uses include description ("crushed bone and hair glued together by chemicals and fat" [1]); comparison and contrast (the description of the canned tuna fish not looking like tuna salad [1–5]); narration ("One time my mother makes . . . [21]); and cause and effect (how the orange soda makes her sick in India [14–15]).

Building Your Word Power, p. 227

1. The similes "like an internal organ" and "like a half-blind bird" in paragraph 3 allow the reader to understand how peculiar and alien the tuna fish must have seemed to Kothari and her mother.

2. The connotation of the word *home* for the author's mother is India, a place where she knows the rules, knows how to take care of and guide her daughter, and feels safe (para. 12). For Kothari, *home* is where she feels comfortable because no one asks why she eats certain foods or who she is (32).

Building Your Critical Thinking Skills: Drawing Conclusions, p. 228

1. As a child, Kothari concludes that her mother is a disappointment because she knows so little about American culture (para. 8–10). This observation adds poignancy to the story because her parents cannot help her navigate life in America in the ways she wishes they could.

2. Kothari concludes that her inability to cook Indian food suggests that she is not really her parents' daughter and, therefore, not really Indian (33). This leads her to further conclude that because she "cannot bear the touch and smell of raw

meat" (33) she is not an American either, putting her in a position somewhere between the two cultures.

Nell Bernstein, "Goin' Gangsta, Choosin' Cholita: Claiming Identity," p. 230

Nell Bernstein uses interviews with California teenagers to explore how cultural ideas about self-definition and identity in America are changing. To many of these teenagers, racial, ethnic, and other identities are flexible, able to be chosen rather than assigned. This essay should prove to be of great interest to first-year students since it contains many references to popular culture and involves their approximate age cohort. Because many of Bernstein's examples contradict or challenge other examples within the essay, her thesis is somewhat complex and nuanced; you may need to help students work through the essay's thesis and examples when evaluating the effectiveness of Bernstein's illustrative techniques.

In class discussion, students might adopt the various stances represented here in order to sift through the logic of Bernstein's thesis that a new generation is "claiming" or "choosing" identities of all kinds. Students might enjoy debating which identities are fixed and which are somewhat malleable (from racial to neighborhood identification). You might also want to use the "Focus on the Topic" activity to guide the discussion toward forms of cultural "claiming" that your students are familiar with, either personally or from pop culture.

Understanding the Reading, p. 235

1. To April Miller, racial or ethnic identity means that a person is whatever he or she chooses to be. According to Bernstein, Miller defines herself by how she dresses, her music, her words, and whatever she pledges "allegiance" to (para. 9).

2. Bernstein proposes the following reasons for why teenagers have developed such attitudes about their racial and ethnic identity: the increasingly diverse population in California (7), media images of pop culture (9), the hybridization of America (10), California's diverse public schools (11), the glamour of gangsta lifestyles (41), a backlash against whites in the state of California (43), the prevalence of interracial marriages in California (45).

3. According to the author and the people interviewed for this essay, rap music plays a role in the formation of cultural identity by making white suburban kids think that ghetto life is glamorous (29–30) and by popularizing urban, inner-city clothing styles.

4. The young people profiled in the essay change their attitudes toward identity as they grow older. As Will Mosley and Adolfo Garcia's remarks show, they gradually

dispense with the "blatant mimicry" of the images shown in rap videos (30), but they maintain a belief that they can "live in a suburban tract house . . . and still call themselves 'city' people on the basis of musical tastes" (30).

Visualizing the Reading, p. 236

Possible answers include:

Teenager(s)	What the Example Illustrates
April Miller (para. 1–9, 53)	She is Anglo but "claims" a Mexican identity; feels that the choice of ethnic identification is hers.
Nicole Huffstutler, Heather, and Jennifer Vargas (para. 15–24)	Nicole (who has Indian blood) and Heather claim a white identity because of "pride" in what they are. Jennifer claims a "mostly Mexican" identity. Nicole and Heather take Jennifer's "claim" of racial identity — despite the fact she is part Caucasian — to be a concession to their community's belief that "white is a bad race."
Will Mosley, Adolfo Garcia, and Matt Jenkins (para. 25–34)	Will and Matt, who are white, and Adolfo, who is Latino, identify with gangsta and ghetto culture. Although they have "outgrown trying to be something they're not," they still identify themselves as "city people" even though they live in a suburb.
Jesse Martinez, Oso Martinez, and Alex (para. 36–40)	Jesse and Oso, who are Latino, and Alex, who is Asian, are in a gang that claims a white gang as its "older generation." They prefer suburban to city culture, "longing for a Beaver Cleaver past" that is a thing of the past.
Andrea Jones (para. 41–44, 52)	Andrea is African American and comes from the suburbs; she believes that appreciating aspects of different cultures is "beautiful" but that using "pop culture stereotypes just to blend" is sad.
Roland Krevocheza (para. 45–49)	Roland is half Mexican and half Eastern European but embraces his white heritage because it is more unusual in the mostly Mexican neighborhood where he lives.

Examining the Characteristics of Illustration Essays, p. 236

1. Bernstein makes the generalization that a new generation believes that people can be whatever they "claim" to be. She supports it with quotations from California teenagers of different races from different areas and different walks of life.

2. Bernstein makes the term *identity* real and understandable by describing how the teenagers in the essay identify themselves through dress ("Her lipstick is dark, the

lip liner even darker" [para. 1]); language ("'nigga' as a term of endearment" [13]); and they way they describe themselves ("city people" [28]).

3. Using the Visualizing the Reading activity, have students rate each example according to how relevant, representative, and striking and dramatic it is. Then encourage students to assess whether the author provides enough examples to support her thesis, and if not, what additional examples they would have liked to see.

4. Answers will vary. Opening and concluding with the example of April Miller is a useful technique to both draw the reader in and bring the essay to a conclusion.

Building Your Word Power, p. 236

1. The figurative expression "sooner or later we'll all get nailed" reveals that April's father believes there is a backlash against white people in California and that NAFTA is taking jobs away from white people.

2. *Claiming* as it is used in the essay means adopting whatever neighborhood, ethnicity, or cultural identity one chooses. The author uses it in various contexts to illustrate its various meanings, such as in paragraph 14, when she explains its meaning through the series of examples.

Building Your Critical Thinking Skills: Alternative Viewpoints, p. 237

1. Will Mosley and Adolfo Garcia offer an alternative to April's views because they no longer "claim" an ethnicity based on clothing, considering their earlier wearing of gangsta clothes to be "blatant mimicry" (para. 30).

2. Andrea Jones views white teenagers' imitation of black culture as "shallow mimicry" (41) and believes that people should be proud of their own culture. Her view contributes to the essay because she does not identify with "city" or ghetto culture, although she is proud of being black (43).

3. Some students may note that because the essay offers only examples from interviews with young people from Califorina, it doesn't offer a true understanding of whether this phenomenon is confined primarily to California or reflects young people all across this country.

Reacting to the Reading: Discussion and Journal Writing, p. 237

You might want to preface class discussion with some remarks about racial tolerance and showing consideration for fellow students, since this issue can be inflammatory.

Dorianne Laux, "What I Wouldn't Do," p. 239

In this poem, Laux uses active verbs and vivid adjectives to conjure up the series of unskilled jobs she held before becoming a poet who teaches writing at the university level. The poem's subject, unskilled and low-paying jobs, should appeal to college students since it may mirror some of their experiences as employees. Combining vivid details with examples, it is a perfect centerpiece for freewriting and discussions on work.

Students might like to write about work experiences from their own point of view, as Laux does from a poet's perspective. Ask students to think about how they might identify themselves—from dancer or musician to video gamer or athlete—and then write about their work experiences with that identity in mind. Invite students to share their work with the class or in pairs.

Understanding the Reading, p. 240

1. The author has held a series of low-paying jobs, such as working in a fast-food restaurant, cleaning houses, making donuts, and cooking in a sanatorium. In addition to paying low wages, all of these jobs require few or no skills.

2. Laux's favorite job was making donuts. She liked it because she worked alone at night "surrounded by sugar and squat mounds of dough" (lines 29–34). She didn't like the *TV Guide* solicitation job because of the disappointment in people's voices when they realized that she was only calling to sell them something (1–3, 35–45).

3. Answers will vary. The author seems somewhat satisfied with her various jobs but not very enthusiastic. Evidence from the poem that suggests this includes low-key statements like "Cleaning houses was fine" (12) and the fact that she "drifted" (18) from job to job.

Visualizing the Reading, p. 240

Possible answers include:

Feature	"What I Wouldn't Do"
Narrator (Who is speaking in the poem?)	The author, Dorianne Laux
Audience (To whom is the poem addressed?)	Laux is not clear on this, though presumably the poem is addressed to anyone who has ever done menial or unskilled labor or to those who share her reluctance to "sell" things to people who haven't asked to be solicited.
Subject (What is the subject of the poem?)	The subject of the poem is working for a living and having to reject certain kinds of work if they interfere with one's values.
Tone (What feelings does the narrator express about her subject?)	The narrator's feelings are somewhat neutral, except in the title and the last few lines. Students may find the overall tone of the poem to be one of melancholy.

Thesis (What main point does the narrator express about her subject?)	The main point is that while the narrator could happily do many kinds of work, she couldn't solicit or disappoint people, even if she needed the money.
Examples (What examples support the thesis?)	1. Telemarketer (selling *TV Guide*) 2. Fast-food worker 3. Working at a laundromat 4. Housecleaner 5. Sanatorium cook 6. Gas station attendant 7. Working in a donut shop

Examining the Characteristics of Illustration Essays, p. 241

1. Laux's theme about the human experience is that even though everyone has to work for a living, there are some jobs that one has to say no to because the work goes against one's sense of what is right. Her unstated generalization about work is that it is possible to find moments of satisfaction and even beauty in most jobs, no matter how menial. Possible alternative interpretations: only work that doesn't exploit others is tolerable (lines 42–45); most work has some element of sensory joy ("all the onion rings I could eat" [lines 4–5] or the "A-minor ping" of the bell in line 18); or Laux will do *almost* anything for money (as suggested in the title).

2. Laux uses a series of six examples of menial, low-level jobs that she has held to explain why she couldn't do the phone solicitation job. Because these types of jobs are probably familiar to younger students, they will likely find Laux's examples to be relevant and representative.

3. Laux appeals to the senses of taste ("all the onion rings I could eat" [4–5]), sound ("A-minor ping" [18]), touch ("plucking bright coins from a palm" [9]), smell ("deep fried burritos" [6]), and sight ("flesh-colored plastic plates" [22–23]).

4. Laux indicates transitions within her poem through phrases such as "Before that" (4); "And at the laundromat" (8); "I drifted," (18); "I liked the donut shop best" (29); and "It wasn't that I hated calling them" (35). The transitions are chronological, but they shift from past to present tense. They are also somewhat obscure, presented without the clear, logical markers that are usually required in an essay.

Building Your Word Power, p. 241

1. The connotative meanings of the word *job* include an occupation and a task, or something that has to be done.

2. The figure of speech "hungry hands" in line 7 implies, literally, the hands of some-one who is hungry, and figuratively, hands like those of starving people or beggars who reach out with their palms cupped in desperation.

Building Your Critical Thinking Skills: Analyzing Poetry, p. 241

1. Laux uses lots of active verbs—such as "grabbing" (line 8), "plucking" (9), and "scooped" (21)—to convey a picture of activity or work. Some of the words in the poem have various shades of meaning. For example, "lazily" (16) describes the bell's clapper but could also apply to Laux as a dreamy, unproductive house-cleaner. Through the use of words like "bright" (9), and "jewelled" (16), Laux's use of descriptive language contributes to her message by illustrating the ways in which she found satisfaction and beauty in her work, no matter how menial the job. Her use of active verbs (see above) also conveys the occasional strenuousness of the work.

2. Students are likely to have different emotional responses to this poem, depending perhaps on their own experiences working. The title conveys an emotional atmos-phere or mood of slight foreboding, but much of the description of Laux's jobs in-dicates relative satisfaction or contentment with the work.

Chapter 8 Process Analysis: Explaining How Something Works or Is Done, p. 243

Process analysis is a simple, direct way of explaining how something is done, step by step. Recipes and directions are good examples of how process analysis is used in or-dinary life. Students enjoy writing these kinds of essays when they are presented as a challenge. You might, for example, want to ask them to explain something as routine as making a peanut butter sandwich in the simplest way possible so that even someone who has never seen or eaten one can make it. Remind students that as in description and narration essays, it is essential to use sensory details and figures of speech to make their writing more compelling, especially if the essay includes technical jargon or outlines a complicated process.

Although it can stand alone, the process analysis pattern is sometimes inserted into the midst of another kind of essay. Writers often incorporate it into essays that are principally defined by another pattern, such as comparison and contrast. When a writer does this, he or she should clearly introduce the transition into process analysis and then transition back into the primary pattern of development.

To begin, you might want to go over all of the characteristics of the process analy-sis essay as outlined in the chapter. Note in particular that such essays usually include an explicit thesis statement. Most of the pieces in this chapter have an explicit thesis statement, so you will have ample opportunity to model for students how to develop explicit thesis statements of their own. The annotated essay, "How the Oscars Work" (p. 244), presents a clear example of process analysis. The graphic organizer on page 252 shows the organizational structure of the essay and presents a model for how students might outline their own process analysis essay. When they begin writing, encourage them to make use of the flowchart on p. 251; it will help them identify and number the steps in their process to make sure that their essay is clear and organized in chronological or logical order.

The process analysis essay should present clearly outlined steps, usually in chronological order. For example, Melissa Russell-Ausley and Tom Harris describe the Academy Award process in chronological order. They simplify the complex processes of nominating and voting and tallying by breaking them into separate steps. David Feige also does this as he describes the legal process of defending a client in "How to Defend Someone You Know Is Guilty" (p. 278). Tom and Ray Magliozzi in "Inside the Engine" (p. 284) use logical order to explain how an engine works — for example, how the oil circulates. In "You and Improved" (p. 262), reporter Matthew Gilbert satirizes the steps involved in TV makeover shows to provide a critique of them.

Process analysis should define key terms, the way Tom and Ray Magliozzi define *crankshaft* and other words that may be unfamiliar to their readers. Process analysis should also provide necessary background information, the way "How the Oscars Work" includes information on the forms, ballots, and equipment involved in Oscar nominations and awards. Public defender Feige also provides background information by describing what he does when he first meets a client, what information he collects, how he decides what defense to use, and so on.

Tom and Ray Magliozzi supply adequate detail, and because theirs is a how-to essay, they anticipate and offer help with potential problems. They instruct the reader to avoid problems by paying attention to warning lights and taking certain actions such as not driving the car once the oil light goes on. Overall, their primary advice is to change the oil and filter every 3,000 miles. Cindy Chupack also advises her readers *buyers beware*, in "Dater's Remorse" (p. 273), humorously outlining problems that women might encounter if they do not shop wisely for a husband.

Analogies are another important component in process analysis. In "Campus Racism 101" (p. 267), Nikki Giovanni compares college with prison in order to emphasize her point that a college education provides an opportunity for more freedom and choice. Chupack uses an extended analogy between selecting men to date and shopping for clothes or furniture. Tom and Ray Magliozzi make humorous comparisons between men checking to see that their zippers are up and car owners double-checking to see if their warning lights work.

Melissa Russell-Ausley and Tom Harris, "How the Oscars Work," p. 244

Melissa Russell-Ausley and Tom Harris (editors of HowStuffWorks.com) make the process of the Oscars accessible and interesting by analyzing the awards' features in a step-by-step fashion. Like most process analysis essays, it provides an explicit thesis statement: "Let's take a look at the organization behind the Oscars, see what the 'Academy' actually is, and learn how Oscars are awarded" (para. 2). The authors explain the process chronologically and provide background information about how the Academy Awards became known as the Oscars.

Kyle Mares, "Creating Your Own Web Site," p. 258

This student essay compiles and illustrates a list of steps for creating a Web site. To emphasize the importance of the process he is going to describe, Mares opens his essay with the idea that posting one's résumé online is a useful tool for both job hunting and connecting with like-minded people online. Mares then outlines a five-step process to create a Web site. Over the course of his essay he defines key terms like *fee-based* and *dedicated*, producing a satisfying, informative essay that students can analyze in terms of their own needs.

Responding to "Students Write," p. 260

1. The writer's thesis statement and introduction explain why making a Web site might be useful and important to readers. Mares's introduction explains that having a Web site and résumé online can lead to jobs and connect someone to others with similar interests, and his thesis suggests that one can "reap . . . benefits" (para. 1) from having a Web site.

2. Potential trouble spots include the drawbacks posed by the unwanted ads and limited storage space of free Web publishing, the "cost" of "fee-based" services, and the very high cost of having one's own Web server (2). Mares also mentions problems such as complaints if the site is poorly designed (5) and the task of keeping it updated (6).

3. While Mares's essay offers an introduction to the process of creating a Web site, the level of detail is probably not great enough to create a Web site using Mares's instructions. Additional detail about how to use HTML or "authoring programs," for example, would be helpful (3). It might be useful to poll Web-savvy students who have created sites before to see if they found Mares's essay useful, and if not, in what areas it is lacking.

4. Mares's conclusion is satisfying because it emphasizes that the process of creating the site is in itself rewarding, and it emphasizes the rewards (9).

Matthew Gilbert, "You and Improved," p. 262

Reporter Matthew Gilbert mocks the TV makeover trend, from homes to bodies and clothes. He questions that "expert" advice can make someone happy, suggesting that all that these programs do is encourage people to criticize themselves. He uses questions that mimic those heard on shows like *Queer Eye for the Straight Guy*, such as "Are you actually going out in public in such infantile baseball caps?" (para. 6) and "Is there a way out of this disgrace?" (7) to mock their style. In a more serious vein, he theorizes that the drive for self-improvement is part of an American tradition.

Because it involves contemporary popular culture, this essay should spark a great deal of interest among your students. You might begin with a discussion of whether it is true that Americans as a group "hunger for transformation" (12). Have students consider also whether makeover shows that use plastic surgery, like *Extreme Makeover*, go too far. Students may wish to write about the idea of self-worth and how it relates to an individual's social image.

Understanding the Reading, p. 264

1. The five steps in the tongue-in-cheek makeover process are (1) scrutinize your home; (2) criticize your appearance; (3) criticize your wardrobe; (4) pause to revise, to rethink, to renovate; and (5) accessorize.

2. According to Gilbert, people like makeover shows because they "suit the traditional American hunger for transformation and self-realization" (12). In the author's view, such shows appeal to people who dream of improving their lives.

3. In Gilbert's opinion, people are especially likely to feel that they need a makeover if they are "dreamers and yearners" (12) and when they have "insecurities" (14) that lead them to want to radically change their lives.

4. Gilbert's purpose for writing is to critique these shows. He thinks that while there is nothing wrong with making something over, people watching such shows lose "perspective" in the transformative power of change, falsely believing that change alone will make them happy (13). Furthermore, according to Gilbert, such shows lead people to compare themselves to "a standard of beauty and behavior that isn't right for you," resulting in "idealized and unreal" visions of how they should look, act, and live (15).

Visualizing the Reading, p. 264

Possible answers include:

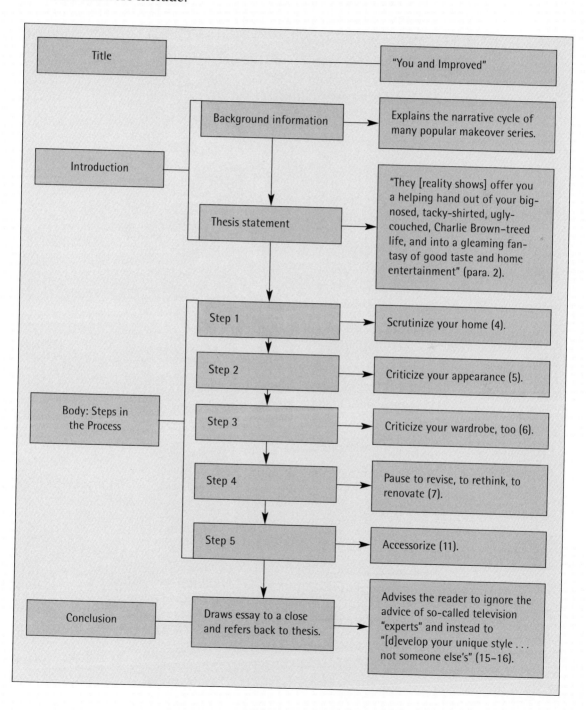

Title	→	"You and Improved"
Introduction → Background information	→	Explains the narrative cycle of many popular makeover series.
Thesis statement	→	"They [reality shows] offer you a helping hand out of your big-nosed, tacky-shirted, ugly-couched, Charlie Brown–treed life, and into a gleaming fantasy of good taste and home entertainment" (para. 2).
Step 1	→	Scrutinize your home (4).
Step 2	→	Criticize your appearance (5).
Body: Steps in the Process → Step 3	→	Criticize your wardrobe, too (6).
Step 4	→	Pause to revise, to rethink, to renovate (7).
Step 5	→	Accessorize (11).
Conclusion → Draws essay to a close and refers back to thesis.	→	Advises the reader to ignore the advice of so-called television "experts" and instead to "[d]evelop your unique style . . . not someone else's" (15–16).

Examining the Characteristics of Process Analysis Essays, p. 264

1. For the author's thesis, see the graphic organizer above. This is a how-it-works essay because it explains how a reality show draws people in, inviting them to "scrutinize" (para. 4) and "criticize" (5) themselves.

2. As background information Gilbert presents the narrative cycle of many makeover series, explaining how popular shows such as *Trading Spaces* and *Queer Eye for the Straight Guy* promise to "eliminate the embarrassing 'before' in favor of the tasteful happily ever 'after'" (2).

3. The organizational technique Gilbert uses is chronological, from "before" to "after" (2). He most likely chose this technique in order to mirror the path used by most makeover shows.

4. The author uses colorful details to humorously describe the "before" person: "your big-nosed, tacky-shirted, ugly-couched, Charlie Brown–treed life" (2). For sensory details, he uses images like "flawlessly glazed turkey" (13) and "fraying Khakis" (6). Figures of speech incorporate gentle humor, as in macaroni and cheese being the "poor man's protein fix" (4).

Building Your Word Power, p. 265

1. *Vintage* as used in paragraph 6 refers to a certain kind of old or second-hand-store clothes that are considered fashionable, unlike other old clothes.

2. The phrase "We are steeped in the tyranny of the glossy magazine spreads" means that the glut of visual images of ideal bodies and homes featured in magazines and advertising has made people aspire to something they cannot ever realistically achieve.

Building Your Critical Thinking Skills: Humor, p. 265

1. Answers may vary. Most students will probably find Gilbert's tone to be somewhat lighter than sarcasm. He uses humor to encourage readers to challenge and reject media definitions of beauty.

2. Gilbert combines humor with process analysis by mimicking the tone and agenda of reality shows. For example, step 4 in his process — "Pause to revise, to rethink, to renovate. Is there a way out of this disgrace?" (para. 7) — would never be spoken as such on a show, but similar subtexts are evident in the tone used by shows' experts. Gilbert also mocks the falsely high-toned language of programs like *Queer Eye for the Straight Guy* when he writes, "Are you ready to select a pocket square, more commonly known as a handkerchief . . .?" (11).

Reacting to the Reading: Discussion and Journal Writing, p. 265

2. The media's role in how people form opinions of themselves is a topic that should lead to some interesting discussion. Forming a critique of the media may be difficult for first-year students, but these kinds of discussions are useful if you guide students by asking questions.

Nikki Giovanni, "Campus Racism 101," p. 267

Giovanni, a professor of English at Virginia Tech, titles her essay as if it were an introductory college course for black students on how to survive racism at a primarily white college, like the one where she teaches. Her process consists of a list of guidelines or rules for how to survive and thrive at a white college. She follows it with a question-and-answer format to effectively illustrate the kind of insensitive questions black students may encounter. Giovanni's tone is one of mildly scolding impatience with the idea that it is better to drop out rather than face racism. But it is clear that Giovanni has high expectations for black students. To better prepare your students, you might want to provide some background material on the history of black education at the college level in the United States before getting into a discussion of Giovanni's tone and guidelines.

Understanding the Reading, p. 270

1. Giovanni thinks her presence is important at Virginia Tech because there are some black students at the school. She also thinks it is important for white students to interact with black people in authoritative positions while in college (para. 2).

2. Some of the challenges that black students may face at predominantly white colleges include being insulted (for instance, being called "nigger" [4]); racist or sexist professors who don't like them (10); and insensitive questions or remarks from white students (13). Giovanni notes that these are all challenges that black students will experience outside of college as well.

3. Giovanni thinks it is important for students to meet and cultivate relationships with their professors because it will indicate that the students are serious about doing well (6).

4. According to the author, a black student's most important job in college is "to obtain an education" (34).

Visualizing the Reading, p. 270

Possible answers include:

Question	Potential Trouble Spot
"What's it like to grow up in a ghetto?" (para. 14)	Racial stereotyping; some students assume all black people lived in a ghetto.
"Can you give us the Black perspective on Toni Morrison, Huck Finn, . . ."(para. 16)	Assumes that a single black student can speak for "all" black people.
"Why do all the Black people sit together in the dining hall?" (para. 18)	Assumes is that a group of white people sitting together is not exclusive, whereas a black group is.
"Why should there be an African-American studies course?" (para. 20)	Fails to acknowledge the important contributions of Africans and African Americans.
"Why are there so many scholarships for 'minority' students?" (para. 22)	Assumes that minorities are unfairly being given easy access through affirmative action quotas and scholarships.
"How can whites understand Black history, culture, literature, and so forth?" (para. 24)	Fails to recognize that black people have historically had to learn white history, culture, and so on.
"Should whites take African-American studies courses?" (para. 26)	Fails to recognize that many courses focus only on the work of white people but are not called "white studies."

Examining the Characteristics of Process Analysis Essays, p. 271

1. The essay title suggests that the author's purpose is to explain the fundamentals of dealing with racism on campus.

2. The essay's thesis statement is implicitly stated in paragraph 4: "There are discomforts attached to attending predominantly white colleges, though no more so than living in a racist world." This thesis identifies the process to be discussed (how to cope with the "discomforts") and suggests Giovanni's attitude toward it (the process is no more difficult than the obstacles that blacks face in everyday life).

3. Giovanni makes readers understand the importance of the process she recommends by comparing college to prison and then explaining how a college education differs because it gives students "a passport to greater opportunities" (para. 4).

4. The background information establishes the author's qualifications for writing about racism by indicating that Giovanni is black and a tenured professor. It also helps readers understand the process that she explains by letting them know that

she cares about her students, even if she is strict in tone. For example, when she says, "We need to quit it," she identifies herself with other black people who have criticized their own race (1).

5. Students' responses may vary. Giovanni's tone is one of impatience with students who are too sensitive to deal with racist comments. She thinks they should have the strength and courage to get an education, no matter what difficulties they face.

Building Your Word Power, p. 271

1. Answers may vary.

2. The different connotative meanings of *discriminate* are: to be selective about something, and to form a bias against someone (for instance, racial discrimination). The former meaning is used by Giovanni in paragraph 10.

Building Your Critical Thinking Skills: Point of View, p. 272

1. Giovanni uses the first person. This perspective reinforces her message to students because it indicates that she is black like them and therefore has an intimate understanding of their difficulties.

2. Answers will vary.

Reacting to the Reading: Discussion and Journal Writing, p. 272

1–2. Be sure to preface any discussion with a few remarks about creating community in the classroom and the need to exhibit tolerance and understanding for everyone's point of view. Questions like number 1 often raise difficult issues, such as what constitutes "preferential treatment" and so on, so it is best to provide some historical background on civil rights and the issue of legal redress. It might also be a good idea to begin with question 2 since it will provide some common ground from which to consider racial differences.

Cindy Chupack, "Dater's Remorse," p. 273

Cindy Chupack creates a humorous analogy between shopping and dating men. Adopting the stance of the experienced and somewhat jaded dater who has made many poor consumer choices, Chupack cautions other women against the types she has encountered, become enamored of, and escaped from. The essay strains its analogies at times as it tries to bring certain ideas together for the sake of humor. To encourage a critical reading of what is likely to be a highly entertaining essay for your students, you might want to assign them to identify and discuss the weakest similes in the piece. After discussing this essay, consider having students try to create a similarly humorous essay about an issue of their choice (for example, traveling with friends or choosing someone to dance with at a party).

Understanding the Reading, p. 275

1. The author's relationship with long distance phone companies relates to the topic of dating because it serves as the basis for an analogy between the choices she has as a long distance phone consumer and the choices she makes in her dating life.

2. According to Chupack, dating someone who is "the human equivalent of a fashion fad" may end up becoming more of an "emotional investment" than expected (para. 4).

3. Chupack uses the analogy between dating and buying furniture to explain how, just like a couch that doesn't go with anything else in the house is an impractical purchase, men who are very different from oneself and one's lifestyle may "mean changing your entire life" (6). Likewise, Chupack advises women to stay away from "fixer-uppers" because they "are more likely to stay forever flawed, no matter what we do" (5).

4. The author assumes that readers are looking for a husband (8).

Visualizing the Reading, p. 275

Possible answers include:

Step	Shopping Analogy	Dating Advice
1	"Go with a classic, not a trend" (para. 4).	Avoid men who are radically different from the types you usually date.
2	"Beware of the phrase 'Some assembly required'" (para. 5).	Avoid men that you have to fix up — they tend to remain flawed.
3	"Make sure your purchase goes with the other things you own" (para. 6).	Don't date someone whose lifestyle is so unlike yours that your entire life will be changed.
4	"Check with previous owners" (para. 7).	If he is older than twenty-five, find out why his other relationships ended so that you don't end up with a lemon.
5	"Caveat emptor" (para. 8).	Be a wise shopper to reduce the number of times it doesn't work out.

Examining the Characteristics of Process Analysis Essays, p. 276

1. Chupack's thesis appears at the beginning of paragraph 3: "The unfortunate truth is that while most of us are savvy shoppers, we're not sufficiently selective when looking for relationships, and that's why we often suffer from dater's remorse."

2. Chupack's essay is not ordered chronologically. While her steps are essentially interchangeable, she does move from advice geared toward women dating men more casually ("Go with a classic, not a trend") to factors that are likely to have long-term implications for women who enter into serious relationships or marriages with the types described ("Check with previous owners").

3. While the author does not offer a lot of detail for the steps in her process, the examples are vivid and compelling, so some students will likely (depending on their own dating experiences) find Chupack's advice useful.

4. Befitting the humorous tone of her essay, Chupack's conclusion ends lightly yet convincingly as she cautions readers, "Caveat emptor" (para. 8).

Building Your Word Power, 276

1. In paragraph 7, *lot,* as in "used car lot," is used figuratively to mean still dating or available, not married.

2. The connotation of *secondhand* and *used merchandise* in paragraph 7 is men who have been in other serious relationships.

Building Your Critical Thinking Skills: Analogies, p. 276

1. Chupack develops her analogy between shopping and dating through the steps in her process. To encourage students to evaluate Chupack's analogies critically, have them go through each step listed above in Visualizing the Reading, examining the details in the text to assess whether all aspects of the analogy are logical and useful.

2. Have students brainstorm in class to discover ways in which shopping and dating differ. Chupack addresses these differences only by saying that "looking for a husband is a bit more complicated than choosing a major appliance" (para. 8).

David Feige, "How to Defend Someone You Know Is Guilty," p. 278

David Feige offers a glimpse into a public defender's emotional response to his clients, even the guilty ones. Feige draws the reader in at the start of his essay with an anecdote about a seemingly unlikable crack addict named Kevin, saying "I loved Kevin" (para. 1). Feige writes like a trial lawyer who uses shock tactics and hyperbole to draw the reader in with statements such as "I rarely bother with 'the facts'" (3). His step-by-step outline of what he does and doesn't do to defend a client becomes even more intriguing when he contends that it is emotion that keeps him committed to his work. Students may find it especially surprising to read that he considers building "trust" (4) with his clients his main task.

In class, it might be useful to note that Feige uses transitional phrases to keep his narrative chronologically consistent, even as the focus shifts between his defense of this individual client and legal procedures in general. Students may like to discuss the idea of a public defender—how the role came about and what it means for the American system of justice. You might initiate discussion by asking questions such as: What would it mean for society if the right to a fair trial and "representation" did not exist? You might also ask students to come up with a scenario—using freewriting—in which they are mistakenly considered a criminal suspect. What if all the "facts" fell into place against them? Would they want Feige to represent them?

Understanding the Reading, p. 280

1. Readers learn that the author will "happily" defend any client, "guilty or innocent" (7). They learn that he defends the guilty for several reasons, including the fact that once he gets to know them he likes them. He also has empathy for them because no one else is rooting for them (9) and because they are "hated" and "desperately need my protection" (11).

2. The author doesn't think too much about the victims of the crimes in which his clients are involved because he is focused on defending his clients. The victims remain "abstract" for the simple reason that the perpetrator is "very human and very real" (9) to him. Just as the prosecutors seek to dehumanize his clients, he too dehumanizes the victims. He can do this because he understands that the victims are being cared for by other lawyers, their families, the police, and so on.

3. Kevin is being tried for buying cocaine from an undercover policeman and then attacking him with a screwdriver. Kevin denies this version of events, saying that he had bought some crack and then "out of nowhere" was shot (7). Feige planned to defend him by saying that the police fabricated the sale of cocaine to cover up the shooting of Kevin (7).

Visualizing the Reading, p. 280

Answers will vary. The primary characteristics in a lawyer that would be of value to the man depicted in this image—according to Feige's essay—would be a willingness to take the time to get to know and understand the man as a person, and an interest in protecting his client no matter what the circumstances of the crime.

Examining the Characteristics of Process Analysis Essays, p. 281

1. Feige uses an implied thesis about why he feels the compelling need to protect and defend suspected criminals. The main process he describes is that of defending a potentially guilty client. Other processes described in this article are Feige's defense of Kevin, the procedures a lawyer and client follow, and how other public defenders describe their reasons for defending guilty clients.

2. The details about Kevin that the author provides are: he has a lengthy rap sheet and a crack addiction, he was shot by the police after supposedly attacking an un-

dercover policeman, and he has a family he loves but is too embarrassed to visit. The rap sheet and gunshot wound are important because they indicate the probability that Kevin was involved in the crime. The details about his family are important because they humanize Kevin. These kinds of details make Feige "really like" his clients (para. 10).

3. The author organizes the steps in his essay chronologically.

4. One potential trouble spot that Feige identifies is how to address the issue of whether his client is telling "the truth" (4). Because Feige knows that the truth "is often the only thing my clients have left," he understands that they will not "part with" it easily (4). His solution to this problem is to accept whatever version of the crime his client gives him, using that as a defense (5). He takes "the defenses as I take my clients—as they are" (5).

5. Answers will vary. Note: Feige does include a brief explanation of the outcome of Kevin's trial in parentheses in paragraph 7.

Building Your Word Power, p. 281

1. "Putting him in a suit would look like a lie" (para. 6) means that a judge and jury will not believe that a homeless crack addict ever wears a suit and that this "lie" won't help persuade them that he is innocent.

2. The author's use of legal jargon, such as "robbery in the second degree" (2) and "plausible defense" (7), contributes to the essay by reminding the reader that most suspects would be lost without the help of a lawyer.

Building Your Critical Thinking Skills: Facts and Opinions, p. 281

1. Fact

2. Opinion

3. Fact

4. Opinion

5. Opinion

Reacting to the Reading: Discussion and Journal Writing, p. 282

1. You might want to consider the issues of race and class as they pertain to *justice*. You might also want to preface the discussion by giving students a little background on how the legal system in the United States has changed over time. Also, some discussion of how the legal rights of women, slaves, and others have been altered over time might be useful.

Tom and Ray Magliozzi, "Inside the Engine," p. 284

The Magliozzi brothers (well known as *Car Talk*'s Tappet Brothers) begin with a brief anecdote about what happens when people don't pay attention to warning lights or gauges in their car. The authors then explain some of the basic features of an engine, such as how the oil circulates. After that, they deliver pointers on the most important signs to pay attention to, the necessity of maintaining and heeding warning lights, and fundamental maintenance procedures to invest in at regular intervals. As they proceed, they explain complex terms and automotive jargon in order to make their how-it-works essay easy to understand, using analogies to familiar things to help their readers understand clearly how certain processes work.

Students will enjoy this essay because it provides essential information made palatable through humor. They may also appreciate its clear and simple presentation and use of simile. The article may spark an interest in writing and sharing some short process analysis essays in class. Ask students to brainstorm a subject about which they know quite a bit and think they could explain step by step (for example, diving or throwing a football). Challenge them to share it and evaluate its effectiveness in pairs before presenting it aloud to the class.

Understanding the Reading, p. 288

1. The customer's car broke down because it had run out of oil. The lesson the authors teach through this example is that the cost of neglecting some basic features of car care may be very high.

2. Oil is very important because it lubricates the car's engine and keeps the metal parts cool (para. 5). A car's oil warning light comes on when the engine has lost pressure, meaning that it is very low on oil and/or the oil pump is not working (14).

3. The problem the authors associate with gauges is that people may take their eyes off the road while they are driving to look at the gauges (10).

4. The authors say the best way to protect a car is to change the timing belt (24) and the oil every 3,000 miles (28).

Visualizing the Reading, p. 289

Paragraph	How-to Advice
13	Shut the engine off if the oil warning light comes on.
16	Make sure that your warning lights work.

17	Don't overfill your oil.
26	Change rubber timing belts every 60,000 miles.
27	Change the water pump when you change the rubber timing belt.
28	Change the oil and oil filter every 3,000 miles.

Examining the Characteristics of Process Analysis Essays, p. 289

1. The Magliozzis' thesis is: "The oil is critical to keeping things running since it not only acts as a lubricant, but it also helps to keep the engine cool" (para. 5). This thesis doesn't state clearly why the process is important to readers, but it implies that if there is no oil, the engine will overheat.

2. The level of detail on the subject of what oil does (5–8) is fairly elaborate, but this seems appropriate because most readers won't have an understanding of this process and will therefore need the sort of detailed explanation that the Magliozzis give.

3. The authors use humor (for instance, the cookies and milk story [3]) and analogies to more familiar things (for instance, checking one's zipper and then one's oil pressure [30]) to make the topic interesting and understandable. The level of knowledge and mechanical savvy the authors assume their readers possess is rudimentary.

4. Potential areas of confusion the authors identify are: paying too much attention to the gauges if one doesn't have warning lights (10); not knowing enough to stop the car if the warning light comes on (13); not making sure that the warning lights work (16); overfilling the oil (17); not knowing that the timing belt should be changed when recommended (25); not remembering to change the water pump when recommended (27); and not remembering to change to the oil and filter every 3,000 miles (28). Answers may vary.

5. The authors use analogy (for instance, the oil pump is like a heart and the oil acts like a cushion to the metal [7]) to make technical terms understandable to readers who lack mechanical knowledge.

Building Your Word Power, p. 289

1. The oil is described as "coursing through the veins of the engine" (para. 7). This use of personification enhances the story by making the mechanism seem more vivid and alive, analogous to a human heart.

2. Answers will vary.

Building Your Critical Thinking Skills: Evaluating Authors, p. 290

1. The authors of "Inside the Engine" are qualified to give professional car advice because they are trained auto mechanics who have owned a garage for many years. In addition, they were both educated at MIT, one of the nation's top institutions for engineering and science, making them both highly qualified to explain complicated processes.

2. The authors generally stick to advice that falls within their realm of expertise. When they do discuss other topics (for instance, radios in cars), the advice is given humorously and is not intended to be taken seriously.

Chapter 9 Comparison and Contrast: Showing Similarities and Differences, p. 292

This chapter should be of great interest to students because *comparison and contrast* is one of the most useful of all essay forms. Students who master this rhetorical mode will have mastered a skill that they can readily utilize in future college papers and on essay exams. You will probably want to devote several sessions to comparison and contrast, explaining that these essays must be organized carefully, point by point or subject by subject. To illustrate the organizational structure of comparison and contrast, it might be helpful to show students the graphic organizers on pages 299 and 300 for subject-by-subject and point-by-point arrangements. As explained on page 298, careful planning and outlining are essential preliminary steps for this mode. It is very important to reiterate that the points of comparison must be significant and similar enough to warrant comparison. Analogies, although useful, must also be accurate in order to be used effectively. Refer students to the Use analogies guideline on page 304 for more on this. To create better-flowing comparison and contrast essays, you will want to emphasize the need for clear transitional words (phrases such as *similarly, in contrast,* and *on the one hand*) as signals or markers for the reader. Have students do revision exercises in order to perfect their ability to guide the reader through the series of points.

The essays included in this chapter present a wide range of examples of the mode for students to analyze, evaluate, and model. Joseph Sobran's essay, "Patriotism or Nationalism?" (p. 293), uses a point-by-point organization very effectively, making this essay a good illustration of how an author compares only "key characteristics." The graphic organizer for Sobran's essay (p. 301) is also very useful for reducing a complex essay to three or four essential points. In "We've Got the Dirt on Guy Brains" (p. 311), Dave Barry humorously argues that differences between men and women are genetically determined. Barry's essay might be compared thematically with "East vs. West" (p. 321), in which Sharon Begley shows how Western and Eastern psychological perspectives of the world differ. Using the point-by-point method, she illustrates that although human thought varies from culture to culture, it can be modified by exposure to new cultures. Jeanne Wakatsuki Houston uses a subject-by-subject organization in "A Taste of Snow" (p. 316), an essay comparing two very different winters from her childhood. Both winters carry symbolic overtones in a subtle way. She begins with her first taste of snow, a happy memory of wonder that took place during an unhappy period when her family was placed in an internment camp during World War II. Then she transitions back to her earlier memories of happiness in winters spent on the California coast, where it never snows. "A Case of 'Severe Bias'" (p. 326), by Patricia Raybon, uses a point-by-point arrangement to support her thesis that media images of black people are inaccurate and damaging. She provides a series of stereotypes, beginning with her own personal experience, and then cites statistical evidence, such as the fact that there are more poor white women on welfare than black women, to counteract the stereotypes of African Americans perpetuated by the media. In "Sex, Lies, and Conversation" (p. 331), Deborah Tannen also uses a point-by-point organization to argue, like Begley, that although differences exist in how men and women perceive communication, they can be modified by learning.

Joseph Sobran, "Patriotism or Nationalism?" p. 293

Joseph Sobran uses a point-by-point arrangement to caution readers against "the seductions of nationalism" (para. 12). He concentrates initially on defining and establishing differences between patriotism and nationalism and then selects key points of comparison, as shown in the graphic organizer (p. 301). Students will benefit from analyzing the way the essay opens with a definition of *nationalism* before proceeding with its persuasive argument against the dangers of nationalism. This topic works well for a discussion of the political climate that followed the events of 9/11. You might like to encourage students to evaluate issues such as the intersection of domestic security and civil rights or the idea of the melting pot in the post-9/11 period. The theme of nationalism in the United States might also be explored historically. Students could, for example, compare and contrast the internment of Japanese Americans during World War II (described in Houston's essay, "A Taste of Snow," which appears later in this chapter on p. 316) with the treatment of Arab Americans after 9/11.

Heather Gianakos, "Border Bites," p. 307

In this student essay, Heather Gianakos skillfully compares Mexican and Southwestern cuisines in a point-by-point style using key points such as uses of corn, chicken, beef, and pork. You might like to assign students to write in-class essays of their own about a particular cuisine, following this essay as a model. You might also review Gianakos's "Works Cited" in class in order to familiarize students with the more extensive research they will do later in the term. Have them discuss which quotes most impress them and how they would evaluate the sources she cites.

Responding to "Students Write," p. 309

1. Gianakos's purpose in writing is to compare and contrast Mexican and Southwestern cooking. She supports her thesis effectively by detailing the "subtle, flavorful differences between the foods featured in Mexican and Southwestern cuisine" (para. 1) through a comparison of the origins of ingredient use, and the uses of corn, chicken, beef, and pork.

2. Gianakos organizes her essay chronologically. She explains the origins of ingredient use and then provides the historical background of each ingredient—the key points of comparison and contrast in her essay.

3. Generally, the author effectively presents details to support each point of comparison. For example, she effectively details how Southwestern cooking often grew out of difficult conditions such as having to pack foods for travel and cook them over open fires on the range (2), whereas Mexican cuisine developed in an environment where there were plenty of fresh ingredients. To describe the differences in cooking styles and tastes, Gianakos relies heavily on sensory details of sight, smell, and taste: "Fried chicken rolled in flour and dunked into sizzling oil or fat" (4); "the richly seasoned, corn- and tomato-heavy style of Mexican food" (7).

4. Gianakos's use of sources contributes to her essay by giving it more authority.

Dave Barry, "We've Got the Dirt on Guy Brains," p. 311

In this essay reprinted from his well-known weekly humor column, humorist Dave Barry lays claim to a scientific breakthrough called "Male Genetic Dirt Blindness" (para. 4). Using pseudo-scientific jargon to compare and contrast male and female perceptions of dirt, he playfully contends that men's reluctance to do housework or communicate with their partners at home may be genetic rather than learned. You might like to use this essay to initiate a discussion of humor and how it works in this instance. Another discussion topic could be generalizations or stereotypes, especially age-old gender stereotypes such as the one Barry treats. You might invite students to provide counter-examples from their own store of anecdotal evidence to the contrary, or to explore the idea that Barry's thesis is dated, not applicable to younger generations now in college. Students might also write an in-class essay that provides a similarly humorous pseudo-theory, but one that takes the woman's point of view.

Understanding the Reading, p. 313

1. The author describes himself as a "modest person" (para. 1), a "journalist" (5), and a husband (7).

2. Barry's original claim regarding men's ability to do housework was that "Male Genetic Dirt Blindness" made them unqualified to do housework because they were genetically unable to perceive dirt. The new proof he offers to back up this claim is a book, *What Could He Be Thinking? How a Man's Mind Really Works*, which states that because men supposedly take in less sensory detail than women, they don't perceive dirt and disorder in the same way (5).

3. The key piece of information cited from the book Barry mentions is that a man's brain "'takes in less sensory detail than a woman's, so he doesn't see or even feel the dust and household mess in the same way'" (5). Another difference involves the "cingulate gyrus," though Barry does not know exactly what this is, leading him to create a hilarious hypothesis of his own to explain this part of the brain. The only other sources quoted in Barry's essay are his own observations about male-female relationships.

4. Two examples of the types of situations in which Barry feels men and women differ in their thinking are: a man would rather lie on the sofa and watch TV than communicate with his mate (8), and a man will think the bathroom is clean when a woman doesn't (3).

Visualizing the Reading, p. 313

Possible answers include:

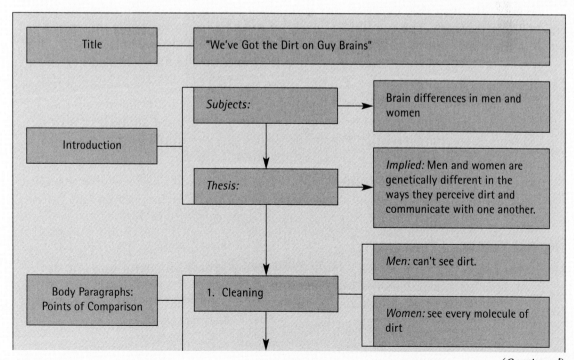

(Continued)

(*Continued*)

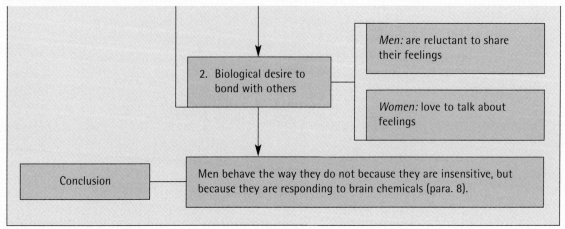

Examining the Characteristics of Comparison and Contrast Essays, p. 314

1. Barry's purpose in writing is to playfully propose that men and women are different because of innate, biological differences rather than cultural influences. His basis of comparison involves the ways men and women perceive dirt (para. 2–5) and communicate with one another (6–8).

2. Barry uses an implied thesis that women and men are genetically different in terms of the way they perceive dirt and clutter and how they communicate and bond with others. The sex-linked characteristics he uses to support this thesis are that men tend not to notice dirt while women do (2) and that women enjoy talking about feelings while men do not like to communicate about feelings (7–8).

3. Answers will vary. Barry does not use many detailed examples to support his thesis, though given that the essay is intended to be humorous, it is unlikely that he is seriously trying to prove his thesis. To encourage a critical analysis of how he explains each characteristic, have students list every example Barry uses and then discuss whether the details are interesting and relevant.

4. Barry organizes his essay point by point. The essay might not be as effective with a subject-by-subject organization because the contrasts between men and women are more humorous when compared side by side, point by point.

Building Your Word Power, p. 314

1. Brad Pitt, as your students no doubt know, is a popular film actor and one of *People* magazine's sexiest men alive. The allusion to Pitt in the first paragraph means that Barry likes to imagine many things about himself that are not true, thereby implying that anything he says should be questioned critically.

2. These images are effective and humorous in the context of the essay because they mimic scientific jargon and the tendency to use fruit metaphors to describe medical conditions (for instance, a grapefruit-size tumor).

Building Your Critical Thinking Skills: Humor, p. 314

1. Barry uses humor in this essay to poke fun at differences between men and women that people often laugh about socially but that are generally treated respectfully and scientifically in our serious, liberal, "p.c." culture.

2. Without humor, the essay would not be as effective because many men and women who are concerned about changing gender roles would not take lightly the idea that genetics determine some men's dislike of housework or difficulties with communication in intimate relationships.

3. Answers will vary.

Reacting to the Reading: Discussion and Journal Writing, p. 314

Issues such as gender roles can lead to heated discussions if they are not properly prefaced with remarks about political tolerance. You might set the tone by discussing the history of gender relations and how they have changed over time. Question 3 might be a good place to start in order to show that many women are messy and many men are neat. Be aware that some younger students may not even understand or subscribe to Barry's humor. They may welcome an opportunity to challenge his humor in view of historical and sociological changes brought about by three decades of feminism.

Jeanne Wakatsuki Houston, "A Taste of Snow," p. 316

Jeanne Wakatsuki Houston compares two very different winters from her childhood. She arranges the essay in a simple subject-by-subject fashion. She opens with a recounting of the first time she tasted snow. This otherwise happy memory occurred in the midst of a stark period in her life, when her Japanese American family was sent to an internment camp in California. Houston then describes her lush, earlier memories of a happy "American" childhood on the California coast, where it never snows. Students might find Houston's use of symbolism (particularly of snow, Christmas and other holidays, and nature) of interest. You might suggest that they read the essay closely at least two times in order to analyze Houston's nuanced use of symbolism. This essay has some thematic overlap with the issue of patriotism and nationalism addressed in Sobran's essay (p. 293). Approaching the two essays in conjunction might generate an interesting discussion and a possible comparison and contrast essay.

Understanding the Reading, p. 318

1. Houston was living in Owens Valley because after the bombing of Pearl Harbor the U.S. government forced many Japanese Americans to relocate to internment camps for the rest of World War II.

2. Houston was interested in the snow because she had never seen it before, having lived previously in Ocean Park, on the California coast where it never snows.

3. Before Houston went to Manzanar, her life was like that of any other California child. She played on the promenades (para. 4), celebrated traditional American holidays (5), and considered her family an American family just like any other.

Visualizing the Reading, p. 318

Possible answers include:

Points of Comparison	Manzanar	Ocean Park
Location	The high desert of Owens Valley, California	Dudley Avenue, a block from the beach
Temperature/weather	cold and snowy	warm and sunny
Impression of landscape	mountains and desert; a "stark landscape of white on white" (para. 3)	ocean and sand
Christmas	An improvised Christmas tree of "a bare manzanita limb embellished with origami cranes" (6)	"a lush, brilliantly lit fir tree" (6)

Examining the Characteristics of Comparison and Contrast Essays, p. 318

1. Answers will likely vary because Houston's intent in writing is not stated overtly. Her purpose in writing this essay may have been to inform others about the existence of Japanese internment camps in World War II, or it may have been simply to express her memories of these very different periods and places in her life.

2. The author uses an implied thesis that she cannot summon memories of her childhood in California without recalling her time at Manzanar (para. 6). Students may have difficulty identifying Houston's thesis. To help them, have them read the essay's conclusion, looking for clues about the significance of the two places that the author contrasts.

3. Answers will vary. The subject-by-subject organization is effective because it creates a child's-eye view of her experience at Manazar that contrasts sharply with her former, sun-filled childhood experience on the California coast.

4. Using the graphic organizer above, have students evaluate the effectiveness of each point of comparison addressed by Houston. She uses highly descriptive language, full of rich sensory details that appeal to taste ("cotton candy, wispy and delicate" [1]); touch ("uncomfortable wetness when the snow melted upon contact" [2]); sight ("orange-flowered dress and white high-topped shoes" [5]); and sound ("the 'kata-kata' clatter of wooden clogs scraping across sand and gravel" [3]).

5. Other patterns of development used by Houston include narration and description. These contribute to her comparison and contrast by providing the rich details that constitute the basis of her contrast between the two places from her childhood.

Building Your Word Power, p. 319

1. Answers may vary. By "beauty had its price to be paid" in paragraph 2, the author may be suggesting that she was already learning that enjoyment in her life would inevitably be followed by pain.

2. When Houston states that the two Christmases exist "like . . . a memory within a memory" (para. 6), she means that the two are so emotionally intertwined that she cannot think of one without the other.

Building Your Critical Thinking Skills: Symbolism, p. 319

1. Christmas symbolizes Houston's memories of these two places. In her memories, the holiday represents a wondrous time of abundance and beauty, whether it comes from nature's splendor during her time of deprivation at Manazar or in the more conventional sense during her time in Ocean Park.

2. Snow appears to symbolize the beauty of nature and its transformative nature, both to alter the world physically and to soften and soothe an otherwise painful time in the author's life. It also suggests the pain of cold, the "price to be paid" for beauty (para. 2).

3. Owens Valley may symbolize a cold, dry (unfertile or sterile) place of exile; it is cut off by mountains and devoid of sunshine. Ocean Park may symbolize the sunny playground of her childhood before she was initiated into the pain of exile. Water represents fertility, so the "ocean" in Ocean Park may also symbolize a place of creativity and abundance.

Reacting to the Reading: Discussion and Journal Writing, p. 319

1–2. These questions provide an opportunity to discuss the idea of community and how celebrations such as the Fourth of July foster a sense of interconnectedness.

A sense of place is often connected to a sense of community. These subjects provide excellent opportunities to have students combine what they have learned thus far about narration, description, and comparison and contrast. Sharing some writing about their home towns or families can also foster a sense of community among your students.

Sharon Begley, "East vs. West: One Sees the Big Picture, the Other Is Focused," p. 321

Science writer Sharon Begley summarizes recent research about how learned cross-cultural differences may affect thinking. Using a wide range of sources, from cognitive psychologists to people who have lived in various cultures, she provides support for her thesis that cultural conditioning influences cognition. Careful to note that these differences are not genetic or fixed, Begley provides examples of people who have learned to bridge cultures. She advocates crosscultural study as a means to attain a new kind of global knowledge and understanding.

This essay provides an excellent transition into argumentation or the research paper. Students will enjoy evaluating the accuracy and reliability of the various sources used in the essay. You might like to initiate a discussion of the use of sources, delineating the difference between anecdotal evidence and serious academic sources. One possible discussion topic is the nature versus nurture debate about genetic versus learned behavior, possibly linked thematically with Barry's pseudo-scientific thesis about male-female differences (p. 311). Another possible topic is the idea of universal as opposed to culturally specific thought. You might make further thematic links in discussing this topic with Houston's essay on Japanese Americans during World War II (p. 316).

Understanding the Reading, p. 323

1. Modern cognitive psychologists assume that the nature of human thought is universal (para. 3), that people think, reason, and perceive their surroundings the same everywhere.

2. The aquarium experiment showed that Asians tend to pay more attention than Westerners to backgrounds and to the relationships between things (7–9).

3. Eastern and Western ways of thinking differ in that Westerners see categories whereas Asians see relationships (6). As illustrated by the aquarium experiment, Westerners' "basic sensory perception" is also different. Westerners pay attention to the "focal object" while Asians attend to the overall background and relationships within it (9). Westerners also attribute causality more to "actors" than to "context" (10). Finally, Westerners and Asians draw inferences differently (12). Westerners "prefer abstract universal principles" while Asians "seek rules appropriate to a situation" (13).

4. According to the author, the thinking patterns of people who live away from their native cultures for some time begin to shift, adapting native thinking patterns and incorporating them into their existing ways of thinking (14). Begley contends that by incorporating cultural diversity and, hence, different ways of viewing issues, businesses may be more likely to "see problems clearly and solve them" (14).

Visualizing the Reading, p. 323

Possible answers include:

Point of Comparison	Supporting Evidence
1. Sensory perception: Japanese remember more background elements than do Americans.	Study conducted in Michigan in which students were shown photos of aquariums
2. Remembering objects:	Taka Masuda's aquarium study in Michigan; psychologist Richard E. Nisbett's book, *The Geography of Thought*
3. Business dealings:	Example of an Australian-Japanese sugar deal that went bad in the 1970s
4. Drawing inferences:	Research study in which Ann Arbor and Beijing college students predicted economic growth rates
5. Abstract principles vs. situational rules:	Research study in the Netherlands in which Easterners and Westerners had to indicate what to do about an employee whose work was suddenly subpar after an otherwise distinguished career

Examining the Characteristics of Comparison and Contrast Essays, p. 323

1. Begley wants to demonstrate that Eastern and Western thought are different but that they are not "hard-wired" (para. 14). She also contends that continued exposure to cultural diversity would create more crosscultural understanding. Her purpose in writing is made clear in her conclusion when she says that these differences can be bridged, leading to deeper cultural understanding (14).

2. Begley's thesis is presented in paragraph 4 through the form of a quotation from a psychologist: "'Human cognition is not everywhere the same. . . . [T]he characteristic thought processes of Asians and Westerners differ greatly.'"

3. The main ideas that make up the basis of Begley's comparison are that new studies prove there are differences in the way Westerners and Asians think and that while these divergences in thinking have led to conflicts in business and politics,

they are not genetic, or hard-wired, so cultural differences can be bridged through cultural diversity and understanding. The details of the various studies add to her comparison by illustrating concretely how different the world views of Asians and Westerners really are, how they can look at exactly the same image and see very different things.

4. For background information about human thought, the author mentions Hume and Locke (seventeenth- and eighteenth-century philosophers) and makes a quick reference to the modern assumptions of "cognitive psychologists" (3). While the references to Hume and Locke are likely to be lost on most students, the explanation by the Harvard University psychologist in paragraph 3, about how cognitive scientists have typically viewed thinking around the world, is clear and easy to understand, so most students will probably agree that Begley provides enough background information.

5. Begley's essay is organized point by point. Answers will vary, but given the complexity of her discussion and the number of points of comparison that she covers, a subject-by-subject organization may not have been as effective.

Building Your Word Power, p. 324

1. The phrase "parse it so finely," as used in paragraph 1, means to explain something by breaking it down into component parts.

2. The idiom "hard-wired" as used in paragraph 14 means genetically determined.

Building Your Critical Thinking Skills: Evaluating Sources, p. 324

1. Using the Visualizing the Reading exercise that lists each source cited by Begley, encourage students to consider each source critically, noting whether the author includes enough information for a reader to track down the original source. Presumably many of these research studies are cited in *The Geography of Thought*, the Nisbett book on which Begley's essay is based, so to find out further information about any of these sources, one would probably want to start with this text.

2. Most of Begley's sources are psychological studies with crosscultural applications. She also uses some examples from business and politics. These examples lend credibility and a serious tone to the author's position.

Patricia Raybon, "A Case of 'Severe Bias,'" p. 326

Raybon begins her essay with a series of media images of black women as welfare recipients, drug addicts, and prostitutes, and then she challenges the validity of these images by describing her own life (as an award-winning writer) and the lives of other "ordinary, hard-working" (para. 13) black people she knows. By illustrating the ways in which popular media images contrast with the reality of most black Americans' lives, the author makes the case for more positive and accurate media imagery of African Americans.

Because Raybon relies on her own research in this personal comparison and contrast essay, it might be useful for students to identify the kinds of examples she uses, evaluating their impact and effectiveness. You might assign students to write a similar kind of essay, using a parallel series of sources, on a topic they are personally familiar with and feel qualified to support with their own observations.

Understanding the Reading, p. 328

1. Readers learn that the author lives in the inner city in Denver (para. 12), is forty years old (1), is not a drug addict or a prostitute (1), and does not fit other stereotypical media images of black women who live in the inner city (1).

2. The media outlets Raybon accuses of being biased are "television . . . newspapers and magazines" (6).

3. Examples of the bias that Raybon describes are: programs about crack, homelessness, and other issues in which all the images are of black people (4); television shows on neutral or positive issues like nutrition in which almost all the images are of white people (4); and film reviews of Spike Lee's film *Do the Right Thing* that contended that a ghetto must have "addicts and drug pushers" for authenticity (11).

4. According to Raybon, negative images of black people are damaging to black people because they must face the "image and perception" created by the media on a daily basis (9). As a consequence, white people regard high-functioning black people as unusual or "different" (10), and "ordinary, hard-working" black people never see themselves reflected in the media (13).

Visualizing the Reading, p. 328

Possible answers include:

Features typical of most black Americans: loving family, middle-class lifestyle, leisure time devoted to the family, suburban lifestyle, enjoying the outdoors, tailgating

Raybon could have used this photo as a contrast to the stereotyped images of black people perpetuated by the media: images of crack addicts, gang members, welfare mothers, and so on. This image of a black family enjoying a picnic outdoors illustrates clearly the author's call for media images of "ordinary, hard-working, law-abiding, tax-paying [black] Americans" (13).

Examining the Characteristics of Comparison and Contrast Essays, p. 328

1. Raybon's thesis is presented in paragraph 3: "Indeed, media coverage of black America is so one-sided, so imbalanced that the most victimized and hurting segment of the black community—a small segment, at best—is presented not as the exception but as the norm." The author is writing to *persuade*. She wants readers to understand that the media portrayal of black people is inaccurate, insidious, and hurtful.

2. The author introduces the subjects of her comparison and contrast essay by listing the things that she—an educated, black, female journalist—is not. She compares herself to the media stereotype of black women as addicts, prostitutes, welfare mothers, and so on (para. 1). The background information she provides by way of contrast is that she is black, forty years old, is married to a man who doesn't abuse her, has children who are not in gangs, and doesn't live in a "tenement" (1).

3. Because students are likely to be very aware of the media portrayal of blacks, most will likely agree that Raybon's technique for contrasting her subject is very effective.

4. The author uses point-by-point comparison. As to its effectiveness, answers will vary.

5. The points of comparison Raybon offers to support her thesis include: imbalanced media images of black people as "poor, criminal, addicted, and dysfunctional" (3); media images of white people as being overwhelmingly healthy, happy, and economically secure; and the way these media images result in ordinary, hard-working blacks being perceived as "different" (10). Raybon concentrates on both differences and similarities. For example, she contrasts the differences between herself as an educated journalist and the image of black women as crack addicts and welfare mothers (1). Raybon concentrates on the similarities between most whites and blacks in describing the neighborhoods where most blacks live: there are "children playing and couples walking their dogs" (12).

Building Your Word Power, p. 329

1. The different connotations of "black America" in the first three paragraphs represent the differences between the media's view of black America (as poor and criminal) and the black community's view of itself (as having working-class and middle-class components).

2. In using the phrase "free press" in paragraph 7, the author refers to the press as being independent of government interference. It is able to "[hold] the mirror on American reality" by reinforcing false images of the black community over and over until they are considered normative.

Building Your Critical Thinking Skills: Cause and Effect Relationships, p. 329

1. According to Raybon, the effect of the "severe bias" in the media is to distort perceptions about the black community.

2. The last paragraph reveals Raybon's hope that her essay will enable readers to see the truth of the black community clearly—"strong people, surviving people, capable people"—rather than through the biased lens of the media.

Deborah Tannen, "Sex, Lies, and Conversation," p. 331

Linguist Deborah Tannen offers a series of examples to illustrate her thesis that gender differences in communication are learned but can also be transformed. Threading throughout the essay an anecdote about a talkative man who describes his wife as the "talker in our family" (para. 1, 22), Tanner deploys extensive evidence from experts and her own research to illustrate that women's and men's expectations about communication differ. She concludes her essay optimistically, arguing that these different expectations and patterns can be transformed using the model of crosscultural understanding.

Thematically, this essay can be linked with Begley's piece (p. 000) on crosscultural differences in Eastern and Western cognition, also learned and also able to be transformed. You might assign students to write a comparison and contrast essay that utilizes the theories about learned versus innate cognition put forth by both Tannen and Begley. Class discussion about learned versus genetic differences might also prove interesting; students could form two panels to support one or the other side of the nature versus nurture debate, using anecdotal or statistical evidence to support their positions.

Understanding the Reading, p. 335

1. The opening anecdote about the man at a women's group illustrates the irony that although men talk more in public, they often talk less at home (para. 2).

2. Observable communication differences between young girls and boys are: girls use communication to "create and maintain friendships," whereas boys' friendships are based more on doing things together and less on talking (9–10); when they do talk, girls face each other and look into each other's faces, whereas boys tend to sit side by side and look elsewhere, except for occasional glances at one another (12); and girls talk at length about a single subject, whereas boys change topics often (13).

3. In conversing, men tend to not face the person they are addressing, while women look into each other's faces directly. Women often perceive this difference in body language as a sign that men are not interested or are not listening.

4. To overcome the communication problems described by Tannen, women and men need to learn to recognize their different communication patterns, coming to a "cross-cultural understanding" and then working to voluntarily alter these patterns to avoid miscommunication (26).

Visualizing the Reading, p. 335

Possible answers include:

Evidence	Purpose
Reference to political scientist Andrew Hacker (para. 3)	Gives legitimacy to the thesis and demonstrates that the thesis is not a new idea
Sociologist Catherine Kohler Riessman's observations from her book *Divorce Talk* (para. 3)	Illustrates the importance of the issue of communication between the sexes, and indicates that women identify "communication" as crucial to intimacy
The author's own research (para. 4)	Illustrates the different expectations about "conversation" that men and women have
American Psychologist article by Stanford University's Eleanor Maccoby (para. 7)	Identifies how children's development is shaped by differences in "peer interaction" in single-sex groups
Psychologist Bruce Dorval's videotapes (para. 12)	Show that physical alignment (face to face or at angles) is different at every age
The author's own research (para. 13–16)	Shows how girls stay on one topic, whereas boys switch topics frequently
Linguist Lynette Hirschman's research (para. 17)	Indicates that women make more "listener noise," whereas men give silent attention
Reference to *Fighting for Life* by Walter Ong (para. 20)	Points out that men use "warlike, oppositional formats to do almost anything"

Examining the Characteristics of Comparison and Contrast Essays, p. 336

1. Tannen's thesis about gender communication is that "although American men tend to talk more than women in public situations, they often talk less at home. And this pattern is wreaking havoc with marriage" (para. 2).

2. Tannen uses a point-by-point organization. A subject-by-subject organization might have been used to good effect, but the types of examples used (for instance,

more anecdotes) would probably need to be altered somewhat to support this type of organization.

3. The points of comparison that Tannen uses to support her thesis include: children's development and peer interactions (7), body language (14), and conversational habits (15–20). The author focuses mostly on differences but does identify a few similarities. Students will likely agree that Tannen treats her subjects fairly and objectively.

4. Tannen's exploration of the causes of these communication differences strengthens the essay because it both serves to illustrate the differences and illuminate her point that because such differences arise through learned behavior, they can be changed.

Building Your Word Power, p. 336

1. The phrase "wreaking havoc" (para. 2) brings to mind the idea of creating chaos.

2. Some examples of linguistic jargon used by Tannen: "peer interactions" (7); "cross-cultural communication" (8); "topical alignment" (13); "listener-noise" (17); and "participatory listenership" (18).

Building Your Critical Thinking Skills: Original Sources, p. 337

This section provides an excellent opportunity to give first-year students some preliminary information about bibliographic research. Explain the importance of learning how to find sources online and in the library. Emphasize its usefulness throughout their academic career. You might want to have students write a short essay in class comparing and contrasting the effectiveness of Barry's and Tannen's use of sources.

Chapter 10 Classification and Division: Explaining Categories and Parts, p. 339

You can easily explain classification and division to students if you define *classification* as grouping things into categories and *division* (closely related to process analysis, Chapter 8) as breaking a single item into parts. Both modes describe types or parts. Each uses only one principle of classification or division, with parts that include all of the members of the group. Judith Viorst's essay on friendship, "Friends, Good Friends — Such Good Friends" (p. 340), provides a familiar subject with which to introduce your students to this rhetorical mode. Since such patterns are sometimes difficult to recognize when they are imbedded in a personal essay like this one, you might like to go through the graphic organizer on page 348 line by line and detail by detail in order to explain the pattern of organization underlying this essay. Likewise, Ryan Porter's annotated student essay, "Motor Heads" (p. 356), will illustrate clearly to students how to craft a thesis statement that includes a "principle of classification" and use concrete examples to aid the reader's understanding.

David Bodanis's "A Brush with Reality: Surprises in the Tube" (p. 360) is a division essay that breaks down an ordinary, everyday commodity—toothpaste—into its various ingredients, describing each in great detail in order to convince readers that toothpaste is not all that it is cracked up to be. Elizabeth Wray's "The Seven Ages of Walking" (p. 366) classifies kinds of walking. She demarcates the life stages at which she thinks a person's experience of walking changes. Scott Russell Sanders, in "The Men We Carry in Our Minds" (p. 372), uses the principle of classification to group men into four categories—laborers, soldiers, bosses, and educated men—in order to explain his sense of alliance with women across class lines. Thematically, you might consider linking Sanders's essay to Tannen's essay (p. 331) on communication between women and men. Also in this chapter, Martin Luther King Jr.'s classic essay "The Ways of Meeting Oppression" (p. 379) uses the principle of classification to identify three responses to oppression. Finally, Cindy Combs's "Profile of a Terrorist" (p. 385) will be of interest to students in the post-9/11 era. In it, Combs classifies terrorists into three groups.

Judith Viorst, "Friends, Good Friends—Such Good Friends," p. 340

Judith Viorst, best known perhaps to students for her children's book *Alexander and the Terrible, Horrible, No Good, Very Bad Day* (1972), here evaluates her friendships according to their degree of intimacy. She uses the principle of classification to distinguish among the various "kinds" of friendship she shares with the people in her life. Viorst's sources are mostly personal observations about a few friends, which makes her piece a personal rather than an academic essay. Students may usefully evaluate whether this essay might be strengthened with evidence such as Deborah Tannen provides in "Sex, Lies, and Conversation" (p. 331). You might also link this essay thematically with Tannen's essay for a discussion about the psychology of women's expectations for intimacy in relationships.

Ryan Porter, "Motor Heads," p. 356

Ryan Porter's student essay is clearly annotated for its thesis statement, details, topic sentences, helpful examples, and other features. In this classification piece, Porter creates somewhat exaggerated "types" of car lovers, dubbing them with titles like "aficionado" and "gear head," but the essay shows how classification can be used to great effect. Students might like to evaluate the effectiveness of Porter's use of vivid details like "glittering external exhaust pipes" (para. 2).

Responding to "Students Write," p. 358

1. Porter establishes the importance of his classification by suggesting that ours is a "car culture" and that everyone cares about cars (para. 1).

2. Other patterns of development Porter used to develop the essay are: description ("dual-cowl phaeton" [2]), narration ("Five weeks later you're stranded on the side of the road" [4]); and illustration ("such as the fabled Duesenberg, Hispano-Suiza, or Bentley" [3]).

3. Answers may vary.

4. Porter's tone is humorous and at times somewhat sarcastic. His audience is primarily those who drive cars and may even love them but generally are not obsessive about them. It is possible that he writes also for the actual "car nuts" he describes, as he notes in paragraph 8 that his reader "may be one yourself." If his audience consisted of serious car aficionados only, his humor would be less effective because "car nuts" might feel mocked by his descriptions of their behavior.

David Bodanis, "A Brush with Reality: Surprises in the Tube," p. 360

David Bodanis scrutinizes the ingredients that go into toothpaste. He uses vivid details and some exaggeration to make his point that toothpaste is neither especially healthy nor worth the price. The section Applying Your Skills: Writing Assignments (p. 364) will be especially helpful to students because it provides writing assignments related to marketing techniques and their effect on consumers. Some discussion about an industry that does not take the health of consumers into account might prove interesting. Students might research or provide more anecdotal evidence about food products such as fast food and how they are regulated by the U.S.D.A.

Understanding the Reading, p. 362

1. The ingredients in toothpaste are: water, chalk, titanium dioxide, glycerine glycol, seaweed, paraffin oil, detergent, peppermint oil, formaldehyde, and fluoride.

2. The author includes information about the origins of chalk ("the crushed remains of long-dead ocean creatures"; para. 3) because it highlights how revolting this ingredient truly is.

3. The ingredient that inhibits the growth of bacteria is formaldehyde (11).

4. As a final thought on the subject, the author offers the idea that "plain water will often do as good a job" (12). The implication is that the author thinks that toothpaste is unnecessary.

Visualizing the Reading, p. 362

Possible answers include:

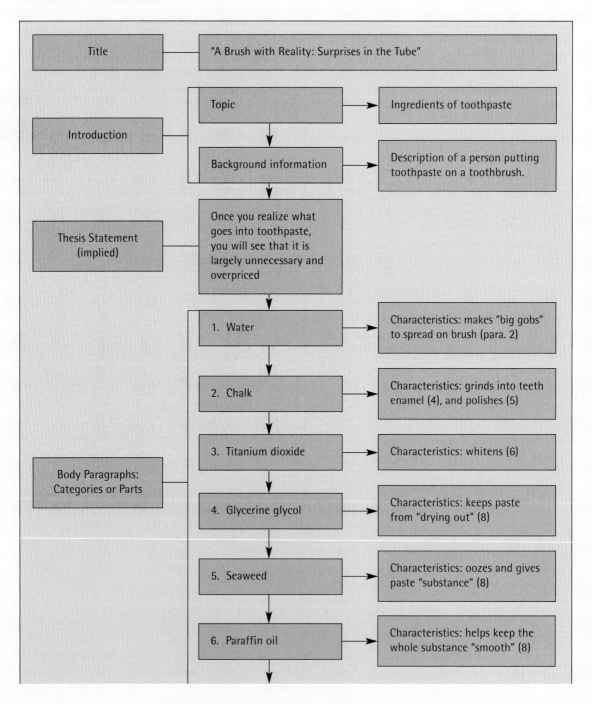

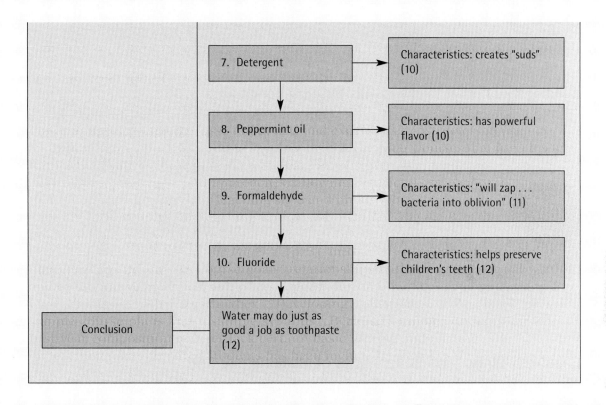

Examining the Characteristics of Classification and Division Essays, p. 362

1. Students may or may not find the author's purpose clear initially, but it should be fairly obvious by the conclusion when the author says water often does as good a job (12).

2. The categories should be seen as fairly complete. Bodanis's categories are clearly defined, and none overlap.

3. Answers will vary. Students will likely choose details that explain the more surprising ingredients, such as titanium dioxide, "the stuff bobbing around in white wall paint to make it come out white" (6) or glycerin glycol, "related to the most common car antifreeze ingredient" (8).

4. Answers will vary. Because the conclusion neatly ties up the essay and clarifies the author's intent in writing, most students will probably find it satisfying.

Building Your Word Power, p. 364

1. The phrase "reassuring white" in paragraph 6 suggests that titanium dioxide serves no other purpose than to make one's teeth white in order to give the appearance of cleanliness.

2. By "finicky distaste" and "host of other goodies" (7), the author suggests that manufacturers engineer an image of toothpaste in contrast to a reality that it is neither appetizing nor healthy.

Building Your Critical Thinking Skills: Drawing Conclusions, p. 364

1. The conclusion the author draws about water being the most plentiful ingredient in toothpaste is that it is lucrative because it doesn't cost anything, allowing large profits on each tube of toothpaste sold. Bodanis also draws the conclusion that because water often does just as good a job on one's teeth, people should save money and just use water to brush their teeth.

2. Bodanis's conclusion about consumers of toothpaste (para. 6, 7, 10) is that they are concerned more about appearances (for instance, the whiteness of their teeth and the taste of their toothpaste) than knowing the facts behind the ingredients.

3. Based on his use of details such as toothpaste being sold for "a neat and account-ant-pleasing $2 per pound" (2) and that it contains inedible ingredients like glyc-erine glycol and formaldehyde, Bodanis seems to be drawing the conclusion that toothpaste is a marketing scam.

Elizabeth Wray, "The Seven Ages of Walking," p. 366

Elizabeth Wray uses classification to develop a series of ideas about walking as a mode of movement whose purpose changes over time. Her stages are based on observations of her extended family and are illustrated with anecdotes and examples. Students may like to critique the comprehensiveness and exclusiveness of her age groups, taking into consideration women who work long hours or don't have children or people who can-not walk because of a disability.

Understanding the Reading, p. 369

1. It will be easy for students to identify the stages of walking because of the head-ings in Wray's essay. The stages include toddlerhood, childhood, teens and twen-ties, thirties, forties and fifties, sixties, and old age.

2. Walking in early life is important, according to Wray, because it offers a way to "reach for" and "discover" the world (para. 4). In later life, walking becomes a way to feel alive and still connected to the world (18).

3. The author reveals a great many details about her personal life and the people who are dear to her: she lives with her extended family in a Victorian in San Francisco (1 and 16), she was a toddler in the 1950s (2), she is now in middle age (3), her mother grew up in Alabama (7), she has a son named Kit (8), she worked as an ed-itor in New York City while yearning for a career in theater (10), she has a daugh-ter named Anava who is in college (10), and her mother died of cancer (17–18).

4. According to Wray, walking is useful because it "gives us a way to be in the world" (4), provides "wonder" (4), makes us "feel good" (6), provides an opportunity for "contemplation" (10), promotes "exercise and meditation" (13), and is "fun" (14).

Visualizing the Reading, p. 369

Possible answers include:

Life Stage	Function(s)
Toddlerhood	To explore the world
Childhood	To move just for the sake of moving (6)
Teens and twenties	To make a social statement by saying "who they are" (9) or to be alone to think (10)
Thirties	To have "contemplative time" (12)
Forties and fifties	To exercise or practice meditation (13) or to walk for a cause (15)
Sixties	To help the very young or very old (16)
Old age	To walk without a goal, just experiencing nature in order to feel alive (17–18)

Examining the Characteristics of Classification and Division Essays, p. 370

1. Wray's thesis is that "[w]alking, like life, has its stages and repetitive patterns" (para. 3). Her principle of classification is age. This principle relates to the author's own life because she has experienced most of the stages herself, either personally or through close observation of family members in those age groups.

2. Students may challenge Wray's categories, citing people they know who are anomalous—for example, physically challenged people who cannot walk.

3. The categories are organized in broad age segments.

4. Other patterns of development used by Wray include: narration (the story of her 84-year-old father getting lost [1]); description ("catalpa leaves patterning the light on the front porch" [4]); process analysis ("a whole repertoire of movement through space: hop, skip, twirl, slide, gallop" [6]); and illustration.

5. The personal details illustrate each of the categories. While some students will find this technique effective, others will feel that Wray's thesis could have been strengthened through the use of more objective examples and details.

Building Your Word Power, p. 370

1. The allusion to the "human condition" in paragraph 5 means that everyone ages and dies.

2. The word *recess* (para. 9) has become childish to the author's son because it suggests play, which he feels is a childish activity.

Building Your Critical Thinking Skills: Analogies, p. 370

1. Wray uses the analogy to the seven ages of man from *As You Like It* as a means of organizing her essay into the progression through the ages as people are "walking through life" (para. 3). The analogy is appropriate because it serves both to explain the organization that the author will follow and to illuminate a familiar phrase of Shakespeare's.

2. Wray's analogy between her mother and an "usher" will probably be reasonably clear to students because the image of a theater usher showing someone the way is familiar and believable.

Scott Russell Sanders, "The Men We Carry in Our Minds," p. 372

Scott Russell Sanders vividly and compassionately describes the different types of men he saw as a boy and how these groups offered glimpses into the different possibilities he might have when he grew up. Along with his close identification with such men came an envy of women because they seemed to enjoy more leisure and to age more slowly. When he attended an Ivy League college on a scholarship, Sanders began to see that the divide between laborers and bosses (para. 1) or men who "ran the world" (10) placed him in alliance with women who sought to gain such power. You might like to provide some background on the women's movement and the class structure in the United States during the 1960s, the time this essay takes place, before initiating a discussion about the laborer and boss divide and how it does or does not play out along gender lines in contemporary society.

Understanding the Reading, p. 375

1. The types of men the author describes are: laborers (para. 1-3); soldiers (4); the men on television (5); and the educated men who "ran the world" (10).

2. Sanders envied women when he was a boy because their lives seemed more "expansive" and freer, and because they seemed to "enjoy a sense of ease and grace" (8). His view of women changed in college because the feminists he met helped him to understand that the "grievances of women" were similar to his own (8).

3. The author was different from many other students at Brown University because he was a scholarship student from a working-class family.

4. As a child, Sanders expected to be a laborer or a soldier when he grew up.

Visualizing the Reading, p. 375

Possible answers include:

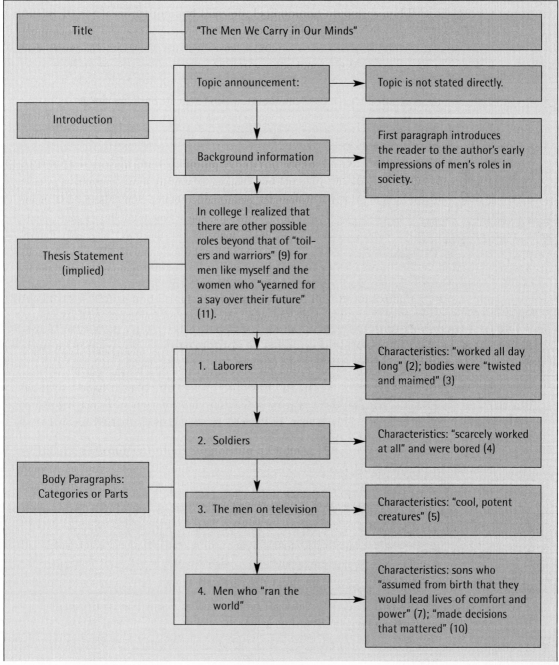

Title	"The Men We Carry in Our Minds"
Introduction	Topic announcement: → Topic is not stated directly.
	Background information → First paragraph introduces the reader to the author's early impressions of men's roles in society.
Thesis Statement (implied)	In college I realized that there are other possible roles beyond that of "toilers and warriors" (9) for men like myself and the women who "yearned for a say over their future" (11).
Body Paragraphs: Categories or Parts	1. Laborers → Characteristics: "worked all day long" (2); bodies were "twisted and maimed" (3)
	2. Soldiers → Characteristics: "scarcely worked at all" and were bored (4)
	3. The men on television → Characteristics: "cool, potent creatures" (5)
	4. Men who "ran the world" → Characteristics: sons who "assumed from birth that they would lead lives of comfort and power" (7); "made decisions that mattered" (10)

(Continued)

(*Continued*)

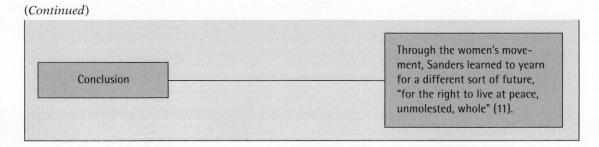

Through the women's move-
ment, Sanders learned to yearn
for a different sort of future,
"for the right to live at peace,
unmolested, whole" (11).

Examining the Characteristics of Classification and Division Essays, p. 376

1. Sanders's implied thesis is included in the graphic organizer above. Sanders's categories are based on the kind of work men do, how it affects them physically, and how much power they wield. He organizes the categories chronologically, reflecting the progression of his awareness of the different possible roles for men as he grows and matures. Answers about the effectiveness of Sanders's choices will vary.

2. Answers will vary.

3. Answers will vary. Some students may find overlap between "the men on television" category and the final category of men who rule the world.

4. Sanders uses other patterns of development in his essay, including: narration ("The first men . . . I remember seeing" [1]); description ("dingy grey-and-black zebra suits" [1]); comparison and contrast (a comparison of the lives of men and women [8]); and illustration (different types of laborers [2]).

5. Because Sanders uses an implied thesis, the conclusion clarifies it more so than reaffirming it. The insight Sanders offers is that he discovers a new-found alliance with women and others who have not "assumed from birth that they would lead lives of comfort and power" (7).

Building Your Word Power, p. 376

1. Some of the descriptive words Sanders uses in paragraph 3 include: *twisted, maimed, ached,* and *creased.* These words emphasize the physical difficulty and danger of factory work and other types of hard labor.

2. Answers will vary.

Building Your Critical Thinking Skills: Evaluating Titles, p. 377

1. The title suggests the different types of men that one encounters in life and how these types are embedded in one's mind.

2. Answers will vary.

Martin Luther King Jr., "The Ways of Meeting Oppression," p. 379

The Reverend Martin Luther King Jr., well known for his civil rights leadership during the 1960s, here argues eloquently for the efficacy of nonviolent resistance to racial injustice in America. Strongly influenced by Ghandi and faced with the growing Black Power movement, King wields the classification mode with great skill, redefining and reinterpreting responses to oppression, using biblical and philosophical truths to support his scholarly and forceful argument. Students may benefit from a discussion of social movements that are characterized by either peaceful protest or the threat of violence, citing as many historical examples as they can.

Understanding the Reading, p. 381

1. According to King, some people prefer to remain oppressed because they have "become conditioned to it" (para. 1).

2. King considers "acquiescence" to be cowardly.

3. Violence is an impractical method for achieving racial justice because it does not bring "permanent peace" and it creates even more social problems (4). According to King, it is also immoral because "it seeks to humiliate the opponent rather than win his understanding," thriving on "hatred rather than love" (5).

4. The "truth" of acquiescence is that "one should not be physically aggressive toward his opponent" (7), and the "truth" of violence is that "evil should be resisted" (7). The principle of nonviolent resistance reconciles these truths by ensuring that "no individual or group need submit to any wrong, nor need anyone resort to violence" (7).

Visualizing the Reading, p. 382

Using King's categories, one would classify the photos as follows: (1) Martin Luther King Jr. at the civil rights march: nonviolent resistance; (2) Black Panthers: violence; (3) Man drinking at a segregated water fountain: acquiescence. An alternative way to classify the pictures would be to group (1) and (2) together as examples of resistance but to put (3) in a category of nonresistance because the individual as shown is not visibly striving to alter his situation.

Examining the Characteristics of Classification and Division Essays, p. 381

1. The thesis statement appears in the very first sentence of the speech: "Oppressed people deal with their oppression in three characteristic ways." Unstated are the three ways—acquiescence, violence, and nonviolent resistance—that King goes on to detail in length in his essay. His thesis does not reveal why the classification is relevant or important; he presents this information later in the essay when he describes "acquiescence" and "violence" as "inferior methods" as he makes his case for nonviolent resistance (para. 8).

2. King most likely presents acquiescence, violence, and nonviolent resistance in that order because it parallels the history of black slavery, the rise of the black power movement, and the civil rights movement.

3. The categories in the essay are exclusive and comprehensive; they do not overlap significantly with one another. King provides a similar amount and kind of detail for each category, making his argument for nonviolence compelling.

4. King uses the following clear transitions to help readers stay on track as they move from one category to another: "One way is acquiescence" (1), "A second way" (4), and "The third way" (7).

5. Other patterns of development used by King include: narration ("Almost 2800 years ago Moses set out" [1]); description ("A voice echoes through time" [5]); and cause and effect ("It creates bitterness" [5]).

Building Your Word Power, p. 383

1. The allusion to everyone being "his brother's keeper" (para. 3) means that one has a moral obligation to care for those in need. "An eye for an eye" (5) means exacting revenge. King uses familiar biblical allusions like these to remind his readers of the ethics involved in the civil rights movement. He relies on biblical allusions because he is a preacher as well as a political leader.

Building Your Critical Thinking Skills: Figures of Speech, p. 383

Answers will vary.

Cindy C. Combs, "Profile of a Terrorist," p. 385

Author of *Terrorism in the Twenty-First Century* (2003) and coauthor of the *Encyclopedia of Terrorism* (2002), Cindy Combs distinguishes kinds of terrorists and their motivations, comparing and contrasting as well as categorizing. Students should find this topic compelling and may want to form small groups to evaluate her categories. The Focus on the Topic exercise on page 385 that asks students to explore their thoughts about terrorism prior to September 11, 2001, will provide a crucial lead-in to a discussion of the essay. Most students before the events of September 11 probably did not perceive terrorism as a threat inside the United States, so their concerns may have changed significantly in the years following that attack.

Understanding the Reading, p. 389

1. According to the author, the differences among "crazy," "criminal," and "crusader" terrorists include (1) their motivations: criminals have personal gain or profit as a motive, crazies' motives are clear only to them, and crusaders are motivated by a "higher cause"; (2) their willingness to negotiate: criminals are more

likely to negotiate for personal gain, whereas crazies may not understand that they may die, and crusaders usually refuse to betray their cause and don't fear death; and (3) their expectation of survival: crazies and criminals have a strong expectation that they will live, whereas crusaders rarely negotiate because they do not care if they die (table, p. 387).

2. The typical outcome for crazies is that negotiation can work successfully if the negotiator can figure out the goal of the perpetrator and if the perpetrator can understand that he or she faces death upon refusing to negotiate (16). The typical outcome for criminals is good because they "will negotiate," "their demands are generally logical," and they have a strong will to live (17). The typical outcome for crusaders is not good because they rarely negotiate and do not fear death (15).

3. The author uses the example of the plane that crashed in Pennsylvania to illustrate how the way the pilots responded to the hijacking, based on a terrorist profile that was different from what they faced, was a "contributing factor to the sequence of events on that day" (para. 20).

4. The author wants law enforcement agencies to know more about terrorists so that they will be able to develop more accurate profiles and respond to terrorist situations more effectively.

Visualizing the Reading, p. 389

Students will have little difficulty identifying Osama Bin Laden as a "crusader."

Examining the Characteristics of Classification and Division Essays, p. 390

1. The author's thesis is that "[u]nderstanding the individual who commits terrorism is vital, not only for humanitarian reasons, but also to decide how best to deal with those individuals *while they are engaged in terrorist acts*" (6). Her thesis does not state the principle of classification used in the essay.

2. Combs names the categories used in her classification in paragraph 7. She provides clear examples and details to explain the "criminal" and "crusader" categories, but gives less attention to and information on "crazies." There is some overlap between crazies and criminals with crusaders, because the acts they commit are all criminal and their motives are often "crazy"; but the author clarifies this by reminding readers that only crusaders are "well trained, well prepared, and well disciplined" (14).

3. Frederick Hacker's table (p. 389) and other references to his work aid in understanding Combs's classification by defining the single figure of the terrorist according to his or her psychological motives, willingness to negotiate, and expectation of survival. The resulting profile of the terrorist's ability and willingness to

negotiate then determines the kinds of strategies that might usefully be employed against him or her.

4. Students may have struggled to identify the author's thesis earlier in the essay but will likely find the conclusion's restatement of the thesis to be more effective. In addition to suggesting why the classification is relevant and important, this restatement more effectively reveals the principle used to classify the topic.

Building Your Word Power, p. 390

1. "Mixed bag" as used in paragraph 9 means confused or jumbled philosophies.

2. "Blind obedience" creates the image of someone following directions as they walk with a blindfold on, unconcerned that they cannot see.

Building Your Critical Thinking Skills: Author's Purpose, p. 390

1. This essay is excerpted from a textbook on terrorism, so presumably the intended audience is college students enrolled in a political science or criminal justice course. The level and tone of this essay are appropriate for this audience.

2. The author attempts to convince readers that this kind of profiling is accurate and important and that negotiating with "crusaders" is probably futile.

3. Combs does not present more than one view on the issue of classifying terrorists. Encourage students to consider whether this one-sided approach weakens her argument.

Chapter 11 Definition: Explaining What You Mean, p. 392

The basic characteristic of a *definition* will be relatively easy for students to grasp. Just as a dictionary explains a term, so does a definition essay explain something, albeit in a longer, extended form. Often, in personal essays or academic papers, a standard dictionary-style definition will serve as a preliminary step or lead-in to a longer exposition on a particular topic. These kinds of expositions are called "extended definitions." For example, in the first essay (p. 393), Mary Pipher, a clinical psychologist, describes *cultural brokers* as having "information on everything," explaining that this occupational niche involves helping immigrants make a smooth transition into a new culture. Student writer Geneva Lamberth, in "Eating Disorders: Serious and Legitimate Illnesses" (p. 407), opens her essay with a standard definition of eating disorders before launching into extended definitions of two of the most common forms of eating disorders: bulimia and anorexia nervosa. By working through the annotations included for these two essays, you can highlight for students visually the key characteristics of definition essays.

The readings in this chapter will expose students to a wide variety of styles and illustrate the effectiveness of definition in writing. In "Spanglish" (p. 411), Janice Castro, Dan Cook, and Christina Garcia define this blend of Spanish and English, giving examples of how it has become widespread in the United States. You may find it helpful to make use of the "Building Your Critical Thinking Skills" apparatus that accompanies this reading in class: It discusses tone (p. 415), something that first-year students often have difficulty understanding. Practice in this area helps them to more quickly and ably discern the nuanced meanings of any essay they read in their courses.

Many of the readings in this section are likely to have strong appeal to today's students. In "One Term Says It All: 'Shut Up!'" (p. 417), Shelly Branch explores the new non-rude definition of "Shut up!" as it transmogrifies into the equivalent of "No kidding?! Are you serious?!" William Plasencia, in "Web Logs Get Personal" (p. 422), uses an extended definition to explain *blogging*, the practice of posting certain kinds of journals or diaries online, and then analyzes the growth of this phenomenon. In "Spinning" (p. 432), Gina Kolata uses an extended definition to explain a form of exercise that has recently grown in popularity.

Explain to students that an extended definition may depart from a standard, dictionary definition. It can also be used to correct popular misconceptions. Gloria Naylor's "The Meaning of a Word" (p. 426), for example, describes the pain she felt when she was called "nigger" as a child and compares that usage with the more contemporary, often positive tone of the word as used by and among black people. She theorizes that words become powerful by "consensus," analyzing how the connotations of the terms shift, depending upon the speaker and the context.

Geneva Lamberth, "Eating Disorders: Serious and Legitimate Illnesses," p. 407

In both her title and her text, student writer Geneva Lamberth defines eating disorders as "legitimate medical illnesses" (para. 1). She first defines the term, then the causes, then the three options for treating eating disorders. Since this is a topic of interest to many students, who may know someone who suffers from an eating disorder (or even suffer from one themselves), they may find it quite interesting to read or write about it in class but be reluctant to openly discuss it. As a more neutral way to address the issue, you may want to initiate a discussion of how media images of beauty contribute to these disorders.

Responding to "Students Write," p. 409

1. Answers may vary. Most students are likely to agree that examples of individuals suffering from eating disorders would have personalized the essay and made the importance of the topic stand out more clearly.

2. Because the different types of treatment are very complex, this section is the weakest part of Lamberth's essay. Terms such as *pharmacological, cognitive-behavioral,* and *psychodynamic* will be unfamiliar to most readers. At the very least, clear definitions of these and other terms used in this section are needed to make the material understandable.

3. Answers may vary. You may want to have students brainstorm aloud in class to develop a more compelling and interesting title for this essay.

4. Answers may vary.

Janice Castro, Dan Cook, and Christina Garcia, "Spanglish," p. 411

Media scholar Janice Castro, along with *Time* writers Dan Cook and Christina Garcia, define "Spanglish," a new blend of English and Spanish, illustrating the many ways that this language hybrid is entering mainstream U.S. culture. You might begin by taking a close look at this essay's organization, analyzing how it moves back and forth among definitions, generalizations, and examples.

Another fruitful way to approach "Spanglish" might be to ask students to describe at least three ways in which this new hybrid language is used, and then compare the essay with "Goin' Gangsta, Choosin' Cholita" (p. 230). Do the two essays provide evidence for the idea that U.S. culture is changing, especially for younger generations such as theirs? Within the context of your discussion about this essay, you might also invite students to form small groups and create a list of other foreign words and phrases that have been incorporated into the English language over their lifetime (for instance, *jihad*). How do immigration and culture influence and shape the English language?

Understanding the Reading, p. 413

1. The addition of Spanish words to the English language has caught on more than that of other languages from Asia or Europe because there are more Latin American immigrants now living in the United States and more Americans take Spanish in high school and college than any other language (para. 6).

2. An example from the reading of an English word that is easier to use than its Spanish equivalent is *income tax* (5). Using English words like this is a benefit to Spanish speakers in America because it saves time (9).

3. Advertisers have used Spanglish to tap into the buying power of Spanish-speaking Americans by "sprinkling" it into their ads. This tactic has created some embarrassing gaffes, such as telling airline passengers that they could fly "without clothes" (when the advertisers meant in "leather" seats) (10), when words are not translated properly or spelled accurately.

4. According to the authors, Latinos react to the misuse of Spanglish with amusement. They might express this in Spanglish as *no problema* (10).

Visualizing the Reading, p. 414

Possible answers include:

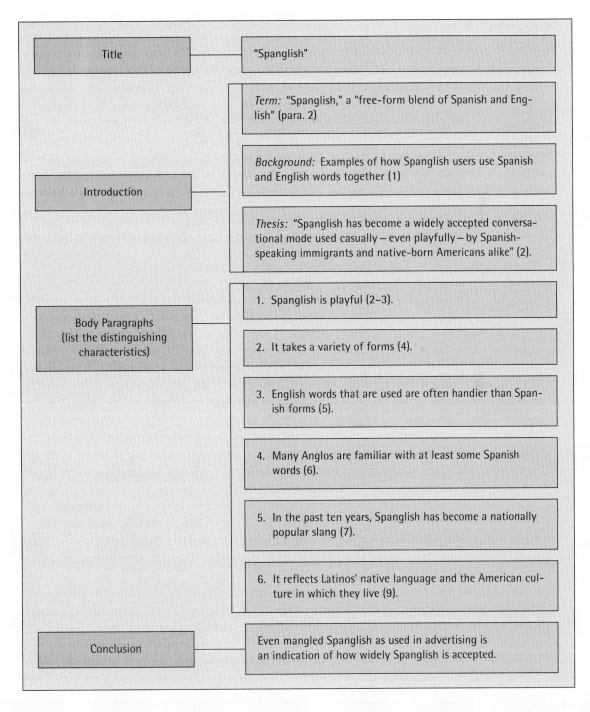

| Title | "Spanglish" |

Introduction	*Term:* "Spanglish," a "free-form blend of Spanish and English" (para. 2)
	Background: Examples of how Spanglish users use Spanish and English words together (1)
	Thesis: "Spanglish has become a widely accepted conversational mode used casually — even playfully — by Spanish-speaking immigrants and native-born Americans alike" (2).

Body Paragraphs (list the distinguishing characteristics)	1. Spanglish is playful (2–3).
	2. It takes a variety of forms (4).
	3. English words that are used are often handier than Spanish forms (5).
	4. Many Anglos are familiar with at least some Spanish words (6).
	5. In the past ten years, Spanglish has become a nationally popular slang (7).
	6. It reflects Latinos' native language and the American culture in which they live (9).

| Conclusion | Even mangled Spanglish as used in advertising is an indication of how widely Spanglish is accepted. |

Examining the Characteristics of Definition Essays, p. 414

1. The standard definition of *Spanglish* appears in paragraph 2. The authors identify the class to which the term belongs (a language) and the characteristics that distinguish it as "common linguistic currency wherever concentrations of Hispanic Americans are found" (2).

2. The main point the authors make about Spanglish is that it is here to stay and consequently worth reading about.

3. The authors expand the definition of Spanglish beyond the second paragraph by identifying the various forms it takes. Answers may vary.

4. Spanglish takes a variety of forms, such as a handy shorthand (5) or "a sort of code for Latinos" (9). These and other details contribute to the extended definition as a whole by illustrating why this language is growing and how it is used.

5. Patterns of development used by the authors include: cause and effect (that the popularity of Spanish is due to the "explosive increase" in the number of Latin American immigrants); classification (the different forms of Spanglish); and illustration (the many examples cited in the essay). These different patterns of development help to clarify the term for readers by illustrating the use and growth of this language hybrid.

Building Your Word Power, p. 415

1. *siéntate*: sit down; *quiero un*: I want a; *cerveza*: beer; *uno dos tres*: one two three; *parquean*: park; *carros*: cars; *ir al*: go to the; *almuerzo*: lunch; *bronco*: rough, coarse.

2. *Explosive* and *collided* as used in paragraph 7 indicate that the introduction of Spanish phrases was somewhat sudden, even jarring.

Building Your Critical Thinking Skills: Tone, p. 415

1. The overall tone of the essay is informative. This tone makes the reader feel that Spanglish is interesting and a worthwhile addition to U.S. culture.

2. The first and last paragraphs contribute to the tone of the essay by suggesting that Spanglish crosses geographical regions, classes, and types of media.

3. Answers may vary. Another kind of tone in the essay is casual—for instance, "Spanglish is as much a part of daily life as sunglasses" (para. 2).

Shelly Branch, "One Term Says It All: 'Shut Up!'" p. 417

Journalist Shelly Branch explores the new definition of "Shut up!" as it becomes a new equivalent of "Are you serious?!" As Branch defines this usage, "Shut up!" now expresses "amazement or disbelief" (para. 4). Branch illustrates the new usage through a series of citations, including the opinions of editors, linguists, and writers. This evidence indicates that through "linguistic . . . amelioration" (5) the phrase is losing its negative associations.

Students should find this essay quite interesting since it deals with a contemporary linguistic phenomenon. You might like to initiate a discussion of how the meanings of words have changed over time, and ask students to think of other words whose meanings have changed in their own lifetime. They might break into small groups to select a word and then trace its evolution for the class. You might also want to have students break into small groups to choose a word that has nuances or associations, depending upon context or intonation, such as *okay, dude, right,* or *sure.* Have them consider why it is different in various contexts — is it the intonation? the context? the speaker? Then have them write about the various meanings of the word, making first a generalization about the term and then providing supporting examples.

Understanding the Reading, p. 419

1. The new use of "Shut up!" is to express "disbelief, shock and joy" (para. 2). Some examples of its different use are a "chief of staff" who uses it with his colleagues (1), an Elantra ad (3), and a character in *The Princess Diaries* (12).

2. The writers for the Elantra ad decided to use "Shut up!" because the more they used it the funnier it seemed. They were initially concerned that it would offend older Hyundai dealers (in their fifties), but when the dealers saw the TV spot they found it very funny (8).

3. The author cites an episode of *Seinfeld* as an example of the use of "Shut up!" on television (13).

4. The history of the phrase "Shut up!" reaches back to sixteenth-century England, where it was figuratively used to mean withholding money or kindness (11). Branch cites the *Oxford English Dictionary* (11) as a source for the evolution of this phrase.

Visualizing the Reading, p. 419

Possible answers include:

Method of Development	Example
Process	Explains how to pronounce the phrase (para. 9–10).
Narration	Provides anecdote about the chief of staff who uses this phrase as an "exclamation point" with his colleagues (1).

Description	Describes of an episode of *Seinfeld* in which Jerry vividly describes how a man "splashed Gatorade on his head, got pneumonia, and dropped dead" (13).
Illustration	Cites other words that have undergone transformation, such as *nice* and *stupid* (5).
Comparison and contrast	Contrasts those who think the phrase is legitimate (for instance, the *New Oxford American Dictionary* editor [4]) with those who find it "rude" (Drew Barrymore [15]).

Examining the Characteristics of Definition Essays, p. 420

1. Branch does not use a standard thesis statement, instead relying on a series of sentences in paragraph 2 to explain both the definition ("People use it as much to express disbelief, shock and joy as to demand silence") and why it is worth reading about ("the term has made its way from schoolgirl chatter to adult repartee and into movies and advertising"). While this is not a formal thesis statement in the style that is expected from your students, Branch does clearly convey both the basic definition of the term and why this new meaning is of interest.

2. Branch's explanation of how to pronounce "Shut up!" (para. 9–10) is important to a full understanding of the current use of the term because how it is pronounced differentiates it from the "rude" meaning.

3. Some of the other ways that Branch defines the term are by giving examples of how people use it, such as in the Hyundai ad (3), and by listing phrases that it replaces, such as "Oh my God!"(2).

4. Answers may vary.

5. Students may find the essay's introduction to be vague because there is no context for how the phrase is used; it is not clear why exactly Hartnagel uses the phrase with his colleagues. Students also may find the conclusion to be vague because the author's choice to quote Drew Barrymore seems arbitrary and may not represent a strong "source" with readers. An editor or writer, or even an actor known for her or his precision with words, might have been a better source for those who "don't like the phrase."

Building Your Word Power, p. 420

1. "Schoolgirl chatter" suggests informal, excitable gossip, and "adult repartee" suggests witty retorts used in informal settings such as parties.

2. Parents are thanking author Meg Cabot "sarcastically" (para. 12) because her use of the phrase in *The Princess Diaries* has caused their children to see it incessantly and because to some ears, despite the new meaning, it still has a negative connotation.

Building Your Critical Thinking Skills: Inferences, p. 420

1. One can infer that Hartnagel's relationship with the California assemblyman he works for is one of younger employee to older boss (para.1). Hartnagel probably refrains from saying "Shut up!" when the assemblyman is around because members of older generations don't use it and would consider it too informal and offensive if they misunderstood it.

2. More than two hundred actresses had to be auditioned for the Elantra spot because they did not understand how to enunciate the phrase correctly so that it was humorous (9).

William Plasencia, "Web Logs Get Personal," p. 422

Plasencia describes blogging, the growing practice of posting the equivalent of journals or diaries online. In his extended definition he provides examples of how people use blogs, from purely personal expression to political discussion, and also praises blogging's potential to finally realize the dream that the Internet would equalize access to information and be free.

First-year students may know quite a bit about blogs and be eager to discuss why people would want to post their personal feelings on the Internet where "anyone" could read them. You might ask them to evaluate what an unwelcome "anyone" might mean, including someone's former friend, girlfriend or boyfriend, parents, and so on. You might initiate a discussion of the difference between this kind of private but public diary and its relationship to other cultural phenomena such as reality TV. If you plan on having students write research papers at some point in the term, you might also assign them to begin by reading and reporting on blogs related to subjects that interest them. They might, for example, present a brief oral presentation on the current material they were able to find about their potential topic.

Understanding the Reading, p. 423

1. According to Plasencia, people create and maintain Web logs in order to express themselves and to receive "responses" from others (para. 2) "without the fear of criticism" (6); to have "a voice" (5); and to find community (6). All kinds of people read them, including homemakers, business executives, and artists (3).

2. Two ways that people use Web logs are: to "vent" (2), and to update "friends and family" (4).

3. The computer requirements necessary to have a Web log are: to use a "hosted service" that provides access to one's Web log, or to set up one's own Web site through a free software program, such as MovableType (3).

4. According to the reading, blogs may allow the Internet to become the "great equalizing medium" it was intended to be (5).

Visualizing the Reading, p. 423

Possible answers include:

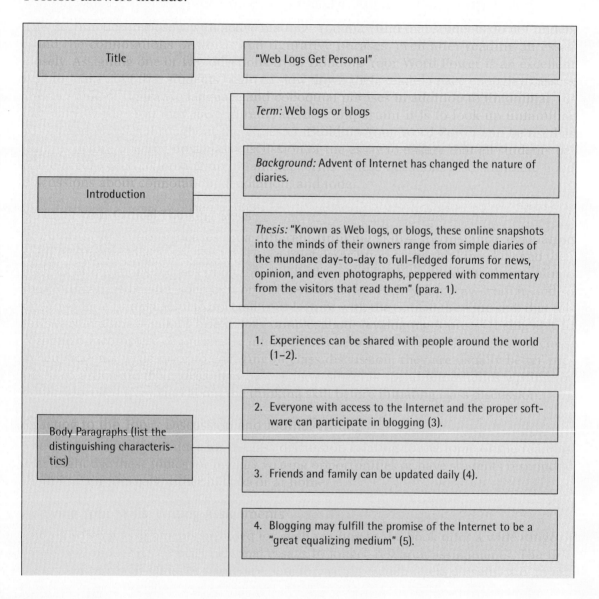

Title	"Web Logs Get Personal"

Introduction	*Term:* Web logs or blogs
	Background: Advent of Internet has changed the nature of diaries.
	Thesis: "Known as Web logs, or blogs, these online snapshots into the minds of their owners range from simple diaries of the mundane day-to-day to full-fledged forums for news, opinion, and even photographs, peppered with commentary from the visitors that read them" (para. 1).

Body Paragraphs (list the distinguishing characteristics)	1. Experiences can be shared with people around the world (1–2).
	2. Everyone with access to the Internet and the proper software can participate in blogging (3).
	3. Friends and family can be updated daily (4).
	4. Blogging may fulfill the promise of the Internet to be a "great equalizing medium" (5).

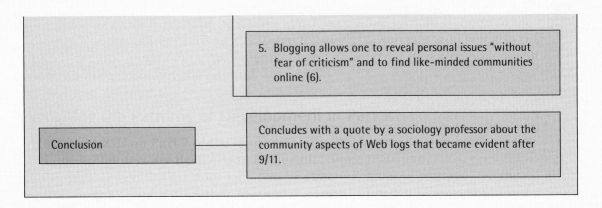

5. Blogging allows one to reveal personal issues "without fear of criticism" and to find like-minded communities online (6).

Conclusion

Concludes with a quote by a sociology professor about the community aspects of Web logs that became evident after 9/11.

Examining the Characteristics of Definition Essays, p. 423

1. See the thesis in the Visualizing the Reading activity above. The author's thesis does not explicitly suggest the importance or usefulness of Web logs. Plasencia instead chooses to address these issues over the course of his essay through the distinguishing characteristics of the term.

2. The author uses a least-to-most-important organizational framework to present the distinguishing characteristics of the term, from the use of the blog for personal expression to its use for political discussion and community building. Answers may vary.

3. Because so much of Plasencia's essay relies on outside sources, it is very important that details about his sources are included.

4. Other patterns of development used by the author include: description ("photographs, peppered with commentary from the visitors that read them" [para. 1]); narration ("Lorena Haldeman . . . updates her Web log every day" [4]); and cause and effect (the effects on blogging after 9/11 [7–8]). These different modes contribute to the essay by clarifying the author's thesis and purpose in writing.

5. The author ends with a reference to 9/11 because the events triggered important community-building via Web logs.

Building Your Word Power, p. 424

1. *Blog* means Web log; *blogging* means the act of writing and posting to a blog; and a *blogger* is someone who writes his or her own blog.

2. *Peppered* means sprinkled here and there.

Building Your Critical Thinking Skills: Evaluating Sources, 424

Students may enjoy the challenge of forming two panels to debate the usefulness and legitimacy of Plasencia's supporting evidence and sources.

Gloria Naylor, "The Meanings of a Word," p. 426

Novelist Gloria Naylor, well known for her novel *The Women of Brewster Place* (1982), here discusses and defines the word *nigger* as she experienced it growing up among her relatives. She contrasts that use of the word with the first time she heard it as an insult from a white boy. This essay is an excellent one to use if you have a mixed-race class. You might talk about the history of insults that have been used against nearly every ethnic group in America at one time or another. You might assign students to classify or divide one of the terms they have heard, much the way Naylor has done with this insult. You might also like to have a group discussion of how words like *queer* or *cripple* can be transformed by a group who uses the term positively. This might also be a good time to initiate a discussion of the meaning of the term *American*, without qualifiers like *black* or *Native*.

Understanding the Reading, p. 428

1. The author thinks written language is "inferior" to the spoken word because words gain power through the senses of sight, sound, smell, and touch.

2. The little boy was prompted to use the word *nigger* because Naylor said something to him about his math grade being lower than hers. While the young Naylor didn't know what the word meant, she was humiliated by its use because she sensed that it was an insult (para. 3).

3. During the author's childhood, weekends were spent in Harlem with a close-knit network of relatives (4).

4. According to Naylor, black people use the word *nigger* to "signify the varied and complex human beings they [know] themselves to be," whereas white people understand it solely to mean degradation or worthlessness (14).

Visualizing the Reading, p. 429

Possible answers include:

Method of Development	Example
Narration	Naylor tells the story of her experience in third grade (para. 3).
Description	Naylor describes the checkers games, babies crying, and grownups gossiping in her grandparents' house in Harlem (4–5).
Illustration	Naylor gives an example of how the word *girl* is pronounced to express praise (11).

Cause and effect	Naylor explains that the way the white boy said the word *nigger* caused her to recognize it as an insult and to ask her mother what it meant (3).
Classification	Naylor classifies the two meanings of the word *nigger* in the black community (6–10).

Examining the Characteristics of Definition Essays, p. 429

1. The author states her thesis at the end of paragraph 2: "Words themselves are innocuous; it is the consensus that gives them true power." Naylor does not include a definition of the term itself in her thesis; however, the thesis relates to the extended definition that follows because the essay explains how the term *nigger* derives negative power from white racist consensus and is rendered impotent through black consensus.

2. Some of the distinguishing characteristics that Naylor uses to explain her extended definition are: the context and tone of how the word is used, and how the sex and number of the person(s) it is applied to influence the word's meaning. So, for example, "that nigger pulled in $6,000 of overtime" (para. 8) is positive because it expresses praise and applies to a single individual male. Naylor includes the detailed descriptions of her own family gatherings to let readers know about the atmosphere in which she first heard this word.

3. Naylor also includes a definition of the term *girl* because it is used similarly to *nigger* when applied to an individual woman (11).

4. Naylor uses her extended definition to dispel the idea that *nigger* can never have a positive connotation. She defines how black people can use the word for praise in the singular (6) or for disapproval in the plural (10), signifying the "varied and complex human beings" that the members of the black community know themselves to be (14).

5. Answers may vary. The last sentence is deeply moving because it acknowledges the racism that all African Americans in America must endure.

Building Your Word Power, p. 429

1. The allusion to the "chicken and egg" dispute refers to the question of whether language shapes human perception of the world or whether everyone sees the world exactly the same way, regardless of language — a question that thus far has not been answerable.

2. The connotation of *bad* as used by Naylor in paragraph 3 is naughty or offensive. The connotation of *hear* (15) in this context is that until that moment Naylor had not really recognized the word as an insult.

Building Your Critical Thinking Skills: Comparison and Contrast, p. 430

1. The author contrasts written language unfavorably with spoken language because the former cannot capture the "richness" and sensuality of life (para. 1).

2. The author's family and friends compared and contrasted hardworking black people with "trifling niggers" (10) who refused to look for work and lacked "self-respect."

3. The black use of *nigger* can mean either praise or disapproval, whereas the white use is only insulting. The black use is characterized by either pride or disappointment, and the white use by hatred.

Gina Kolata, "Spinning," p. 432

New York Times science writer Gina Kolata gives an extended definition of the sport of "spinning," a form of group aerobic exercise using special stationary bicycles. Kolata uses a number of rhetorical modes, including narration, cause and effect, division and classification, and comparison and contrast, to illustrate how she and her husband became intrigued by and eventually addicted to spinning. Students might like to try using a number of techniques to describe their own favorite hobby, beginning with definition. Sharing informative, personal essays with the class may foster a sense of understanding and camaraderie among the students.

Understanding the Reading, p. 436

1. The author's husband, Bill, prefers road biking to other kinds of exercise (para. 3).

2. Bill attributes his annual depression to his inability to ride outdoors when it gets dark too early or the weather gets too cold and icy (3).

3. Kolata describes the bicycles that are used for Spinning as set in metal frames, with only one flywheel, with adjustable seats and a resistance knob (6). A bike should fit so that the seat is high enough for the rider to extend her or his leg with a foot on the pedal and the handlebars only one or two inches above or below the seat. When extended, arms should not be locked at the elbows (7).

4. One increases or decreases the resistance on a Spinning bike in order to get a less strenuous or harder workout.

Visualizing the Reading, p. 436

Answers may vary. While some of the riders in the photo appear to be working very hard, others look relaxed, as if they are listening to the instructor, like the people described in paragraph 10 who just pedal along at "a low resistance."

Examining the Characteristics of Definition Essays, p. 437

1. Answers may vary. One possible thesis is that this sport allows people to get an excellent workout but they have to put the effort into challenging and exerting themselves to test their limits.

2. The distinguishing characteristics of Spinning are that it is conducted indoors, on stationary bikes; workouts are done to music with an instructor in a darkened room; and friction created by resistance knobs maximizes or minimizes the workout. Answers may vary.

3. Kolata uses an extended definition to explain heart-rate monitors (para. 14). Answers may vary.

4. Other patterns of development include: narration ("the cold evening in November of 2000 when I first stepped into a Spinning room" [1]); cause and effect (how effort increases heart rate [17]); and description ("in a darkened room, on stationary bikes that look remotely like road bikes" [4]). The author distinguishes Spinning from exercising on stationary bikes like LifeCycles by first describing how boring they are and how they "do not look or feel like a real road bike" (3). She then explains how, in a Spinning class, participants "do more than simply sit back and pedal their bikes" (4).

Building Your Word Power, p. 437

1. The word *funk* as used in paragraph 3 means depression. Words like *downcast, discouraged, glum,* and *grey moods* provide clues to its meaning.

2. Answers may vary.

Building Your Critical Thinking Skills: Author's Purpose, p. 437

1. Kolata's book title, *Ultimate Fitness: The Quest for Truth about Exercise and Health,* suggests that the author's purpose in writing may be to dispel misinformation about exercise and health. The use of the word *quest* implies that the book is likely to be personal in nature.

2. Answers may vary.

Chapter 12 Cause and Effect: Using Reasons and Results to Explain, p. 439

Because *cause and effect* (also known as causal analysis) is fairly straightforward and logical to explain, you should be able to cover the material with ease. It is especially helpful to explain how cause and effect works by reviewing the graphic organizers included in this chapter. Be sure to caution students to clearly identify the difference between causes (reasons that something happens) and effects (results of the things that happen) in order to keep the chain of events clear. Note too that the cause and effect essay is usually informative or persuasive (rather than expressive). The three types of cause and effect essays are outlined in the chapter in both print and visual formats (through graphic organizers): causes and effects, a chain of causes and effects, and multiple causes and effects.

You will likely find it useful to begin discussion by analyzing the annotated essay "How Nature Heals Us" by Deb Aronson (p. 440). It uses a "most to least" order that starts with familiar and obvious kinds of contact with nature and moves toward less obvious kinds of contact. Aronson seeks to inform readers about the healing effects of nature and to dispel assumptions about what relieves stress. The graphic organizers on pages 446–448 will be useful tools in showing exactly how a cause and effect essay is constructed. Nathan Nguyen's "Gambling on Our Future" (p. 456), is clearly marked and highlighted to guide students through his argument. He speculates that a chain of events has led to an increase in problem gambling, citing statistics and providing expert opinions to support his views.

The remaining essays in this chapter offer a wide range of types, from personal pieces to journalistic accounts to research writing. You might want to initiate a discussion of Clive Thompson's "The Honesty Virus" (p. 460) by exploring its thematic relationship to "Web Logs Get Personal" in Chapter 11 (p. 422). In his essay, Thompson discusses how online communication differs from oral communication in that people are less likely to lie online than in person. "When the Plug Is Pulled on the Digital Age, the Basics Black Out" (p. 466) offers more insight into the effects of technology in modern life as the authors explore the effects of the massive power outage that much of the northeastern United States experienced in August 2003. Ruth Russell's deeply moving essay, "The Wounds That Can't Be Stitched Up" (p. 472), about the effects of a drunk driving accident that severely injured Russell's family members, illustrates how an essay can be both persuasive and personal. Another personal essay included here is "Changing My Name after Sixty Years" by Tom Rosenberg (p. 477): The author explores the journey he took to change his name, explaining both the causes behind his decision to change his name legally and the effects of his decision on his friends and family. The final reading in the chapter, "The Clan of One-Breasted Women" by Terry Tempest Williams (p. 482), offers an account that is both personal and scientific, as it traces the long-lasting effects of the atomic bomb testing that was conducted in the author's home state of Utah in the 1950s.

Nathan Nguyen, "Gambling on Our Future," p. 456

Nathan Nguyen's research paper theorizes that a series of events has led to an increase in problem and addictive gambling in the United States. This paper on a current social problem provides an excellent model to explain not only cause and effect but also the use of research to support ideas with academic opinions and impressive statistics.

Responding to "Students Write," p. 458

1. Answers may vary.

2. Answers may vary. Alternative ways to introduce the topic might involve including a question that cites a statistic about gambling's increase over the past few years or an anecdote illustrating the effects of addiction on someone of interest.

3. Answers may vary.

4. Nguyen might have ended by offering a story about a program that is helping people to stop gambling or by offering some solutions to the problem.

Clive Thompson, "The Honesty Virus," p. 460

Writer Clive Thompson explores the recent claim by a Cornell University professor that people lie less frequently online than in person. Thompson uses a series of examples to contend that rather than being deceptive online because of a sense of anonymity, as predicted in the early days of the Internet, people are actually more forthcoming, expressive, and truthful online. You can use this reading to start a class discussion about why people might feel more comfortable sharing their feelings and being honest with total strangers than with those they meet face to face. What social and psychological factors, for example, might lead to such behavior?

Understanding the Reading, p. 463

1. The results of Jeffrey Hancock's study of his students' online behavior indicated that his students were more honest online than in person or on the phone (para. 1).

2. According to Thompson, the "digital age is tough on its liars" because email records are never erased and can be brought back to "haunt" liars (5).

3. Thompson speculates that what causes people to be honest when they are online is that they fear they might be caught (4) or that they are "disinhibited" (9).

4. Online communication differs from offline communication in that it does not entail "face-to-face" contact (9), it is recorded in email memory (6), and it can be anonymous and geographically distant (9). People communicate differently on the Internet because nothing is forgotten (6) and they feel geographically distant and almost invisible (9).

Visualizing the Reading, p. 463

Possible answers include:

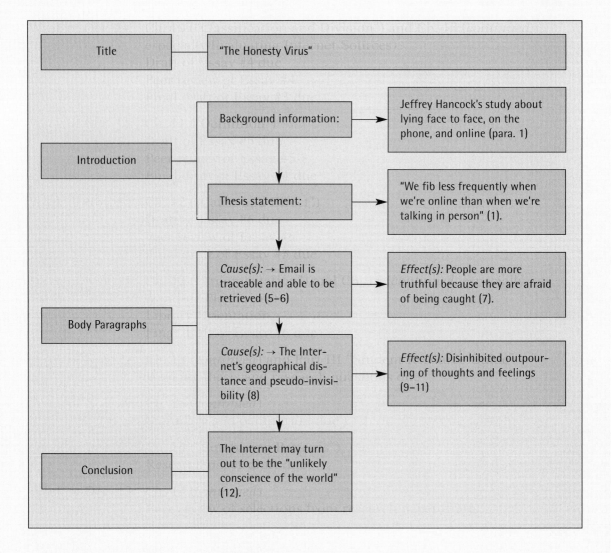

Title	"The Honesty Virus"

Introduction
- Background information: → Jeffrey Hancock's study about lying face to face, on the phone, and online (para. 1)
- Thesis statement: → "We fib less frequently when we're online than when we're talking in person" (1).

Body Paragraphs
- *Cause(s):* → Email is traceable and able to be retrieved (5–6) → *Effect(s):* People are more truthful because they are afraid of being caught (7).
- *Cause(s):* → The Internet's geographical distance and pseudo-invisibility (8) → *Effect(s):* Disinhibited outpouring of thoughts and feelings (9–11)

Conclusion
- The Internet may turn out to be the "unlikely conscience of the world" (12).

Examining the Characteristics of Cause and Effect Essays, p. 464

1. The author's purpose in writing is both informative and persuasive. He gives background information about early expectations that the Internet would allow for rampant deception and then argues (using evidence gathered by scholars and others) that anonymity and distance are causing the opposite of what was expected.

2. Thompson's thesis statement is expressed through the statements: "We fib less frequently when we're online than when we're talking in person" (para. 1) and that we are more truthful online because "We're worried about being busted" (para. 4).

3. The types of evidence the author uses to support his thesis are: academic studies (1); examples ("Even Microsoft was tripped up by old e-mail messages" [5]); and quotations from experts ("50 percent of those who write in via e-mail express suicidal feelings, compared with only 20 percent of those who call in" [9]).

4. The popular assumption about the Internet that Thompson is seeking to dispel is that it encourages lying. Depending on students' personal experiences online, they may or may not find Thompson's case effective.

5. Other patterns of development used by Thompson include: definition (explanation of *disinhibited* [9]); narration ("Remember when George W. Bush first met Vladimir Putin . . .? [11]); and illustration (examples of how technology records and saves information [6]).

Building Your Word Power, p. 464

1. The prefix *pseudo* means false. By *pseudo-invisibility* as used in paragraph 8, the author means that they people online are seemingly invisible in the sense that no one can see them face to face but they are in fact traceable and able to be found.

2. Three synonyms for *lying* in the essay are "fib[bing]" (para. 1), "mishandled the truth" (1), and "prevarications" (11).

Building Your Critical Thinking Skills: Tone, p. 464

1. Answers may vary, but some words or phrases that contribute to the overall tone of the essay are "fib" (para. 1), "scary zone" (3), "busted" (4), "unless you're talking to Linda Tripp" (4), "although he told me that on the phone, so who knows?" (5), "gotcha politics" (6), and "punk" (7). The essay's tone might be described as casual and slangy.

2. Answers may vary.

3. The author's tone toward conservative politicians is irreverent and skeptical. It may reveal that his political opinions are fairly progressive.

Susan Warren and Melanie Trottman, "When the Plug Is Pulled on the Digital Age, the Basics Black Out," p. 466

Journalists Susan Warren and Melanie Trottman describe the effects of the August 2003 massive power outage on much of the northeastern United States. The effect of the blackout, which many of your students may recall or personally experienced, was great because of our culture's dependency on electricity to run everything from cash registers to hotel card keys. Such dependency has deepened over the past ten years, which the authors are careful to point out, suggesting that events like this one must not be forgotten. Students may like to write about and discuss the increasing reliance on technology that they have observed in their own lifetimes.

Understanding the Reading, p. 469

1. This power outage differed from the widespread outages of the past because the Electronic Age had made people more reliant on electricity (para. 2).

2. Some of the more difficult aspects of the blackout for the shopkeepers were that electronic cash registers (2), electric hair trimmers (11), and credit cards (16) didn't work.

3. Cell phones worked but couldn't be recharged, and many networks were jammed (12). Cordless phones also didn't work, leaving the only working phones those that were plugged directly into a wall (18).

4. In addition to candles, employees at one hotel used glow-sticks to guide people down the halls (14).

Visualizing the Reading, p. 469

Possible answers include:

Cause →	Effects Become Causes →	Effects
Northeast Blackout of 2003	1. Company cash registers wouldn't work.	1. Employees had to make do with paper and pencils.
	2. Electronic keycards and locks wouldn't work (para. 2).	2. Hotel staff had to discharge guests or use master keys to unlock hotel rooms
	3. Stoves with an electric ignition didn't work (10).	3. People had to eat cold food.
	4. Electric hair trimmers didn't work (11).	4. People had to leave the barbershop with hair half trimmed.
	5. Cell phones worked but couldn't be recharged (12).	5. People couldn't make phone calls or had to find a phone plugged into the wall.
	6. Cordless phones didn't work (12, 18).	6. People drove in cars to re-charge phones, but then needed gas and couldn't get it because gas pumps weren't working.

Examining the Characteristics of Cause and Effect Essays, p. 469

1. The authors' purpose in writing is not overtly stated, but given the number of examples, one can assume that their purpose is to warn readers about Americans' overreliance on electricity.

2. The essay's thesis appears as a series of sentences in paragraph 1: "For the better part of a decade, the digital dream has been a wireless, cashless, instantly connected society. But . . . [w]hen you're unplugged, even very simple tasks bec[o]me impossible."

3. To explain the causes and effects of the blackout, the authors use vivid examples of ordinary people trying to make do without electricity. The examples support the thesis by illustrating how helpless people were rendered by the loss of electricity.

4. The other pattern of development is narration. This technique contributes to the essay by making the story of the effects of the blackout vivid and immediate.

5. Answers may vary. Students might say that a final sentence such as "Next time, we'll be prepared" would make the ending feel more conclusive.

Building Your Word Power, p. 469

1. The phrase "digital dream" means a "wireless, cashless, instantly connected society" (para. 1).

2. The phrase "plain-Jane model" means a basic, old-fashioned, plug-into-the-wall phone (18).

Building Your Critical Thinking Skills: Identifying Assumptions, p. 470

1. The *Wall Street Journal* targets the business community, so the authors might have assumed that their readers would be most interested in the potential financial losses that businesses can experience as a result of widespread electrical outages.

2. Examples targeted toward business people include: companies with electronic cash registers (para 2); electronic keys and lights in hotels (2, 14); electronic tools used extensively in restaurants (3); electronic scales in grocery stores (7); and electric trimmers in hair salons (11).

3. Students might enjoy having a discussion of the "digital dream" of a wireless and connected society and what it means in terms of the environment. Have them break into groups first to come up with three points each.

Ruth Russell,"The Wounds That Can't Be Stitched Up," p. 472

Ruth Russell narrates the story of the drunk driver who hit her family's car when she was young and then spent very little time in jail. Years later, she saw him again driving drunk and was motivated to write this story. She wonders why he wasn't blamed by local people and tells the reader how the town's attitude in excusing the drunk driver and "blaming the victim" (her family who didn't have seat belts on) affected her life. Students may like to analyze the underlying feelings that the writer does not address directly. Do they agree, for example, that she has made a strong case by presenting her family as further victimized by their town?

Understanding the Reading, p. 474

1. Her mother's car was hit head-on by a drunk driver who was in the wrong lane with no headlights on (para. 7). Her mother lost several teeth and her face was se-verely cut up, her sister almost died with a "fractured skull" requiring surgery that left a permanent scar (6), and her youngest brother was traumatized with a black eye.

2. The man who hit the author's family was jailed for the weekend and lost his li-cense for thirty days (10). The local people in Russell's town like the drunk driver and excused his behavior because he is a "war hero" who had a hard family life (12).

3. The man who hit Russell's family ended up living in her apartment building (13). Russell meets him when he is drunkenly speeding past and then reversing into the apartment building's parking lot (14).

4. The title refers figuratively to the author's memories, which cannot be erased.

Visualizing the Reading, p. 474

Possible answers include:

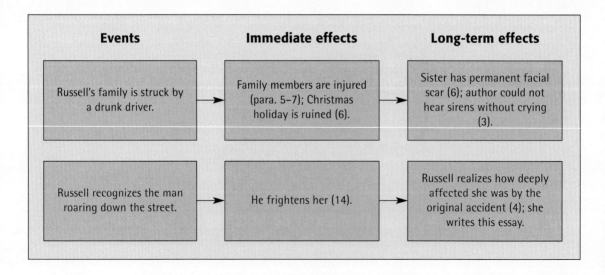

Events	Immediate effects	Long-term effects
Russell's family is struck by a drunk driver.	Family members are injured (para. 5–7); Christmas holiday is ruined (6).	Sister has permanent facial scar (6); author could not hear sirens without crying (3).
Russell recognizes the man roaring down the street.	He frightens her (14).	Russell realizes how deeply affected she was by the original accident (4); she writes this essay.

Examining the Characteristics of Cause and Effect Essays, p. 474

1. The author's thesis appears in paragraph 4: "Twenty-three years have passed, but only recently have I realized how deeply affected I was by events caused by a drunk driver so long ago." Her essay focuses on effects such as physical scarring and long-term fears.

2. Russell organizes her essay according to chronology, from the original devastating accident to the time she sees the drunk driver years later.

3. To fully explain the effects of the accident, the author uses details such as the effect of the sirens on her for years afterwards (para. 3) and her sister's scars (6).

4. The pattern of development used to organize the events in this essay is narration. This pattern contributes tension to the essay and illustrates how the accident eroded the author's sense of safety in the world.

Building Your Word Power, p. 475

1. The "power" that the author refers to in paragraph 3 is the force of the memory that caused her to feel sorrow for years afterwards.

Building Your Critical Thinking Skills: Author's Purpose, p. 475

1. Although twenty-three years have passed since the accident, the author seems to still be bothered by the fact that the drunk's behavior was excused in the community because he was a well-liked war hero (para. 12), and that he was not "accused" the way her family were for not wearing seat belts (11). The trigger for writing is the event when she runs into him years later, after he swerves drunkenly into her apartment parking lot.

2. The transition, "Sometimes when I tell this story" (11), indicates that the author's purpose in writing is to explore why the drunk driver was forgiven by locals. In the same paragraph she defends her family, perhaps because she feels that they have been blamed more (for not wearing seat belts) than the drunk driver was for hitting them.

3. Russell's treatment of the drunk driver suggests that she still doesn't think he has paid for his crime. She seems justifiably incredulous that he is still allowed to drive.

Tom Rosenberg, "Changing My Name after Sixty Years," p. 477

Tom Rosenberg speculates about the reasons his family Anglicized their name after leaving Germany and its effect upon his life, trying to deny or hide his Jewishness. He also explores his decision years later to take back his Jewish surname out of pride and in response to political repression in the wake of 9/11. Students might find it useful to first freewrite about what it would mean to have to hide the origins of one's name out of fear. They could then form small groups to discuss how Americans of various ethnic groups have sought to Anglicize their names and what that decision means in terms of America's ideal of the melting pot.

Understanding the Reading, p. 479

1. The author's parents may have been motivated to change their name by "fear, a desire to assimilate or a combination of both" (para. 2). Other immigrants' names were often changed by "an immigration bureaucrat" upon arrival at Ellis Island (2).

2. The author has been associated with "Theta Chi" (5), a Christian fraternity, and has attended a Unitarian church and a Jewish temple (7). The religious affiliations contributed to the way he raised his children by allowing him to express "tolerance" (7) and to acknowledge his Jewish background to a greater extent than he had in the past.

3. The author decided to change his name because he felt that he was still denying his background and he wanted to express "pride" in his Jewishness (15).

4. The rabbi proposed that the author take a Hebrew first name as well (10). The author was initially shocked because he thought it would mean becoming more religious (11), but he now sees it as a way to express "pride" (15).

Visualizing the Reading, p. 479

Possible answers include:

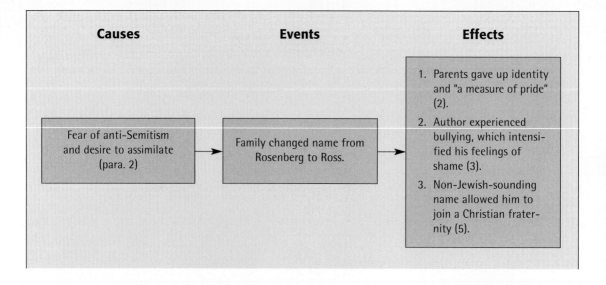

Causes	Events	Effects
Fear of anti-Semitism and desire to assimilate (para. 2)	Family changed name from Rosenberg to Ross.	1. Parents gave up identity and "a measure of pride" (2). 2. Author experienced bullying, which intensified his feelings of shame (3). 3. Non-Jewish-sounding name allowed him to join a Christian fraternity (5).

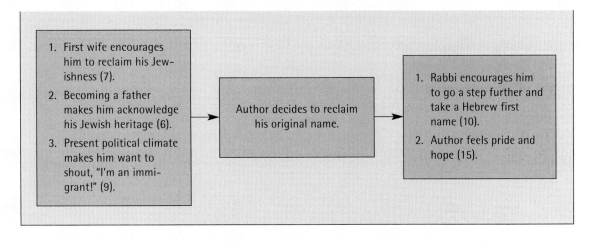

Examining the Characteristics of Cause and Effect Essays, p. 479

1. Rosenberg's essay is expressive, informative, and persuasive. He wants to express his "shame" and denial (para. 4), to inform people about the history and effects of anti-Semitism (1), and to persuade people that it is best to embrace one's heritage (15).

2. His implied thesis is that it is best to embrace one's heritage rather than hide it or try to deny it.

3. The inclusion of different causes and effects relates to Rosenberg's thesis and purpose in writing by indicating the serious reasons behind his decision to change his name. The author includes personal details about his marriages and religious practices because having a Christian wife in his first marriage was a positive experience that helped him to reconnect with his Jewish heritage. Having children made him reflect upon how damaging his parents' hiding was and inspired him to embrace Jewish culture and spirituality.

4. Answers may vary.

5. Rosenberg uses narrative dialogue for his conclusion. Answers may vary.

Building Your Word Power, p. 480

1. The connotation of the word *baggage* as used in paragraph 1 is guilt.

2. The expression "continued to dog me" as used in paragraph 10 means that the author's memories continued to bother him.

Building Your Critical Thinking Skills: Inferences, p. 480

_____ 1. Rosenberg joined a predominately Christian fraternity because Jewish fraternities would not accept him.

_____✓_____ 2. Rosenberg would approve if his children wanted to change their names.

_____✓_____ 3. Rosenberg's relationship with his first wife contributed to his decision to change his name.

_____✓_____ 4. Rosenberg is an active member of his temple.

Terry Tempest Williams, "The Clan of One-Breasted Women," p. 482

In this personal essay Terry Tempest Williams describes her childhood in Utah, seeing generations of women in her family die from or have surgery for breast cancer. She writes this essay in response to her uncovering the possible cause, nuclear testing in the desert in the 1950s, which radicalizes her and drives her to develop a new attitude toward authority of all kinds. The issues in this essay about personal authority and challenging unjust authority are central ones for college students. The essay should provide interesting discussion combined with freewrites and personal essays about your students' own experiences with issues that galvanized them to action.

Understanding the Reading, p. 488

1. The recurring dream cited by Williams at the start of the essay is of a flash of light in the sky. Her father tells her that it was a nuclear test that she actually watched as a young girl.

2. According to Williams, the cancer in her family was caused by exposure to the fallout from nuclear testing.

3. The factors that made it easy for the government to conduct nuclear tests in Utah in the 1950s and 1960s were a conservative political climate in which opposition to nuclear testing was unacceptable and an attitude that "[p]ublic health was secondary to national security" (para. 20–21). The government responded to the rise in cancer rates years later by denying that there was any "basis" to believe there was a cause and effect relationship between the two (22).

4. The dream at the end of the essay is of powerful women joining together to protest the violation of the earth (42). In real life, Tempest Williams and other protesters trespass on military property to protest the Nevada test site (49).

Visualizing the Reading, p. 488

Answers may vary. Encourage students to consider the "visible" effects of the nuclear fallout shown here with the more "invisible" effects of military tactics, which indicate a similar attitude toward civilians. Just as policymakers decided to drop the atomic bomb on innocent civilians in Hiroshima, so too does the U.S. government ignore and deny responsibility for harming innocent civilians during the nuclear bomb tests of the 1950s.

Examining the Characteristics of Cause and Effect Essays, p. 489

1. The author makes her main point toward the middle of the essay in paragraph 37: "Tolerating blind obedience in the name of patriotism or religion ultimately takes our lives." Her purpose in writing is to emphasize that it is important to challenge authority when that authority is unjust.

2. The causes and effects discussed in Williams's essay are nuclear fallout and cancer. Williams suggests that the nuclear testing caused breast cancer in her family but acknowledges that she can't prove it (35). The fact that the court case *Irene Allen v. The United States of America* was initially won (though later overturned) suggests that there is ample evidence to suggest a direct connection but that it may fall short of a direct causal relationship.

3. Williams's use of descriptive language and sensory details provides vivid images of the landscape she grew up in, the nuclear test she witnessed as a girl, and the effects of cancer in her family. Examples from the essay include: "the sandstoned landscape, bare-boned and beautiful" (para. 12); "this golden-stemmed cloud, the mushroom" (16); "as they vomited green-black bile" (32).

4. Other patterns of development include: description ("the way she held herself in a purple velvet robe" [9]); narration ("They were taken to a white, square building on the other side of Mercury" [46]); and illustration ("Mrs. Allen's case was the first on an alphabetical list of twenty-four cases" [23]). These patterns enhance the causal analysis by showing how the author's individual family experience was also part of a larger historical event.

5. Williams's conclusion reinforces her main assertion through the example of how she and women like her decided to no longer tolerate "blind obedience" and instead challenged the government. Answers may vary.

Building Your Word Power, p. 489

1. Doublespeak such as "low-use segments of the population" (para. 20) and "virtually uninhabited desert terrain" (38) mean that although people reside in that area, the government considers them insignificant.

2. The meaning of the metaphor "becoming a midwife to the rebirth of their souls" (32) means that she helped them to die.

Building Your Critical Thinking Skills: Facts and Opinions, p. 489

Facts (F) or Opinions (O).

___F___ 1. "Most statistics tell us breast cancer is genetic." (para. 4)

___O___ 2. ". . .living in Utah may be the greatest hazard of all." (4)

___F___ 3. "Within a few minutes, a light ash was raining on the car." (16)

___F___ 4. "Irene Allen lived in Hurricane, Utah." (24)

___O___ 5. "Tolerating blind obedience in the name of patriotism or religion ultimately takes our lives." (37)

___F___ 6. " Ours was an act of civil disobedience." (52)

Reacting to the Reading: Discussion and Journal Writing, p. 490

2. The notion of blind obedience put forth by Williams is likely to generate interesting class discussion. Have students form two panels, pro and con, and then have
them present their material to the class as a whole to stimulate discussion and
questions.

Chapter 13 Argumentation: Supporting a Claim, p. 491

Many college students are eager to enter into political and social arenas, to vote and
debate issues and have a voice in their broader community. Learning how to write and
think critically and to formulate arguments is critical to that transition. As shown
here, *argument* has three basic parts: an issue, a claim, and support. This chapter
clearly defines each aspect of argumentation, and students should quickly grasp the
basic stance required for it. At some point in their papers, students should also
acknowledge and refute opposing viewpoints. The list of Guidelines for Refuting Evidence (pp. 505–506) will assist students in acknowledging and refuting their opposition
in a step-by-step fashion. You will note that the graphic organizer for argumentation is
more flexible than those for other modes because it does not designate the order in
which an argument is presented and it leaves space to begin with a claim or evidence
or even opposing views. Because the form of an argument can be so variable — drawing
as well on other modes of development — you will need to stress the importance of the
thesis and clearly supported claims.

A number of contemporary controversial issues are covered in this chapter. Wilbert
Rideau, in the annotated essay "Why Prisons Don't Work" (p. 493), makes the claim
that prisons don't make society safe, using induction to dismiss the various arguments
in their favor. Studying Rideau's essay in conjunction with the annotated student
essay, "Ethnic Definitions Hinder Society's Enlightenment" by Rudy De La Torre (p.
511) will show students visually how successful arguments are structured. Euthanasia
is movingly discussed in Carol Bernstein Ferry's "A Good Death" (p. 515), a letter by
the author in support of her own right to a "painless death" with emotional appeals
about the pain that her prolonged suffering would cause her family. Frank DeFord's
"Athletics 101: A Change in Eligibility Rules Is Long Overdue" (p. 520) deals with the

amateur rules governing eligibility to play college and professional sports. This topic is likely to be of interest to many students, particularly at institutions where sports play a large role in campus culture. Martin Luther King Jr.'s "I Have a Dream" (p. 524) offers students a chance to analyze a classic speech, breaking it down to appreciate how King effectively uses language and argument to argue for civil rights.

This chapter also provides pairs of arguments for and against organ donation, with Bruce Gottlieb's "How Much Is That Kidney in the Window?" (p. 531) in favor and Gilbert Meilaender's "'Strip-Mining' the Dead" (p. 538) against; violent video games, with Dave Grossman and Gloria DeGaetano's "It's Important to Feel Something When You Kill" (p. 545) against and Gerard Jones's "Violent Media Is Good for Kids" (p. 554) in favor; and the Patriot Act, with Zara Gelsey's "Who's Reading over Your Shoulder?" (p. 560) against the library surveillance provision and Ramesh Ponnuru's "Fears about the Patriot Act Are Misguided" (p. 566) in favor. These pairs of essays will provide students with an opportunity to use what they have learned about synthesizing and evaluating arguments.

Rudy De La Torre, "Ethnic Definitions Hinder Society's Enlightenment," p. 511

Student Rudy De La Torre's essay questions why people need to ask about a person of color's ethnicity when they first meet that person. De la Torre speculates what would happen if someone said, "What difference would it make?" He argues that people should be evaluated on the basis of their actions, by what they have contributed to society rather than by their ethnic heritage. This essay may lead students into a discussion of the meaning of ethnicity in America.

Responding to "Students Write," p. 512

1. Have your students brainstorm a list of title ideas and then vote on which one best conveys Torre's thesis in a catchy and interesting way.

2. Even though Torre's historical responses to "What are you?" provide food for thought, depending on one's understanding of world history they may or may not be clear to the reader.

3. Answers may vary.

4. Many students are likely to find this conclusion to be fitting because it encapsulates Torre's claim that racial classification is reductive and limited.

Carol Bernstein Ferry, "A Good Death," p. 515

Carol Bernstein Ferry, a wealthy benefactor and advocate for euthanasia, here defends the right to die "a good death," as she calls it in her title. She wrote this article after she was diagnosed with cancer, and she committed suicide three months after it was published. Arguing that euthanasia is the right of any sane adult, she deftly anticipates and acknowledges her opponents. Issues such as euthanasia are important ones for students to consider. They may like to express their personal feelings in journals before engaging in more logical debate. Students may enjoy debating the pros and cons of euthanasia, using religious, medical, and humanitarian arguments. You might ask them to do some preliminary research on the subject and then have them present their findings to the class. In discussing this essay, remind students that it is important to try to remain somewhat neutral in order not to become swept up in one's feelings during debate.

Understanding the Reading, p. 517

1. Ferry plans to commit suicide because she is terminally ill with emphysema and advanced in age, at seventy-six years of age.

2. No one will be assisting Ferry in her death because they could be legally implicated in her death (para. 3).

3. Ferry is happy about the life she has lived. She views the time she has left as a "gift" (3).

4. According to Ferry, the barriers to dying in peace are the legal restrictions on assisted suicide that say that she has to do it alone. She could be more "certain" that she would die peacefully if she could have the help of a second person (3). Ultimately, through her letter, Ferry hopes to change the attitude in the United States that cannot accept each person's life as his or her own (5).

Visualizing the Reading, p. 517

Possible answers include:

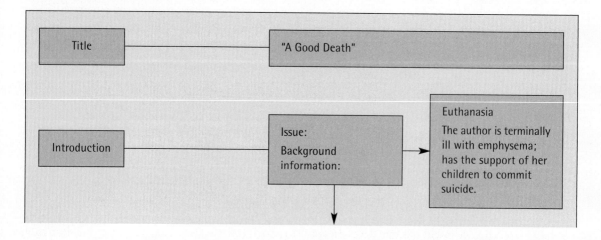

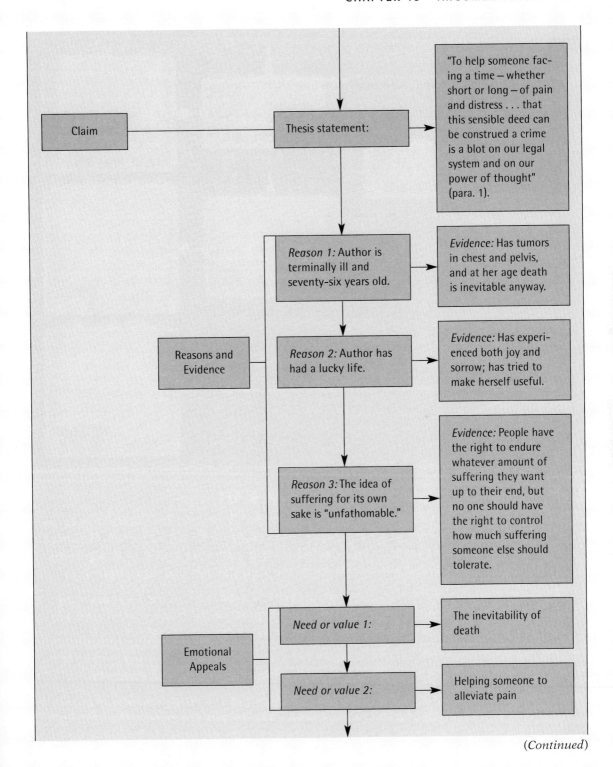

Claim —— Thesis statement: → "To help someone facing a time — whether short or long — of pain and distress . . . that this sensible deed can be construed a crime is a blot on our legal system and on our power of thought" (para. 1).

Reasons and Evidence

Reason 1: Author is terminally ill and seventy-six years old. → Evidence: Has tumors in chest and pelvis, and at her age death is inevitable anyway.

Reason 2: Author has had a lucky life. → Evidence: Has experienced both joy and sorrow; has tried to make herself useful.

Reason 3: The idea of suffering for its own sake is "unfathomable." → Evidence: People have the right to endure whatever amount of suffering they want up to their end, but no one should have the right to control how much suffering someone else should tolerate.

Emotional Appeals

Need or value 1: → The inevitability of death

Need or value 2: → Helping someone to alleviate pain

(Continued)

(Continued)

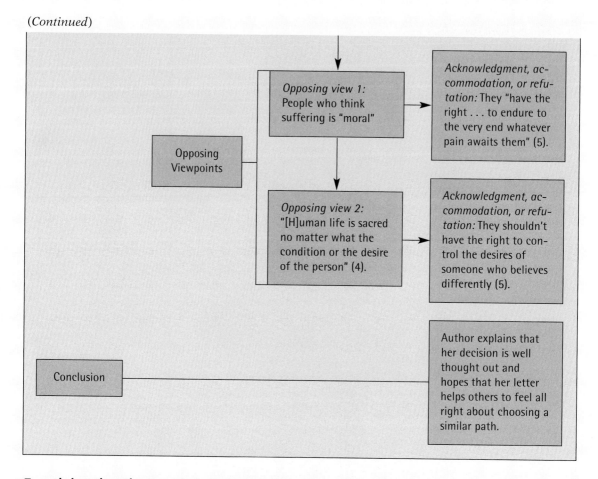

Examining the Characteristics of Argument Essays, p. 517

1. The type of audience Ferry is writing for is probably neutral or wavering because her letter was submitted to a newspaper that reaches a broad audience. However, elements of her letter seem to be directed toward a smaller group of disagreeing people, the religious and political leaders she views as her primary opponents.

2. Answers may vary. Ferry qualifies her support of assisted suicide by explaining how medical help for the terminally ill is useless and how much sorrow and anxiety the family and friends of someone who is dying must undergo.

3. The reasons that Ferry uses to support her claim are: she has the support of family, she is going to die soon anyway, and she has lived a long and good life.

4. Ferry addresses opposing viewpoints by questioning the religious view that sees a moral beauty in "suffering for its own sake." She refutes the notion that "human life is sacred no matter the condition or the desire of the person" by explaining

that people who feel that way can do what they will with their own life, but they have no right to decide for others who feel differently. Answers may vary.

5. Ferry uses inductive reasoning to order her argument by working from the facts of her own situation toward the overarching idea of euthanasia. Her method of organization is logical in that it moves from her personal situation to public views.

Building Your Word Power, p. 517

1. The connotative meaning of the word *death* as used by Ferry is suicide because that is what she means by "painless death."

2. The idiom "put up roadblocks" as used in paragraph 5 means to oppose or place obstacles in the way of someone's progress.

Building Your Critical Thinking Skills: Evaluating Letters, p. 517

1. Some of the opinions Ferry expresses are that "each person's life is his own" (para. 5) and that politicians and religious leaders should not interfere with an individual's right to die peacefully. In support of her view, she presents her own case for taking her life.

2. The bias she reveals is that she is in fact terminally ill and suffering and that she plans to end her life.

3. The letter is addressed to a general audience. Answers may vary.

Frank Deford, "Athletics 101: A Change in Eligibility Rules Is Long Overdue," p. 520

Frank Deford, a staff writer for *Sports Illustrated* and a TV and radio commentator, defines the "antiquated amateur rules" as outdated and something that should be discontinued, especially since they unfairly advantage the privileged. He compiles a list of examples to support his views, including the idea that in many other fields interns are encouraged to gain professional experience and earn money if they can. Students may enjoy debating this issue since they would be going to school with "professional athletes" if this rule changed. Have them break into groups to discuss the issues involved. Then have them form panels in favor of the amateur rules and against them.

Understanding the Reading, p. 521

1. According to the author, educators, the NFL, and the NBA care more about the eligibility of basketball and football players than the eligibility of golfers and tennis players because basketball and football are the only sports that attract "big-ticket crowds and rich television contracts for the universities" (para. 2).

2. In support of changing eligibility rules, Deford offers the following reasons: they are antiquated, and they unfairly disadvantage college athletes.

3. The author compares students who serve as radio station interns to college athletes in order to show that many interns can make money in their profession — and are even encouraged to do so — and still remain amateurs, whereas athletes cannot (5).

4. According to Deford, the eligibility rules were originally established to protect upper-class athletes from having to come into contact with "young working men" (8).

Visualizing the Reading, p. 522

Possible answers include:

Example	What It Contributes to the Argument
Tiger Woods	Shows that the golf community is not concerned about the issue of amateur rules.
Pete Sampras, Andre Agassi, and Venus and Serena Williams	All dropped out of college to play professionally but no one cared, showing that people are only concerned about athletes for college sports that draw big-ticket crowds and television contracts.
Baseball prospects abandoning school for the minor leagues	Shows that no one cares about athletes leaving school to turn pro unless it is for a college sport that generates a lot of money.
Radio internship	Shows that amateurs in other fields are able to make money.
College singer making money in a dance band	Shows that amateurs in other fields are allowed and even encouraged to make money in their field.
Chris Young of Princeton	Shows the irrationality of a system that punishes an amateur for being good enough to play professionally.

Examining the Characteristics of Argument Essays, p. 522

1. People who are interested in sports of all kinds read *Sports Illustrated.* DeFord urges the readers of the magazine — presumably fans of college basketball and football — to take action to rid the schools of this policy by using examples to show how irrational and nonsensical amateur eligibility rules are.

2. Deford's claim in stated in paragraph 3: "Throw out all the antiquated amateur rules." While his position on the issue is clear and specific, his thesis is not very effective because it doesn't explain why this would be a good thing to do.

3. Deford cites examples both from other sports where amateur rules don't generate much fuss and from non-sports-related instances involving university students who are praised for earning money relating to their field of study. Through these examples, DeFord exposes the hypocrisy of the current system.

4. DeFord appeals to the value and need for fairness as he exposes the hypocrisy in eligibility rules.

5. Deford refutes the view that athletes who are paid bonus money will "goof off and do nothing but play their sport" by explaining that wealthy students with "huge trust funds" do this all the time but no one cares about them (para. 7).

Building Your Word Power, p. 522

1. By "cries of academic anguish" in paragraph 2 the author means that universities hypocritically pretend to be concerned about the athletes' education when their motives are actually about profit.

2. The idiom "big-ticket crowds" means that people will pay a lot to see these athletes play, and "box-office appeal" means that the athletes' names are well known enough to draw a crowd (para. 2).

Building Your Critical Thinking Skills: Tone, p. 523

1. Deford describes the eligibility rules in college athletics as *antiquated, nutty,* and *idiotic*. These informal words contribute emotional suasion to the tone of his argument.

2. Deford uses sarcasm to discredit the people who support eligibility rules in the essay's opening sentence: "As the NBA draft approaches, there is, anew, a great deal of weeping and wailing and gnashing of teeth about the poor basketball players who will be deprived of more higher education." He also uses sarcasm through the words he italicizes in paragraphs 4 and 5.

3. Answers may vary.

Martin Luther King Jr., "I Have a Dream," p. 524

Martin Luther King Jr. gave this powerful civil rights speech at the 1963 March on Washington for Jobs and Freedom. Although it contains many of the rhetorical devices commonly used in speeches, it also holds up well as a piece of writing. You may like to provide some background on the civil rights era, let students listen to the speech on a tape recorder if possible, and have them examine it closely for persuasive elements. Some historical background on the Emancipation Proclamation (and the fact that the speech was delivered at the base of the Lincoln Monument) and the Declaration of Independence (which some of the students may like to provide historical information about) would also be useful as a preface.

Understanding the Reading, p. 527

1. According to King, one hundred years after the signing of the Emancipation Proclamation African Americans still face many types of discrimination and therefore are still not free.

2. Using the analogy of a bad check, King contends that America has defaulted on a check, a promissory note "that all men would be guaranteed the unalienable rights of life, liberty, and the pursuit of happiness" (para. 3).

3. King urges his followers to return to Mississippi, Alabama, and other communities to agitate for social change.

4. In order for America "to be a great nation" (21), all people must have freedom. King's dream is that America will make good on its promise to give black people equal opportunity.

Visualizing the Reading, p. 527

Possible answers include:

Figurative Expression	Meaning
". . . we have come to our nation's Capitol to cash a check." (para.3)	Implies an obligation between the words of the Constitution and the Declaration of Independence and the rights of the Negro. Use of this analogy gives the cause a sense of importance and legitimacy.
"*Now* is the time to lift our nation from the quicksands of racial injustice to the solid rock of brotherhood." (para. 4)	Through the analogy of racial injustice as quicksand, King suggests the urgency of the cause and the ultimate solidity of the goal.
"The whirlwinds of revolt will continue to shake the foundations of our nation until the bright day of justice emerges." (para. 5)	Suggests that civil rights agitation will not end until equality has been achieved; strengthens his argument because it shows how determined they are in their struggle for civil rights.
"Let us not seek to satisfy our thirst for freedom by drinking from the cup of bitterness and hatred." (para. 6)	Cautions black people not to hate white people because of the injustices they have suffered. This figurative expression warns of the wrong path toward freedom.
"You have been the veterans of creative suffering." (para. 8)	Suggests that the history of inequality is a long one and that black people have endured many kinds of suffering.
"With this faith we will be able to transform the jangling discords of our nation into a beautiful symphony of brotherhood." (para. 19)	King is describing a nation with potential; like a symphony that can overcome bad notes to make beautiful music, so too can racial intolerance be overcome to create a better world. Lends his cause hope of peaceful coexistence and racial harmony.

Examining the Characteristics of Argument Essays, p. 528

1. Because King's audience that day was overwhelmingly in agreement with him, he did not to have to address dissenting opinions at great length. He acknowledges his opponents but concentrates on the shared dream of his audience members: equality for black people in America.

2. King's claim is that America still owes black people true equality (para. 3). He presents it by citing the promises made in the Constitution and the Declaration of Independence (3) and the Emancipation Proclamation (1).

3. His reasons and evidence are: that the founding fathers intended true equality for all as stated in the Constitution and the Declaration of Independence (3); that black people are still living in poverty, as "an exile in his own land" (2); that "[t]here will be neither rest nor tranquility in America" until blacks are truly free (5); and that blacks will not be satisfied as long as they are subjected to police brutality, cannot gain lodging in motels and hotels, and cannot live where they like (7). Answers may vary.

4. The values that King appeals to in his speech are fairness and human decency. Answers may vary.

5. To acknowledge opposing viewpoints King mentions the state of Georgia, where he hopes that "the sons of former slaves and . . . of former slaveowners will be able to sit down together at the table of brotherhood" (12), and he alludes to Alabama, where the governor's "lips are presently dripping with the words of interposition and nullification" (16). He counters these opposing viewpoints by presenting a positive view of a future where the opposition will no longer hold sway over the lives of blacks.

Building Your Word Power, p. 528

1. The "symbolic shadow" (para. 1) refers to Lincoln, whose monument the crowd is standing beneath and who signed the Emancipation Proclamation. The Proclamation liberated the slaves in states that had seceded, giving the "light of hope" (1) to black people. The "long night" refers to slavery, and "daybreak" to that moment when the slaves were freed (1).

Building Your Critical Thinking Skills: Evaluating Speeches, p. 529

1. King captures the attention of his audience by opening with an echo of the Emancipation Proclamation (para. 1), repeating various words such as *now* (4), and using vivid imagery such as "lonely island of poverty" (2).

2. Repeated words and catch-phrases are "now" (4), "I have a dream" (10–18), and "let freedom ring" (21–27). In addition to engaging the listener, this device helps build King's argument as he moves from the situation that black Americans have had to endure to a vision of the future for both blacks and the United States that he is arguing for.

3. The conclusion appeals to both the American political idea of "freedom" and the religious ideal of freedom. It projects into the future by talking about speeding up "that day when all God's children" will be free and urges listeners to take action by letting "freedom ring."

ORGAN DONATION: SHOULD PEOPLE BE ALLOWED TO SELL THEIR ORGANS?

Bruce Gottlieb, "How Much Is That Kidney in the Window?" p. 531

Lawyer and freelance writer Bruce Gottlieb outlines and dismisses a series of arguments against legalizing the sales of kidneys for transplants, using various persuasive techniques, including emotional appeals. This article is worth reviewing closely with students to evaluate the effectiveness of the author's tone, examples, statistics, and so on. As an argumentative essay, it must meet a certain standard of proof in order to be effective; students will enjoy critiquing it and the next article about organ donation, based on what they have learned.

Understanding the Reading, p. 534

1. Gottlieb favors organ sales because it offers a solution to a situation in which people are dying.

2. The author thinks that kidney sales should be the only type of organ sales to be legalized because they are unique in that "somebody with just one can live an almost entirely normal life" (para. 8).

3. Black and Hispanic populations (who represent, respectively, 35 and 12 percent of the people on the waiting lists) would be most affected if there were an increase in available kidneys (7).

4. The doctors mentioned in the article changed their minds about kidney sales because the shortage "became more acute" (9).

Visualizing the Reading, p. 534

Possible answers include:

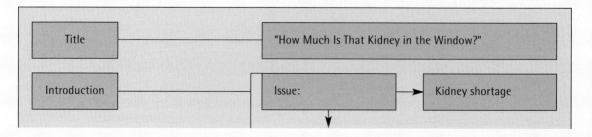

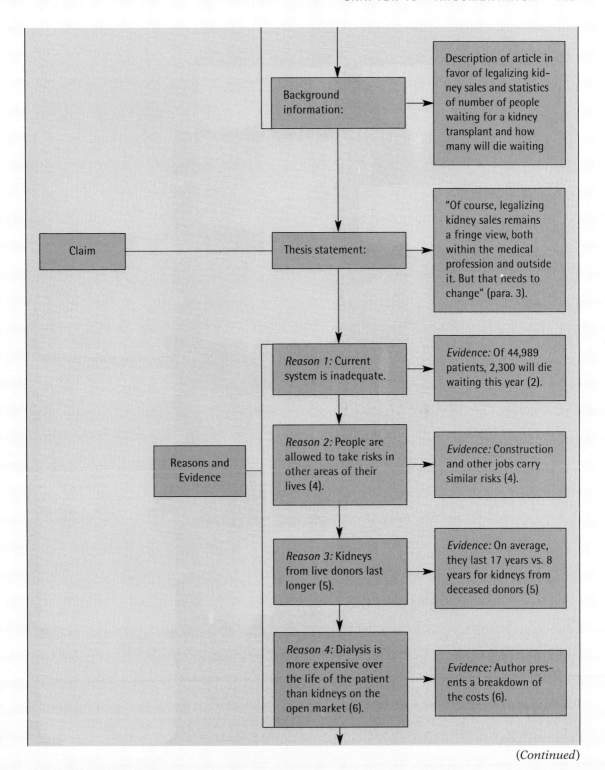

Background information: Description of article in favor of legalizing kidney sales and statistics of number of people waiting for a kidney transplant and how many will die waiting

Claim — **Thesis statement:** "Of course, legalizing kidney sales remains a fringe view, both within the medical profession and outside it. But that needs to change" (para. 3).

Reason 1: Current system is inadequate. — *Evidence:* Of 44,989 patients, 2,300 will die waiting this year (2).

Reasons and Evidence

Reason 2: People are allowed to take risks in other areas of their lives (4). — *Evidence:* Construction and other jobs carry similar risks (4).

Reason 3: Kidneys from live donors last longer (5). — *Evidence:* On average, they last 17 years vs. 8 years for kidneys from deceased donors (5)

Reason 4: Dialysis is more expensive over the life of the patient than kidneys on the open market (6). — *Evidence:* Author presents a breakdown of the costs (6).

(Continued)

(*Continued*)

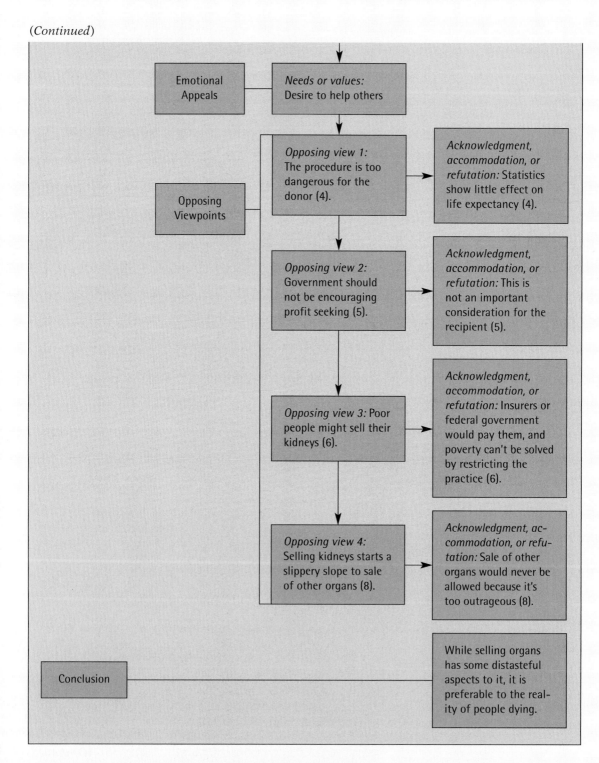

Examining the Characteristics of Argument Essays, p. 534

1. Answers may vary.

2. The author's claim is one of value because he says that saving the lives of those awaiting kidneys is more important than the problems that may arise if poor people sell their kidneys for money.

3. Gottlieb arranges opposing viewpoints in order of importance from least to most serious objection. Answers may vary. Gottlieb refutes opposing viewpoints with clear logic and evidence.

4. The author's uses of statistics—such as the number of years that a kidney from a live as opposed to a dead donor lasts (para. 5), and how little donation affects the life span of the donor (4)—offers compelling evidence that may affect the reader's acceptance of his argument. The mention of a controversial figure like Jack Kevorkian is a curious beginning to what is otherwise a clear and effective argument. The inclusion of this anecdote may hinder Gottlieb's arguments because Kevorkian is known as "Dr. Death" and is currently serving a prison sentence.

5. Answers may vary. More emotional appeals might have been more effective.

Building Your Word Power, p. 536

1. The idiom "slippery slope" means that if one thing is allowed to happen, related things will follow inevitably. One's "gut reaction" is one's instinctive reaction to something.

Gilbert Meilaender, "'Strip-Mining' the Dead: When Human Organs Are for Sale," p. 538

Gilbert Meilaender, an editor and member of the President's Bioethics Council, contends that people's objections to the sale of human organs are instinctive and profoundly moral. Moving through the arguments that have been used to encourage or "pressure" people into reconsidering the idea of selling organs, he questions the use of the hyperbolic words *tragedy* and *catastrophe* (para. 4). This issue provides lively student debate, pro and con, taking first one side and then the other. Have your students freewrite first, then break into small groups to strategize their arguments, and then present their ideas as a panel.

Understanding the Reading, p. 542

1. Meilaender's reasons for opposing human organ sales are: it is morally repugnant (para. 5); the body should be respected (12); certain things are not to be bought and sold (6); and placing organs on the market would undercut human society (10).

2. Describing transplantation as "a noble form of cannibalism" means that even though the goals for organ transplantation may be ultimately noble, the act itself is as morally unacceptable as cannibalism.

3. Meilaender seems to approve of organ donation because it is still "connected with the one who freely gave it, whose person we continue to respect" (5).

4. The policy the state of Pennsylvania enacted in the spring of 1999 was to "[pay] relatives of organ donors $300 toward funeral expenses" (8). According to the author, this policy does not affect "the organ-donation system currently in place" (10).

Visualizing the Reading, p. 542

Possible answers include:

Element	Questions	Answers
The claim	What is the author's claim? Is it stated or implied?	Stated: "It's not hard to understand our national reluctance to permit the buying and selling of human organs for transplant, for it expresses a repugnance that is deeply rooted in important moral sentiments" (para. 5).
The support	What facts, statistics, expert opinions, examples, and personal experiences are presented? Are appeals made to needs, values, or both?	Examples include: Leon Kass quote, "a noble form of cannibalism" (5); C. S. Lewis on trees (5); Michael Walzer on buying replacements in Civil War (7); eBay already had bidding on kidney (10).
		Appeals are made to the basic needs of fear (of having one's body "salvaged" [2] after death) and the repulsion toward organ selling and to the value of knowing that "certain things . . . may not be bought and sold" (6).
Purpose and audience	What is the author's purpose for writing? To whom do the reasons, evidence, and emotional appeals seem targeted?	The author is writing to a general audience to convince them that the sale of organs is immoral.
The writer's credibility	Is the author qualified and knowledgeable? Does he establish common ground with readers?	The author seems to be qualified only to write on the subject from the religious and moral perspective. He establishes common ground by listing the difficult questions facing society (2–3).

The strength of the argument	Does the author supply several reasons with relevant evidence to back up the claim? Does he use fallacies or unfair emotional appeals?	Answers may vary. Depending on one's religious views, the section on the corpse as "mortal remains" might be construed as an unfair emotional appeal (12).
Opposing viewpoints	Does the author acknowledge, accommodate, or refute opposing viewpoints with logic and relevant evidence?	Answers may vary.

Examining the Characteristics of Argument Essays, p. 543

1. Answers may vary.

2. Meilander uses deductive reasoning to dispel the idea that the kidney shortage is a "catastrophe." Answers may vary.

3. The analogy between the Civil War draft exemption and organ donation is that wealthy people can buy themselves "life," in effect, by offering money in exchange for what could be the potential of physical harm, or even death, to the "seller."

4. The reference to the Grimm Brothers tale about the ability "to shudder" is effective because it appeals to shared human instincts, emotions, and values.

Building Your Word Power, p. 543

1. The connotative meaning of the word *salvage* as used throughout the reading is to pick over or save from the scrap heap.

2. The author puts the words *tragedy* and *catastrophe* in quotation marks in paragraph 4 because he feels that they are used hyperbolically.

Analyzing the Arguments

Building Your Critical Thinking Skills: Synthesizing Sources, p. 544. Class discussions of this section should prove very useful. Have students write comparison and contrast essays about the two articles before entering into class discussion or breaking into panels to support one or the other article.

THE EFFECT OF MEDIA ON CHILDREN: IS VIOLENT MEDIA HARMFUL?

Dave Grossman and Gloria DeGaetano, "It's Important to Feel Something When You Kill," p. 545

In this well-researched argument, Dave Grossman, the director of an organization that studies the effect of killing and violent behavior on society, and Gloria DeGaetano, a writer on children and the media, argue against violent video games using as support data from a series of compelling studies that illustrate just how directly video games impact the real-life ability and desire to kill. The authors' most important evidence may be that the military uses similar video games to teach soldiers to kill. This issue is one that students will probably find very engaging because they have grown up with interactive video games, may play them frequently, and are familiar with stories of Columbine and other school killings.

Understanding the Reading, p. 551

1. According to the authors, the popularity of interactive video games may be traced to their realism; that the user can control the action; and stimuli that keep players' "excitement high" (para. 21).

2. Violent video games alter players' attitudes toward killing by fostering more aggressive thoughts (8) and teaching players to look someone in the eye as they kill (12). The physical effects of violent video games include raised heart rate, dizziness and nausea, and manifestation of "more aggressive thoughts" (8).

3. The military and the police teach trainees that sometimes the best strategy is not to shoot (20–21).

4. The authors use the incident of a fourteen-year-old boy killing five fellow students at his school as support in their argument because the boy shot the students much as one would shoot a target in a video game: He didn't move his feet or body, fired only once per target, aimed for the head (awarded extra points in video games), shot everything in sight, and had excellent aim even though he had never before used a real handgun (18).

Visualizing the Reading, p. 551

Answers may vary. The boys have a detached, cold expression. Their interaction with the video game supports the authors' claims that video games offer "an active participatory role for the child" (para. 7); that due to their physical nature, certain "'games' are actually killing simulators" (11); and that when kids play video games, "[t]here is never an incentive not to shoot" (21). Possible places in the essay where this image might be used to effect include the paragraphs cited above. For the final segment of this activity, you may wish to have students break into two groups, parents and the boys, and then have them role-play their responses for and against playing violent video games.

Examining the Characteristics of Argument Essays, p. 552

1. The authors' claim is that because interactive video games very effectively teach and encourage killing, they are dangerous and should not be used by children.

2. The main reasons the authors give to support their argument are: military uses games like Doom to teach soldiers how to kill (para. 20); these games provide hands-on simulation of killing (11); and children's "brains and response mechanisms" are not fully developed and are therefore more impressionable (10). Answers may vary.

3. The authors cite many psychological studies (9–12) and analyses of individual cases like the one at Paducah (16–18). Answers may vary.

4. This is likely to be construed as a weak spot in an otherwise well-supported essay, particularly as some students are likely to be gamers, or know gamers well, and they will have likely seen or experienced little increased propensity for violence.

5. Other patterns of development include: narration ("Hostility and cardiovascular reactivity were examined after subjects played" [9]); description ("pistol grip joystick" [20]; cause and effect ("developing the will to kill by repeatedly rehearsing the act until it feels natural" [20]); and illustration (Paducah and Columbine).

Building Your Word Power, p. 552

1. The phrase "riding the technology curve" means that children are adapting to and changing more quickly in response to the rapid shifts in technological advances.

2. *Splatter* as used in the final paragraph suggests killing and blood.

Gerard Jones, "Violent Media Is Good for Kids," p. 554

Comic strip writer Gerard Jones founded the organization Media Power for Children and serves as adviser to the Comparative Media Studies graduate program at the Massachusetts Institute of Technology. In this essay, he goes against the popular view that media violence has a bad effect on children, describing it instead as cathartic and even psychologically beneficial. This issue is one that students may be familiar with and may enjoy debating. Have them freewrite about violent programs that they have watched, especially any that they think may have helped them to deal with or even overcome emotional or personal problems. Then have them debate the Jones and Grossman/DeGaetano articles, pro and con, analyzing the effectiveness of each one's use of evidence.

Understanding the Reading, p. 557

1. The reasons Jones presents in support of his claim that children need violent entertainment are: it helps them to integrate their public and private psyches (para. 5); through violent stories, they learn to be human (9); through violent entertainment, they learn to accept parts of their selves (9); violent entertainment fosters

developmental functions (11); and violent games and stories can provide a tool for mastering rage (12).

2. Reading comic books like the Hulk allowed the author to find a "fantasy self" (4) and to deal with his feelings of rage. He read his son Tarzan comics to overcome the boy's fear of climbing trees (6).

3. The author feels that it is beneficial for children to be exposed to "creative violence" because it helps them to "engage the rage they've stifled" (12).

4. According to the author, experiencing violent cartoons or video games helps children through developmental stages by allowing them a "dual identity" with which to negotiate the conflicts between their public and private selves (11).

Visualizing the Reading, p. 557

Possible answers include:

Type of Evidence	Example from the Essay
Personal experience	1. Reading comics as a boy helped the author gain confidence and eventually led him to become an action movie and comic book writer (para. 1–5).
Expert opinion	Stories are how we learn what it is to be human (clinical psychologist, 9).
Media examples	The author's love of the Incredible Hulk as a young boy (2–5); Ice T's "mythologized street violence" helped a girl to become well adjusted (15).

Examining the Characteristics of Argument Essays, p. 558

1. The author's claim is that violent stories offer tools for children to master their rage. Answers may vary.

2. The story of Jones's son imagining himself as a dinosaur supports his idea that stories can help children to integrate aspects of their psyche (para. 6). The story of the girl who acted out violent fantasies shows that they helped her to become "socially competent" (14). The final example is of a girl who used gangsta rap as a means to escape a difficult family situation (15). Answers may vary.

3. Jones appeals to the needs of adolescence: fear, anger, desire for power, and rage. The author also addresses the value holding violence to be bad, but here he suggests that we as a society are sending confusing and mixed messages about this value to children because of the natural aggression that we all harbor.

4. Jones recognizes the opposing viewpoints of "pop psychologists" who say violent stories are "junk culture" (7). He refutes them by quoting "clinical psychologists" who say such stories are valuable.

5. Jones uses a sentence fragment to isolate and emphasize the idea of violence because it is so central to his thesis.

Building Your Word Power, p. 558

1. The metaphor "then the Incredible Hulk smashed through it" means that the author had been sheltered from pop culture and its violence until he was introduced to the Hulk.

Analyzing the Arguments

Building Your Critical Thinking Skills: Synthesizing Sources, p. 559.
Class discussions of this section should be lively and interesting. To increase their skills in synthesizing sources, you might have students write comparison and contrast essays about the two articles before entering into class discussion or breaking into panels to support one or the other article. Based on the readings, have students break into two groups and then debate each other using the two readings as sources for their position, pro or con.

CIVIL LIBERTIES: DOES THE PATRIOT ACT GO TOO FAR?

Zara Gelsey, "Who's Reading over Your Shoulder?" p. 560

Writer Zara Gelsey evaluates the legitimacy of the FBI's policy of monitoring library records without "probable cause" under the Patriot Act. Gelsey argues that the right to privacy is being violated in unprecedented ways. This issue is a very important one for students to inform themselves about and debate. You might like to assign them to research and report on the changes in civil liberties brought about by the Patriot Act. Initiate a debate about when, if ever, these changes are likely to be reversed, given that the War on Terrorism appears to have no deadline. Students could debate the value of the Patriot Act, pro and con, after breaking into small groups.

Understanding the Reading, p. 563

1. According to the author, the freedom of thought and the freedom to read are interrelated because if one feels intimidated or inhibited one is likely to censor oneself (para. 13).

2. The author thinks that the FBI is using the Patriot Act to evade the First Amendment by "threatening readers rather than prohibiting what they read" (13).

3. The outcome of surveillance of what someone reads might be similar to a classic sitcom plot line in that a series of "unrelated details" are pieced together to "construct conclusions" that are untrue (5).

Visualizing the Reading, p. 563

Possible answers include:

Reasons	Evidence (list)	Effectiveness (explain)
Secret monitoring of library records is "ripe for potential abuse" (para. 3).	It intimidates patrons (3).	Details about a case in which a researcher was mistaken for a terrorist would strengthen this idea.
What one reads indicates different things to different people.	Analogies to a classic sitcom plot line (5); hypothetical example of the FBI concluding you're a terrorist because you are doing research on suicide bombings (6); makes the FBI "predisposed to find suspicious facts" (7).	Fairly effective, though an actual case of "mistaken identity" would have made for more compelling evidence.
"[S]urveillance always spreads beyond its original purpose" (para. 9)	War on Drugs was tied to the War on Terrorism (10).	Weak because the single example is not well explained.
Surveillance will cause self-censorship.	Reference to George Orwell's *1984* (12); circumvents the First Amendment (13).	Again, could be made stronger with a concrete example.

Examining the Characteristics of Argument Essays, p. 564

1. Gelsey's claim appears toward the end of her essay: "Thus, the FBI circumvents the First Amendment by threatening readers rather than prohibiting what they read" (para. 13).

2. Answers may vary. Using examples from fiction like the novel *1984* (12) does not seem as effective as an example of a real researcher taken for a "suspect" would be.

3. One of the emotional appeals Gelsey makes is evident in her description of the FBI as "peering over my shoulder" (1). She appeals to the need for privacy and the value of freedom of thought.

4. Gelsey acknowledges the broader need for protection from terrorists in paragraph 9, but she doesn't address any opposing viewpoints relating specifically to library surveillance.

Building Your Word Power, p. 564

1. The allusion to the Garden of Eden means that knowledge can be used for good or evil. The allusion to George Orwell's *1984* refers to a novel in which the government became dictatorial, violating its citizens' rights.

Ramesh Ponnuru, "Fears about the Patriot Act Are Misguided," p. 566

National Review editor Ramesh Ponnuru expresses skepticism that the Patriot Act poses a threat to American civil liberties, citing legal precedents prior to 9/11, dismissing fears expressed by those on both the right and the left, and arguing that the end justifies the means. He acknowledges that without such outcry the Patriot Act might have violated many more civil liberties, but he still dismisses the idea that such gradual infringements of civil liberties might lead to a less democratic society. This is an important issue for students to consider. Ask them to do some research in advance of class discussion in order to be prepared to defend their position. Have students adopt positions pro and con on the introduction of the Patriot Act, and ask them to consider when and if it should expire.

Understanding the Reading, p. 569

1. According to Ponnuru, concerns about the Patriot Act are misguided because: there were already legal precedents for the use of roving wiretaps (para. 9); Internet surveillance requires a court order (10); the Act hasn't shifted the balance between privacy and security (11); and the feds already had the right to break into someone's house for a "sneak and peek" before the Act was established (14). On balance, the author believes that "legal laxity" would be worse (17).

2. According to the author, the coalition of left- and right-wing groups working against the Patriot Act has received favorable publicity because the press finds this oddly bipartisan coalition "irresistible" (5).

3. The example Ponnuru cites to explain how terrorists regard the Patriot Act is Jeffrey Battle, who complained that it had reduced the "financial support" terrorists had received from individuals because of their fear of reprisal (18).

4. Ponnuru explains the controversy surrounding the Patriot Act by suggesting that the opposition has not read it and is merely hysterical over misunderstood and imagined infringements (20).

Visualizing the Reading, p. 569

Possible answers include:

Patriot Act Provision	Opposing Viewpoint	Refutation
Roving wiretaps (para. 9)	Violation of civil liberties	They have been used since 1986 and are not new.
Internet surveillance (para. 10–12)	Allows for "spying on the Web browsers of people who are not even criminal suspects" (10).	Patriot Act requires a court order and has privacy provisions as strong as those for phone calls, stronger than for mail.
Computer hacking (para. 13)	The definition of terrorist activity includes non-lethal acts like computer hacking.	Such a definition is misleading because only specific kinds of hacking, like taking out a power grid, would be considered terrorism.
Sneak and peek (para. 14)	ACLU says that the government can secretly enter your home and search it.	This can be done, but only with a search warrant and you must be notified that it happened after the fact.
Library records (para. 15)	Federal agents can "commandeer library records" (15).	Traditionally, such records could be accessed by law with a subpoena.

Examining the Characteristics of Argument Essays, p. 570

1. Ponnuru's claim that some of the provisions of the Patriot Act are reasonable occurs in paragraph 8 when he says that "most of the concerns about the Patriot Act are misguided or based on premises that are just plain wrong."

2. The types of evidence Ponnuru uses to support his argument are: quotations from legal experts (para. 10); quotations from the coalition against the Patriot Act (12); and an example of how terrorists have responded to the Act (18). Answers may vary.

3. Ponnuru organizes his essay by least to most important, culminating in the response of a terrorist to the Act. Answers may vary.

4. Ponnuru accommodates some of the civil libertarians' objections to the Patriot Act, such as the idea that "Internet gambling" should be excluded and acknowl-

edging that they did manage to insert some necessary restrictions on the Act (16). Answers may vary.

5. Ponnuru's conclusion suggests that the opposition is hysterical and has not read the Act closely. It supports his argument by suggesting that a calm look at the facts will prove that people are reacting irrationally to legislation that doesn't infringe on civil liberties any more than they were before and in the end does much good in the nation's War on Terrorism.

Building Your Word Power, p. 570

1. The metaphor "the lion and the lamb lying down together" in paragraph 5 means that political enemies are on the same side against the Act.

Analyzing the Arguments

Building Your Critical Thinking Skills: Synthesizing Sources, p. 571.
The Patriot Act topic is controversial and certain to generate a heated discussion. Because much of the controversy circles around hearsay for the simple fact (as Ponnuru points out) that few people have taken the time to read the Act, it would be useful to assign groups of students to read the parts of the Act mentioned by these two authors and then report their findings to the class. If possible, have the same groups look into some of the claims made by Ponnuru to see if his information about certain tenets of the Act being in place before the Act was enacted are indeed true. Armed with this additional information, are students still swayed by one or the other argument, or do they find themselves changing positions based on their own research? Once students have tried to winnow out the truth in these two essays for themselves, you might want to open up the discussion to the larger issues associated with argument and the possibility of abuse of spreading misinformation through writing.

Chapter 14 Combining Patterns: Using Variety to Achieve Your Purposes, p. 573

This chapter represents the culmination of the semester's work, when students can combine the patterns they most enjoy using to create a varied, skillful piece of writing with various kinds of arguments and evidence. In general, one rhetorical pattern should predominate, but other modes can be used to supplement and enliven the piece as needed. Because the formats of essays that combine modes are so variable, a general graphic organizer for this type of essay is not included. Encourage students who find this organizational tool helpful to create their own, modifying its structure according to the patterns used. You might find it helpful to refer students back to the basic structure of the graphic organizer showing the key elements to include on page 14 of Chapter 1.

The essays in this chapter represent a wide variety of styles and approaches; analyzing the different modes used by these authors will illustrate for students the wide range of writing choices they have now that they have mastered each of the individual modes discussed in this book. Anna Quindlen primarily uses argumentation in her 9/11 story, "We Are Here for Andrea" (p. 574), but supplements it with other modes. Her essay is annotated to show the different modes and is represented visually with a graphic organizer (p. 580) that can be used to take students through the essay point by point. Student writer Robin Ferguson uses narration to tell her story, "The Value of Volunteering" (p. 583), but also uses process analysis, cause and effect, and other modes. Her story too is annotated for students who need some assistance identifying these patterns. Lars Eighner, in "On Dumpster Diving" (p. 586), uses primarily process analysis to explain eloquently how someone becomes a professional scavenger; and John Leo, in "The Good-News Generation" (p. 591), uses predominantly definition to distinguish among the various generations. Chitra Divakaruni, in "Houseguest Hell" (p. 596), uses narration to tell her story about inconsiderate guests who descend upon her San Francisco home year after year. In "Naked Terror" (p. 604), Jeffrey Rosen uses an extended example to support his thesis that airport security in the wake of 9/11 is largely designed to give the "appearance" of security. And Shirley Jackson's short story "The Lottery" (p. 609) is a much-anthologized piece that uses narrative as well as process analysis to describe a cruel rite practiced in a little New England village.

Robin Ferguson, "The Value of Volunteering," p. 583

In this section, students can review and evaluate the final version of student writer Robin Ferguson's essay about her experience working as a literary volunteer. Students were introduced to Ferguson in Chapter 3, and they may find it interesting to refer back to the earlier prewriting that she did before turning in this final, more polished version. Told as a personal narrative, Ferguson's essay also combines cause and effect, description, illustration, and other modes to explain the positive impact of volunteering on her life. Her experience helping Marie, a single mother, to read proved more rewarding than she had anticipated. Students will enjoy comparing Ferguson's experience to their own experiences as volunteers. Sharing what they write will also serve as a way to get to know each other even better.

Responding to "Students Write," p. 584

1. Answers may vary. Ferguson could have made her introduction more engaging by creating some suspense—for example, by opening with a phrase such as "Little did I know."

2. The transitions that suggest narration are: "I began working" (para. 1); "When I first" (2); "As we worked together" (4); and "As time went by" (5).

3. The use of narration contributes the feeling of a story to the essay (for instance, the plot of how Ferguson came to appreciate what she was learning, the character of Marie, her hard-working single-mother student). The use of cause and effect explains the reason why volunteering was meaningful to Ferguson. Process analysis explains how Ferguson acquired learning strategies in her volunteer training. Illustration explains the effects of illiteracy on her student. Description makes the story more vivid, drawing the reader in and personalizing Ferguson's experience. The use of comparison and contrast contributes to a sense of what the teacher and student had in common, such as being single parents. Finally, Ferguson concludes her essay with argument, calling for action to help illiterate people to reclaim full lives.

Lars Eighner, "On Dumpster Diving," p. 586

Lars Eighner, a sometimes homeless fiction and essay writer, describes in exquisite detail the stages of becoming a scavenger, breaking down the process of scavenging vividly as if he needed to teach his readers how to do it themselves. Using first-person narration and an informative tone, Eighner quickly makes his intelligence and radical worldview clear, but his reasons for remaining homeless, are mysterious. Students may find it difficult to understand why someone so obviously talented and educated would be homeless, but they will be fascinated by the world he shows. You might like to preface the class discussion with some information about homelessness, in particular contributing factors such as the "deinstitutionalization" of the mentally ill in the United States.

Understanding the Reading, p. 588

1. According to the author, the stages people go through before becoming "professional" dumpster divers are: feeling shame and self-loathing (para. 5); coming to the realization that people throw away "a lot of perfectly good stuff" (6); trying to acquire everything one comes across (7); and restricting oneself to acquiring only those things with immediate utility (7).

2. The principal risk associated with dumpster diving is "dysentery" (para. 12).

3. Eighner has learned two lessons from dumpster diving: to take only what he can use and leave the rest; and to acknowledge "the transience of material being" — that is, ideas are longer lived than material objects.

4. The attitude the author shares with the wealthy is that there is always plenty more where something comes from, so it's unnecessary to collect "gaudy bauble[s]" (16).

Visualizing the Reading, p. 588

Possible answers include:

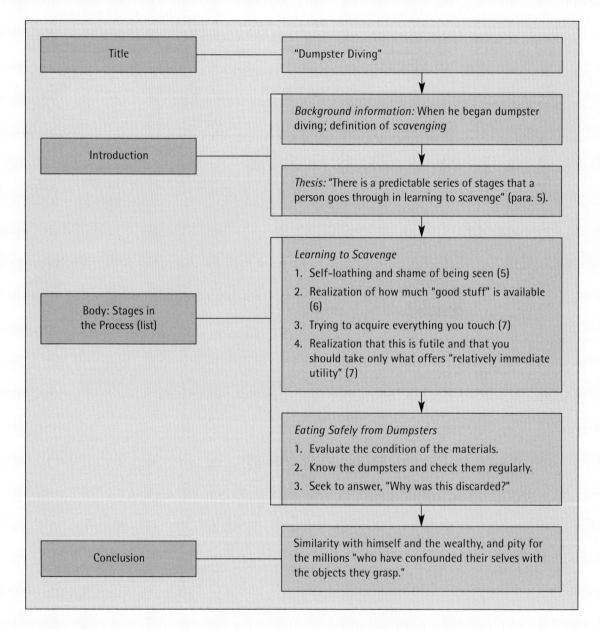

| Title | "Dumpster Diving" |

Introduction

Background information: When he began dumpster diving; definition of *scavenging*

Thesis: "There is a predictable series of stages that a person goes through in learning to scavenge" (para. 5).

Body: Stages in the Process (list)

Learning to Scavenge
1. Self-loathing and shame of being seen (5)
2. Realization of how much "good stuff" is available (6)
3. Trying to acquire everything you touch (7)
4. Realization that this is futile and that you should take only what offers "relatively immediate utility" (7)

Eating Safely from Dumpsters
1. Evaluate the condition of the materials.
2. Know the dumpsters and check them regularly.
3. Seek to answer, "Why was this discarded?"

Conclusion

Similarity with himself and the wealthy, and pity for the millions "who have confounded their selves with the objects they grasp."

Examining the Characteristics of Essays That Combine Patterns, p. 589

1. In addition to process analysis, other patterns used in this essay include: narration ("I began dumpster diving about a year before I became homeless" [para. 1]); defi-

nition (dumpster diving); comparison and contrast (scavenging vs. foraging [2–3]; relationship between himself and the wealthy [16]); description ("pristine ice cream, still frozen" [6]); division (types of food to be found in dumpsters [10–11]); and cause and effect (getting dysentery [12] and lessons learned [13–14]).

2. Eighner includes sensory details relating to sight, touch, and taste, including "running shoes that fit and look and smell brand-new" (6); "[r]aw fruits and veg- etables with intact skins" (10); and "desire to grab for the gaudy bauble" (16).

3. Distinguishing characteristics Eighner presents to define dumpster diving are: living from the refuse of others (3); eating from dumpsters (9); and risking illness (12).

4. The author's main point is that dumpster diving has some drawbacks but is a valid way of life that has taught him larger lessons about life. He supports this point through examples of the "perfectly good stuff" he uses that would otherwise go to waste, and the ultimately "valueless" nature of material possessions (such as love letters and rag dolls).

Building Your Word Power, p. 589

1. According to Eighner, the difference between *scavenging* and *foraging* is that scav- enging involves picking over other people's refuse whereas foraging is specifically a matter of gathering things like nuts and berries.

2. The phrase "gaudy bauble" means anything that is shiny and desirable but ulti- mately worthless.

Building Your Critical Thinking Skills: Bias, p. 589

1. Answers may vary.

2. Answers may vary.

John Leo, "The Good-News Generation," p. 591

John Leo, a writer for *U.S. News & World Report,* discusses the new generation known as "millennials," born between 1977 and 1994. Although he gently mocks the new sci- ence of generations, he acknowledges that he is encouraged by the generalizations about millenials, also known as generation Y. Students should find this subject inter- esting and may like to contribute their own observations about each of the generations they are familiar with. Encourage them to systematically evaluate the categories, adding new elements in accordance with their own thesis. You might have them create new categories within categories—dividing, for example, gen Y into two or three kinds of gen Y-ers. They might also like to compare and contrast gen X and gen Y, or speculate about what gen Z might be like.

Understanding the Reading, p. 593

1. The generations described in this article are: silents ("duty, tradition, loyalty"); baby boomers ("individuality, tolerance, self-absorption"); gen X-ers ("diversity, savvy, pragmatism"); and millenials ("authenticity, authorship, autonomy") (para. 1).

2. The millenials represent the largest birth group in American history.

3. When Clurman says millennials are "pluralistic" (para. 3–4), she means that they overlook differences such as race, ethnicity, and gender (4).

4. The groups that have close family relationships are millenials and their boomer parents (7).

Visualizing the Reading, p. 593

Answers will vary.

Examining the Characteristics of Essays That Combine Patterns, p. 593

1. Leo's thesis appears in paragraph 2: "The comic overtones of dividing and labeling everyone this way are hard to miss, but there is some sense to it, too." He reveals the importance and relevance of this topic through his details about each generation.

2. The primary pattern of development in Leo's article is classification. He also uses definition (of each group); comparison and contrast (with other generations); illustration (the distinguishing characteristics for each category); and description ("an ordinary looking, midriff-free, nondancing singer" [7]).

3. Classification: supports the thesis; comparison and contrast: supports the thesis and adds details; illustration: adds details; description: adds variety and interest.

4. The distinguishing characteristics of millennials are that they are "family oriented, viscerally pluralistic, deeply committed to authenticity and truth-telling, heavily stressed, and living in a no-boundaries world" (3). Generation X-ers are characterized by "diversity, savvy, pragmatism" (1). Silents are characterized by a sense of "duty, tradition, loyalty" (1). And baby boomers are characterized by "individuality, tolerance, self-absorption" (1) and are developing close bonds with their millennial children (7).

Building Your Word Power, p. 594

1. Baby boomers being characterized by *self-absorption* means that they devote time primarily to their own mental and physical well-being; generation X-ers having *savvy* means that they are worldly-wise and sophisticated; and millennials having *authorship* means that they like to take individual responsibility for their work.

2. The phrase "over-the-top cultural products" means products that are elaborately and dramatically conceived, reproduced, and advertised. It has a somewhat negative connotation.

Building Your Critical Thinking Skills: Evaluating Sources, p. 594

1. Answers may vary. Ann Clurman is described as a "generation-watcher" (1) and Leo reinforces her reputation by adding that she is "one of the best," but he does use a disproportionate amount of information from her company, Yankelovich Partners, including quotations from the president of that same company. A Gallup poll is reputable (6), as is a Harvard poll if it is formally connected with the university, although this one is not identified as such (8).

2. Answers may vary.

Chitra Divakaruni, "Houseguest Hell," p. 596

Award-winning novelist and essayist Chitra Divakaruni has published numerous essays, poems, and short stories in the *Atlantic Monthly* and other magazines. In this personal essay, Divakaruni complains about her frequent houseguests from India, speculating about why she can't seem to say No to her guests' demands. Her yearly dilemma will likely amuse students and introduce them to a culture that they may not be familiar with.

Students should enjoy finding the various, underlying reasons that Divakaruni uncovers for not being able to say No to her guests. To identify her reasons, have them outline the essay using a graphic organizer. You might like to lead a discussion about Divakaruni's complex motivations as a busy writer with American needs for privacy and scheduling and feminist expectations about freedom from excessive hosting. Evaluate these other influences in her life in light of her close ties to India and her memories of how her mother delighted in entertaining guests.

Understanding the Reading, p. 600

1. Indian relatives come to visit Divakaruni each late spring until the end of summer. They are a lot of trouble because they expect Divakaruni to entertain them and take care of them. As she so aptly puts it, "they require Maximum Maintenance" (para. 2).

2. The guests expect her to cook Indian foods like rice and lentils (4) and to prepare hot tea. Her guests also expect her to entertain them by personally accompanying them on shopping and sight-seeing trips. It is hard for Divakaruni to meet these expectations because she has a busy schedule as a writer and because she does not have the servants she would have had in India to do all of the cleaning and housework.

3. Divakaruni's way of entertaining is different from her mother's because her mother found visits from relatives and friends to be a delightful experience that she anticipated with a "smiling sense of holiday" (11). Their experiences are similar in that they both feel an obligation as women to entertain and to be a "caretaker" (10) to their guests. But the experiences are different because Divakaruni is a writer and a feminist who lives in America and has worked hard not to have to cater to people's needs, whereas her mother was a traditional wife in India who had the help of servants. Her mother didn't mind having her "daily routine" interrupted, whereas Divakaruni does (11).

4. The author might make the visits easier on herself by ordering take-out food, taking guests to restaurants, and serving them "Special K and Lipton's tea bags" (9) instead of cooking traditional foods. She could also send her guests off on the subway or buses instead of driving them or having her husband take them "sightseeing over the weekend" (9). She plans to suggest these things in the future with "firm charm" (16).

Visualizing the Reading, p. 600

Possible answers include:

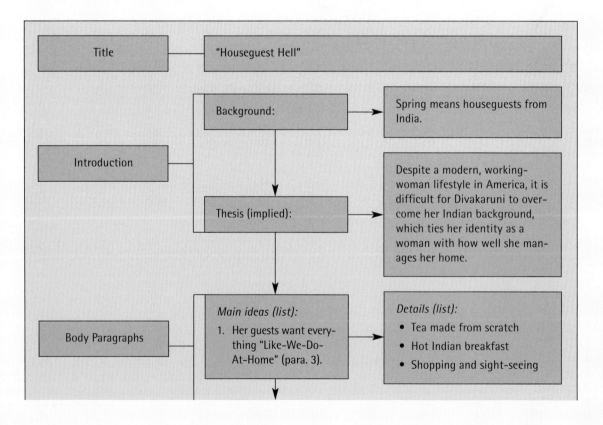

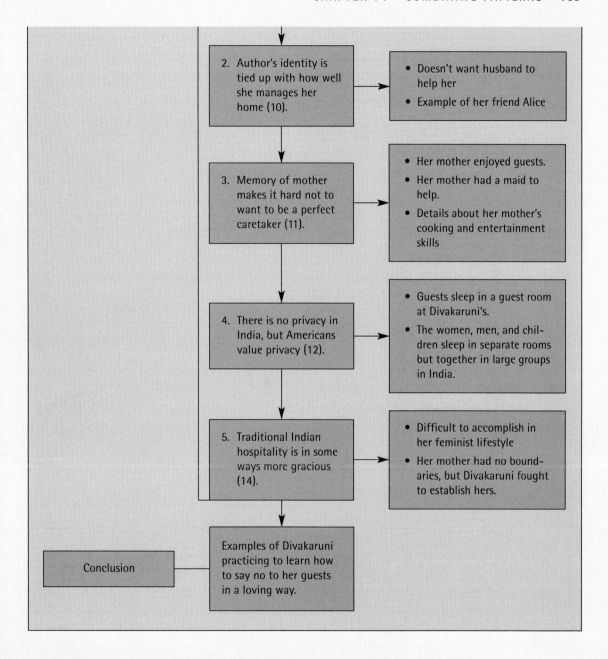

Examining the Characteristics of Essays That Combine Patterns, p. 601

1. Divakaruni uses conflict and tension to build toward a resolution by mysteriously referring to the arrival of her dreaded guests as something she cannot prevent and by describing herself as a "twenty-four-hour captive" (para. 2). Her use of dialogue, especially the disembodied questions that relatives ask repeatedly, contributes

significantly to her narrative by giving the reader some sense of the entitled attitude of her guests. For example, "Surely you've been to Saks?" (5) and "Ah, wouldn't it be nice to have a hot cup of tea" (5).

2. Divakruni's details about Indian food contribute to the larger picture of her houseguests by showing that traditional foods like tea take a long time to prepare and require a lot of clean-up, which her guests do not offer to help with. The same preparation occurs in India, but in the world where she grew up the servants did all the clean-up and prep work.

3. Divakaruni uses first-person point of view. The questions to the reader contribute to this approach by revealing the author's emotional reaction to being a host, for example, "Guess who's spitting mad by the time she gets into bed . . .?" (7).

4. The author uses comparison and contrast techniques most importantly to analyze her situation as compared to her mother's (11). She also uses comparison and contrast when discussing her friend Surekha (2) and Alice, her "senior executive" friend (10).

5. Answers may vary.

Building Your Word Power, p. 601

1. "Maximum Maintenance" means that the author's guests require a lot of personal attention, entertainment, and caretaking because they do not offer to help out with chores or cooking or anything else.

2. The connotation of "Like-We-Do-at-Home" is that the guests expect Divakaruni to entertain them in the style they are accustomed to in India, where a guest is considered "God come to visit" (para. 14). In India, however, many women do not work outside the home, and in upper caste families the servants help with cooking, cleaning, and so on.

Building Your Critical Thinking Skills: Identifying Assumptions, p. 602

1. Based on details in the essay, presumably Divakaruni assumes that her audience does not know a great deal about India. She explains, for example, that "rice and lentil mix for idlis has to be soaked overnight" (4). She also seems to assume that the reader can understand and appreciate the dilemmas she faces as a feminist American working woman with a very traditional heritage.

2. The author assumes that her houseguests will not help themselves if she does not wait on them and that they expect to be treated exactly as they are in India. When they say, for example, "Ah, wouldn't it be nice to have a hot cup of tea," she gets up to make it (5).

Jeffrey Rosen, "Naked Terror," p. 604

Jeffrey Rosen teaches law, is a radio commentator, is the legal affairs editor at *The New Republic,* and has written articles about law for the *New York Times,* the *Atlantic Monthly,* and the *New Yorker.* He argues that irrational demands for airport security have led to an invasion of privacy in the post-9/11 era. He contends that fear creates a vicious cycle in which citizens demand solutions to problems that cannot readily be fixed. Instead, people are given solutions that only "appear" to solve the problem and in fact can serve as an invasion of privacy. Students could usefully discuss how media images post-9/11 frightened them and how they now feel about solutions to the threat of terror.

Understanding the Reading, p. 606

1. Rosen regards the public response to the threat of future terrorist attacks as irrational because it is emotional, leading people to "miscalculate" the probability of threat (para. 4).

2. The difference between the Naked Machine and the Blob Machine is that one shows the outline of the naked body and the other distorts and disguises it (3). According to the author, some people prefer the Naked Machine because they have "abandoned all hope of privacy," or they "have nothing to hide," or they are more concerned about *"feeling* safe than being safe" (3).

3. According to Rosen, the two "institution[s] of democracy" that affect Americans' psychological vulnerabilities are TV and politicians (6).

4. Americans can break the cycle of exaggerated risks and the demand for poorly designed laws and technologies by finding better leaders (7).

Visualizing the Reading, p. 606

Possible answers include:

Pattern	How It Supports the Thesis.
Comparison and contrast	Compares the "Naked Machine" to the "Blob Machine" (para. 2–4). Illustrates the irrational choices that people make in response to remote threats.
Cause and effect	Watching images of 9/11 caused post-traumatic stress in viewers outside New York City (5). Supports his argument for turning off the TV.
Illustration	The World Trade Center images crowd out "less visually dramatic risks in the public mind" (4). Supports his point that people are prone to disproportionate panic instead of understanding that mundane threats like strokes are far more likely to cause harm.

Description	Used to describe the Blob and Naked Machines, providing interest and clarifying his comparison and contrast of these two devices (2–4).

Examining the Characteristics of Essays That Combine Patterns, p. 607

1. Rosen's thesis statement is: "The public responds emotionally to remote but terrifying threats, and this leads us to make choices about security that are not always rational" (para. 1). Rosen provides clear support for his thesis.

2. Answers may vary.

3. The predominant pattern of development used in the essay is cause and effect.

4. Rosen cites a study of the psychological response in New York and elsewhere after the 9/11 attacks to illustrate the impact of TV in creating "psychological vulnerabilities" (5).

Building Your Word Power, p. 607

1. The allusion to Rudolph Giuliani is a reference to the former New York mayor who encouraged the citizens of New York to overcome their fears in the wake of 9/11.

Building Your Critical Thinking Skills: Facts and Opinions, p. 607

___F___ 1. ". . . the Naked Machine bounces a low-energy X-ray beam off the human body." (para. 2)

___O___ 2. "The Naked Machine promises a high degree of security, but it demands a high sacrifice of privacy." (para. 2)

___F___ 3. ". . . 17 percent of the American population outside New York City reported symptoms of post-traumatic stress related to 9/11." (para. 5)

___O___ 4. ". . . our success in overcoming fear will depend on political leadership that challenges us to live with our uncertainties rather than catering to them." (para. 6)

Shirley Jackson, "The Lottery," p. 609

Writer Shirley Jackson is best known for this chilling short story about a New England village. In her fable, the villagers kill one person every summer because it has long been a tradition, although the origins of the tradition have been forgotten. Students may enjoy speculating about the meaning of this story, especially if it is conjoined with some discussion of group psychology, historical mass movements, and peer pressure.

Understanding the Reading, p. 616

1. The setting of this story is in a rural village square in June.

2. Old Man Warner's scoffs at the news that the north village is considering giving up the lottery, suggesting that it is a foolish decision (para. 32).

3. Tessie Hutchinson wants her married daughter and son-in-law to take part in the drawing to maximize the chance that she herself will not select the wrong slip of paper. It is an inappropriate suggestion because as a mother she should want to protect her daughter.

4. Tessie draws the paper with the black spot on it, and the vollagers stone her to death (79).

Visualizing the Reading, p. 616

Possible answers include:

Details	Importance
"They stood together, away from the pile of stones in the corner, and their jokes were quiet and they smiled rather than laughed." (para. 3)	Suggests a sense of foreboding and dread of what is to come.
"The black box grew shabbier each year; by now it was no longer completely black but splintered badly along one side . . ." (5)	Suggests that the ritual is very old.
"The people had done it so many times that they only half listened to the directions; most of them were quiet, wetting their lips, not looking around." (20)	Suggests that people are familiar with this annual ritual and, although compliant, are nervous and anxious about it.
"They do say . . . that over in the north village they're talking of giving up the lottery." (31)	Suggests that they could discontinue the ritual, that some people don't believe the lottery is necessary anymore.
"It had a black spot on it, the black spot Mr. Summers had made the night before with the heavy pencil in the coal-company office." (72)	The black spot signifies death.

Examining the Characteristics of Essays That Combine Patterns, p. 616

1. The main theme in "The Lottery" is the idea that many traditional societies require human sacrifices or scapegoats (in this case, to ensure a good harvest). This idea is supported by the way that no one protests having to stone Tessie in the

end. Another possible interpretation is that if overpopulation ever became a problem, people might have to "thin the herd" just like farmers do. This is suggested
by Mr. Warner's comment that if it weren't for the lottery, they'd "all be eating
stewed chickweed and acorns" (para. 32).

2. Other patterns used in the story include process analysis (how the lottery works
[4–79]) and description (the "faded or stained" black box [5]).

3. Answers may vary. For example, the way that people laugh nervously indicates
that they are anxious about the lottery, setting an ominous and foreboding tone.

4. The central conflict in "The Lottery" is who will pick the black-spotted slip. Jackson builds and sustains tension by drawing out the lottery process through dialogue and by the fact that although indications from the story suggest that the lottery is not a happy affair, readers do not truly know what the black dot represents
until the first stone is cast at the end of the story.

5. The distinguishing qualities and characteristics of the main characters are that
Mrs. Hutchinson fights the process up until her end, complaining that it isn't
"fair" (45), Mr. Hutchinson is compliant and uncomplaining even in the light of
the impending doom within his family, and Mr. Summers is conservative and formal and insists upon following the traditional ways.

Building Your Word Power, p. 617

1. The significance of the phrase "pack of crazy fools" as used by Old Man Warner is
that the force of tradition is what is important with the lottery, and those who
don't believe in the tradition are therefore foolish.

2. The connotation of this phrase in the context of the story is that the lottery is a
fair system, anonymous and rule-bound, and that Mrs. Hutchinson is a poor sport
since she is the only one to complain that it isn't fair.

Building Your Critical Thinking Skills: Symbolism, p. 617

1. The black box might symbolize death because it is coffin-like and black. An alter-
nate interpretation would be that it symbolizes Pandora's Box. The color and condition of the box might be important because they show how old the tradition is.

2. The name "Mr. Summers" may suggest the summer harvest which is what the
townspeople are sacrificing someone for; "Mr. Graves" suggests death; "Old Man
Warner" suggests a town crier or cautioner.

3. The lottery itself may stand for or represent the desire for a social scapegoat.